Fear and What Follows

FEAR
AND WHAT
FOLLOWS

The Violent Education of a Christian Racist

A MEMOIR

Tim Parrish

University Press of Mississippi   Jackson

www.upress.state.ms.us

The University Press of Mississippi is a member
of the Association of American University Presses.

First printing 2013

Library of Congress Cataloging-in-Publication Data

Parrish, Tim.
  Fear and what follows : the violent education of a Christian
racist, a memoir / Tim Parrish.
     pages cm (Willie Morris books in memoir and biogra-
phy)
  ISBN 978-1-61703-866-2 (cloth : alk. paper) — ISBN
978-1-61703-867-9 (ebook) 1. Parrish, Tim. 2. Authors,
American—Homes and haunts—Louisiana—Baton Rouge. 3.
Racism—Louisiana—Baton Rouge. 4. Baton Rouge (La.)—
Race relations—Biography. I. Title.
  PS3566.A7575Z46 2013
  813'.54—dc23
  [B]   2013003013

British Library Cataloging-in-Publication Data available

For my family

"The potent poison quite o'ercrows my spirit."
  —Hamlet

"I remember being the dark."
  —Beth Ann Fennelly

Contents

Foreword

In this book, I've strived to be true to my memory of relevant events from my young life. I have also tried to reveal as thoroughly as possible my emotional and psychological journey and to render other characters as fully and honestly as I am able. That said, because of memoir's inherent reliance on memory, this book is an imperfect record. To state the obvious, memoir is not reportage; memoir is a literary genre.

My primary goal has been to accurately portray my experience during a specific time and cultural context. In order to accomplish this goal and to create a more linear, streamlined narrative than exists in life, I have taken a fiction-writer's license both in rearranging some events and in writing scenes with dialogue that is based on what I remember, but which I do not claim to be factual transcription. However, I have not contrived any of the remarkable coincidences, such as reappearances by certain characters at particular moments or recurring appearances of objects that may seem to be placed in order to create fictional motifs. I have invented some minor scenes to dramatize my emotional and ethical process and to more fully, and I hope fairly, characterize people around me. In creating these minor scenes, I fully believe that I have not misrepresented, exaggerated or ameliorated any aspect of a real person. I don't claim to accurately remember everything that happened or was said, but I have tried my hardest to honestly depict myself and the characters here. As for my representation of actual people, some of the characters are composites of several people, and all but my family's and a few others' names have been changed. It is not my intent to malign or compromise anyone, but rather to get at truths about my upbringing and myself. I look forward to hearing from anyone who thinks I got something wrong.

Fear and What Follows

Prologue

June 2006

"Get ready for your balls to pop sweat," my brother Robert said. He grinned, his belly pressing out against a thread-worn shirt, his shorts too short on his white legs. A beige brace wrapped his injured wrist, the latest in his line of perpetual damages. In his good hand he held a tiny, antennaed TV to keep up with LSU baseball through a nebula of static.

"I thought I told you to order me some cool," I said.

"Hey, I'm trying to get you ready for hell."

I gave him a hug, the odor of cigarettes engulfing me, and then we headed toward the tiny, Baton Rouge airport exit.

"Yeah," Robert said, "Daddy's been going on how I better stop listening to you or I'll go to hell too."

"I'm still sending *you*? How's that work? You're the older brother."

"And you're a godless professor."

"And Alan still gets a pass."

"He's got money. God don't send you to hell if you got money."

This conversation was almost a ritual, but usually there was more of an interlude before we performed it. Robert was joyfully torqued.

The doors slid open, and we stepped into air like a super-heated membrane. I tried to ease into the heat, let it ease into me and loosen my tight shoulders, breathe like my girlfriend had reminded me before I left Connecticut. In the parking garage, we plopped into Robert's car. He lit a cigarette, rolled down his window, and blew hard.

"Yeah," he said, "me and Daddy were riding to the produce market and he was going on about how cousin Jack got a TV for refereeing football for such and such years, and I said, 'Good, he can hook the wires to his ears and say, Nigger, nigger, nigger.'" Robert pulled his chin in to imitate Daddy's deep Mississippi drawl. "He goes, 'What the hell you talking about, son?' and I go, 'The N-word's all he says,' and Daddy says, 'Your brother's putting all that nonsense in your head. You don't watch out, he's gone take you to hell with him.'"

Daddy is a loving, generous man, a master storyteller, my friend, and a father who still sometimes calls me "Sugar," but lately, every time I came home, he hit me with his old fears that I was damned, that the country was falling apart, that Muslims were out to kill us, that blacks were still the root of many problems.

"Here's the good part," Robert said. "I say to him, 'I don't remember the Book of N in the Bible,' and he looks at me and goes, 'What's wrong with you?' and I go, 'That's all you good Christians say is 'N-this and N-that. Where's that in the Bible?'" Robert flicked ash out his window, fumbled with one of the several refilled water bottles in the car and took a swig. "He gives me that old, 'It was different when I was growing up,' and I say, 'I grew up with y'all saying it around me all the time. How's that different?' 'It's different,' he says. So I say, 'How many you ever had shoot at you? When I was a cop, I had blacks shoot at me and I don't go around saying the N-word all the time.' He shakes his head and goes, 'Well, you sure turned around. I remember how you was. You don't do nothing Tim don't say.'" Robert pointed his cigarette at me and grinned. "So it's all your fault. You made me think about not saying it and now you got me pointed at hell."

I was proud of Robert. One weekend fifteen years earlier, Robert had been throwing the N-word around in front of my band mates, and when I told him it bothered me, he cockily asked them if it bothered them too. They all said yes. His face fell. Soon after, he stopped saying it. Robert on the road to Damascus.

We ramped onto I-10 near where in the mid-eighties I'd taught at a mostly black, solidly middle-class high school. Weekends I'd sung in punk/new wave and post-punk bands, pissed off at everybody but my students, alienated by Reagan and the attitudes of men I'd grown up around and emulated.

"You got your outfit picked for the reunion?" I asked. "I don't want you looking sloppy like you did at the twentieth."

"You're just jealous how pretty I am. I ain't wearing a tie, though. Like a tourniquet on your throat. Yek."

At the previous reunion, Robert had worn a nametag on which I'd written "Asshole." As always, he was a hit. He'd graduated seven years before me, two years after our oldest brother, Alan, but he knew a lot of the people from my high school days because he'd been a cop then.

We cruised along the raised interstate, the Mississippi hidden behind the Exxon refinery and the chemical plants to our right. I peered left toward our old neighborhood a mile distant, now inhabited almost completely by African-Americans. Our most successful neighbors had been cops, state employees, and plant workers like Daddy. Others struggled to get by. The street itself was so low that hard rains rose in the road and up into the yard, twice so high that water slipped beneath the front door and across our living room floor, warping the wood. After the storms, my friends and I waded through the dark oily floods, our eyes scanning for fire ants riding leaves and for whirlpools from the drains our parents warned would suck us under. When the floodwater was deep enough, people paddled flat-bottomed bateaus down the street. Once, a bass boat motored past sending its wake against our front door, causing Alan to scream curses from the porch until they throttled back. But still, for a while, our street had seemed a small, calm island.

I glanced at the refinery again, a place that still mesmerized me. As a kid, from the bunk above Robert, I'd watched the flare stacks spit flame, the fat burn-off clouds pulsing salmon on the horizon. Very young I'd turned the fires symbolic. By age seven, the flames conjured the approaching apocalypse and holy war our pastor invoked at least every fourth Sunday. Later they were the threat of blacks moving toward our neighborhood and the war that sent Robert overseas. Still later they were the terror, malice, and violence that saturated me after I was attacked and stalked.

"Look," Robert said, and pointed. A thick white cloud billowed from a stack and drifted across the road. My nostrils and eyes stung like the time Robert had maced me as a joke. We coughed and laughed. "Benzene," Robert said. "Breathe a good lungful. Visit Louisiana and leave a lung."

June 2006

We hit the curve past low, gray Memorial Stadium where I'd played and watched football and where I'd been in my first race riot. "I want to walk from our old house to Prescott Junior while I'm home," I said.

Robert spit smoke and coughed. "Are you crazy?"

"I want to walk it."

"Prescott Mohican Crossover is crack central killing zone."

"Nothing's going to happen if we go during the day."

"Bullshit."

On my trip home the previous summer, he and I had strolled around our old elementary school ground, still bucolic land shaded by huge oaks. But Prescott was a quarter mile in the opposite direction from our old house. "You really think somebody'd mess with us?" I asked.

"Two white guys walking in that neighborhood, they'll think we're either trying to buy drugs or figure they can take some money off us. Why you wanta walk that?"

"I've been thinking about Dyer and Jarreau and all that crazy shit after I fought Lassiter. I wanted to walk past where I fought him again."

"Huh. I ain't thought about all that in years."

"The reunion's got me thinking about Dyer."

"He wasn't in your class, was he?"

"A year ahead."

"You think he'll show?"

"I doubt it. It's just got me churned up."

Robert flicked his smoke out the window. "Well, you better call for some go-gettin' jets if you wanta walk that."

Through a low-grade depression, I'd been imagining the walk for weeks. For some reason I needed to cross the parking lot where Lassiter's knife had come out and punctured my sense of safety, where the older Jarreau had risen as a menace and truly began my tumble into terror and rage. But I knew what Robert was saying was true. Two people had been murdered in separate events in our childhood home. Even if nobody messed with us, the walk would be hot, tense, and unpleasant rather than clarifying.

"I guess we could just ask Daddy if he wants to drive by and see the old house," I said.

"That'll work. Now how 'bout we eat."

I nodded and stared straight ahead. I'd just begun writing this book, 9/11 and the war in Iraq having triggered emotions I'd tried to bury for years. I'd begun the book thinking my own story could explain the country's mindset in following Bush to war, but I knew not long after I'd started that it was still mainly my story, a story about what fear made me, made us, do. As a kid I had gotten scared and looked to a brute to protect me, looked for some convenient other to vilify and attack in order to regain a sense of security and masculinity. My whole life I'd heard the yearning for a holy war, for apocalypse, and had wrestled with my own yearning for them, for the clarity of them. And as the Bush administration used fear and jingoism to take us to Babylon, the memories of my own fear, racism, and struggle to prove myself a man came up like glass swallowed decades before. I couldn't simply spit it out. I had to try and chew it into shape.

Book One: Fear

1958–1966: The Family Backdrop

My daddy sailed into Nagasaki Bay a month after the bomb. He only told me once about being loaded into a truck bed and driven with other sailors through the flattened wasteland of rubble and dazed Japanese. I think it was because he didn't like the sadness and vulnerability exposed by telling that story. What he liked to tell was the part about two Japanese men rowing up in a small boat and pointing a tiny cannon at Daddy's destroyer. "We yelled and waved our arms at 'em to go on till they went," he drawled, his storyteller's smirk on his face. "They rowed on over to a big old carrier and then a battleship and all over all day, pointing that itty bitty cannon, till they just give up and went on back to shore." As with most of his stories, he delivered this one with irony that provided some distance from the dismal futility, focusing on the laughable absurdity. But no matter what the subject matter or tone, darkness and conflicted emotions from whatever source—fatigue from plant work; worry over the future; Christian guilt—often underpinned his telling.

Daddy grew up on a Depression-era farm in Mississippi, the son of a volatile man who used a razor strop on his boys whenever they "gave him nonsense." Daddy's skin was dark from years of work in the sun and from the Cherokee blood in his background. He was thin with sinewy arms, high cheekbones, black hair, and brown eyes that glinted with intensity. When he worried we would turn out wrong, he took a belt to our behinds, but his unreadable sternness and unclear expectations were much worse. And yet the stories defined him, self-deprecating stories about courage, revenge, character, defiance, and mischief: the story of loosening the band on an insufferable supervisor's hard hat so that when he plopped it onto his head it dropped over his eyes; the story of Daddy popping his own kneecap back into place during a high school football game; the story of Daddy and another plant operator rescuing a coworker knocked out by phosgene gas; the story from his first day in chow line on a new ship. In the latter story, he had been working on Midway and was dressed in a nonstandard camouflage uniform when the server refused to give him any potatoes. "Feller kept on smartassing me how I wasn't gone get none, so I just reached over and grabbed his collar and snatched him across that counter. I said, '*Boy, you best give me some taters fore I whup your ass.*'" Daddy laughed and held his flat belly. "He started going, 'Yes, sir, yes sir,' and give me a big old heap. Word went around I was some kinda commando 'cause of them camouflage clothes and I got all the taters I wanted after that." How could I see him as scared?

Before I was old enough to understand, he had switched us to a country church twenty miles outside of town. The Southern Baptist pastor in the church two blocks from our house had suggested that the church take a vote on whether blacks should be allowed to attend, and even though no blacks yet lived within a mile of our church, and none would have tried to come, just the consideration drove Daddy away. If work allowed, he went to church three times a week. He returned thanks to Jesus before every meal, read the Bible often, and demanded we be good Christians so we wouldn't burn in hell. How then to make Christian sense of his worry about "niggers taking our neighborhood" and his saying that black "agitators" should be shot dead in the street? When footage of blacks being bitten by dogs and hosed and beaten by police came on TV, his rage heated the room almost as if *he* were inflicting the punishment. Worst of all, although I wouldn't realize it until much later, he was something close to glad when the Kennedys were assassinated and said of Martin Luther King that he was faking his death and would rise in three days saying he was the new black Christ.

And yet he would also tell the racially contradictory story about his train trip home from the war, one of the stories that didn't often emerge from his repertoire. His journey from the Pacific had brought him back to California, and from there he and thousands of other returning servicemen were loaded onto a giant train that would travel for days across the southwest, Texas, Louisiana and on, dropping Daddy and the other Mississippians not far from home. The lightness and joy fell away when he told this story, his voice growing serious. "We heard they's beating Jews and niggers at the other end of the train—this was a long train—but we hadn't seen none of that in our cars. About the third day these nigger boys showed up in our car where they wasn't supposed to be and they was scared to death. They was going, 'They's beatin' people bad back there and they's workin' their way down heah.'" His impersonation of their accent was heavy. "They was four of 'em, just old farm hands from Mississippi like us, so we put 'em up in our bunks, even let 'em sleep in there with us, head to foot while these sonsabitches kept going up and down the aisle all night asking if we'd seen any niggers. When we got to Jackson, them boys got off and they was going, 'Thank you, sirs, thank you, thank you.'"

I didn't comprehend the fearful roots of his fury, but I sensed the contradictions in him as a hum in my subconscious. It was this contradiction between being a man with an urge toward race violence and being a tolerant Christian that would eventually be my struggle.

Alan, my oldest brother by nine years, started a riot during a basketball game in the paper mill town of Bogalusa. None of our family was there, but Alan's teammates and an aunt and uncle who had driven over from Mississippi confirmed the story. Alan had been a chubby kid who shot up to be a six-foot-five, two-twenty menace on the basketball court. He wasn't a good player until he graduated from high school, but he could rough up just about any other big man and intimidate opponents as a rebounder until he quickly fouled out. In Bogalusa, Alan was getting ready to shoot a free throw when an opposing guard clapped his hands behind Alan's head. Alan spun and decked him. Other opponents charged him, but as soon as they came within reach of his long arms, he poled them too. Then the fans attacked. "They were running toward us in their street shoes," Alan said, "so when they tried to stop they started sliding and we busted their asses." The packed gym continued to rush Alan, his street-tough teammates, and their former Golden Gloves coach. The Istrouma team clustered together like a Roman war turtle, lashing out as they moved toward the locker room. "I finally rared back and this hand grabbed my wrist. I went to hit him with my other fist and it was this big state trooper who said, 'Get in that locker room, son.' The amazing thing is we went in and started wiping off all this blood and none of it was ours."

As the oldest, Alan caught the brunt of Daddy's moods and discipline during the lean days of unsteady employment or working two jobs. Alan was ultra-conservative and ultra-successful academically, but like Robert (whom we called Olan until he came home from Vietnam) and me, he dreaded Daddy's disapproval. Still, he rebelled. One night when he was in high school, he came home after curfew. Olan and I were in our bunk beds and heard Daddy meet him at the front door. "What I tell you about being late?" Daddy said. Alan began to explain, but Daddy told him he didn't want to hear it. I leaned over the edge of my bunk to see Olan's grinning face. "He's gonna get it," he said gleefully. We heard the whack of the belt, Alan's yelp, and footsteps as Daddy chased him. They careened into our room from the short hallway, then into the kitchen, back into the living room, down the hall, and into our room again. Olan and I were both propped up, laughing. Daddy stopped and shook the belt at us. "Y'all want some of this?" "No, sir," we said and lay flat, still giggling. We reveled in Alan's misery because Daddy's anger had filtered through Alan down to Olan. Alan bullied him, sometimes forcing Olan and his friends to box each other in the front yard or else be bloodied by Alan. Olan also thought that Alan condescended to him and made fun of his average grades.

Mostly, though, Alan turned his feelings and his energy toward overachieving in academics and school politics. He had a need to prove himself smarter than everyone else, and he studied extra to show up his teachers. Once when Alan was in junior high, Daddy told me, he and Momma were called to the principal's office to meet with a veteran history teacher. She started crying during their meeting. "I don't know what to do," she said. "He's smarter than me and he humiliates me in every class." Alan got Daddy's belt for that, but it didn't seem to faze him. He laughed easily, charmed people, and was as nice and supportive as someone so preoccupied could be. But I always felt bossed around and impatient when he tried to help me with my math homework or he told me to shine his shoes for a quarter or wash and wax his car for a dollar and gave me strict instructions on how to do it, then criticized my work and made me redo it. Nonetheless, Alan wanted to protect me, even if the message of that became jumbled.

For class in third grade, I'd put together a Revolutionary War battle scene on a snowy field made of flour. That morning Momma had driven me to school to make sure the wind didn't blow the snow and coat my soldiers in white, but that afternoon she was at work at J. C. Penney's. I walked with my friends across the large playground, carrying the display like a cigarette girl's tray. The low-sided rectangular box Daddy had built was unwieldy no matter how I held it. At the street corner stood a big, red-headed, sixth-grade patrol boy, his white belt diagonal across his chest like a bandolier, his flag held like a rifle on his shoulder. He stopped us with the flag and sneered, "Aw, he's got his little men." He lowered the tip of the flag beneath the edge of my box and flipped it. The flour exploded upward into my face. I bent at the waist, coughing, and shook my head. I dropped the box and brushed at my eyes until I could see. I was white all the way down my front. The kid doubled over laughing. My friends glanced between the patrol boy and me. Normally they would've laughed, but I think they were stunned that this big kid we didn't even know, and a patrol boy no less, had gone after me. I thought for a second about going after him, but his size intimidated me. I knelt, collected my plastic soldiers from the ground, and piled them into the box. The patrol boy stepped into the street, his face bright red from laughter, and gestured with his head for us to cross.

When I walked into the house, I caught sight of myself in the mirror on the living room wall. I looked like a white raccoon, my head coated except for where I'd brushed the flour from my eyes. It was exactly the kind of joke that Olan and I loved from the Three Stooges, and it would have struck me as funny if the big stranger hadn't done it. I looked away. "What happened to you?" Alan said from the kitchen table. My ears heated. I hadn't seen him, and I didn't want to tell him what had happened since I hadn't fought back. He stood. "I said what happened?"

"The patrol boy knocked this box in my face."

Alan shoved his chair back. He grabbed a rag from the kitchen counter and nudged me toward the door. "Let's go."

"I want to clean my—"

"No, *he's* gonna clean it. Put that box and your book sack down."

We didn't speak as we tromped the short block to school, his hand lightly on my back, both comforting me and pushing me along. My cheeks were so hot it felt as if the flour might bake, but I didn't say anything. When we were about fifteen yards away, the patrol boy's flag drooped to the ground. Alan moved up close and placed me between him and the kid. "You do this to my little brother?"

"Yes, sir," the patrol boy said, his voice shaky.

Alan produced the kitchen rag and held it out. "Wipe it off."

"Sir?"

"*Wipe it off.*" I cringed then looked down when I caught the terror and embarrassment in the kid's eyes. He took the rag and hesitated. "Wipe it." He gently cleaned my forehead, my eyes, my cheeks, and my neck. Then he brushed at my shirt, my skin shrinking from him. "That's enough," Alan finally said, and the kid's hand fell to his side. "I oughta do something like this to you," Alan said. "Would you like that?"

"No, sir."

"I'll bet you wouldn't. Listen here, if you do anything like this to him again, I *will* do something."

"Yes, sir."

"Now tell him you're sorry. Look at him, Timmy." Alan laid his hands on my shoulders. I forced myself to meet the kid's eyes, teary and squinched.

"I'm sorry."

"Good," Alan said and took the rag back. "Let's go home."

The short block back to the house seemed like a mile. Alan's long legs stretched so that I had to stretch to keep up. "You got to learn to take up for yourself," he said. "You can tell me if it's somebody who's not your size, but you still got to take care of yourself. You understand?"

I nodded. I understood. No matter what the size of someone picking on me, if I didn't fight back, I was weak and cowardly. Understood that humiliation was worse than any physical pain.

From the time he was a kid, Robert Olan wanted to be a cop. As Robert the Adult, he would have as reasons the desire for power and for approval from Daddy, but as Olan the Kid the original catalyst came from the TV channel Times, Tunes, and Cartoons, which provided exactly what it promised, plus news bulletins. One night while he was watching, a bulletin went out for all Baton Rouge Police to report to duty immediately because, as Robert remembers, a flying saucer had landed. It turned out the saucer was actually a chemical plant pop-off valve that had been blown a number of blocks into someone's yard when the pressure in a pipe had gotten too high. But what had actually happened didn't matter to Olan. All that mattered to him was the men with guns, badges, and uniforms were the first called to the most exciting event on Earth.

Olan lived in Alan's shadow. When he arrived for classes taught by the same teachers Alan had two years before, they would ask if he was like his brother. Olan didn't know if they meant the brilliant student or the troublemaking bully. Either way he didn't want to be like him, so he didn't know what to say, something that must have made him feel invisible. At school he was a shy, skinny kid who wore thick black-rimmed glasses to correct his terrible eyesight and wrote with his left hand, which made his intelligence suspect in the late fifties and the early sixties.

Despite Olan's being seven years older than I was, we were allied in all things. On Saturday mornings we got up early together, poured bowls of Cheerios and watched *The Three Stooges*. When they were replaced by *The Mickey Mouse Club*, Olan created a petition that expressed our hatred of Mickey and the Mouseketeers and our strong desire to have the Stooges reinstated. He enlisted some of his friends and me to sign it, but he also forged a number of signatures in his scrawly hand before he sent it off to "Walt Disney Company, Hollywood, California." Several weeks went by, and one day while Olan, Momma and I were visiting our relatives just north of town, the phone rang. "Rachel, it's Hollis," Aunt Evelyn said. Momma took the phone, raised her eyebrows and lifted her hand to her throat as she listened. "All right, we'll come right on home." She hung up and looked at Olan. "Your daddy says there are some men at our house from Walt Disney."

Olan glanced at me, his face stricken. "They're at the house?" he asked. "With Daddy?"

She nodded. "Did you write some kind of letter?"

Olan didn't say much on our way home, but I was exultant. We'd defied the intrusion of the saccharine Mouse Clubbers and had forced a showdown with the company. Olan and Momma didn't appear to share my enthusiasm.

Olan trudged from the car to the living room, where Daddy met him with a grimace. Two men in suits stood from the couch as we came in. "This is Gordon Ogden," Daddy said. "He owns the Gordon Theatre. This man is a lawyer from the Disney Company. They tell me you wrote a letter and some kind of petition." I stepped up close behind Olan, hoping he would tell them off, demand that justice be done, even though Daddy's scowl and the bizarreness of Disney men in suits visiting our house was straightening my spine.

"Yes, sir," Olan said. "I wrote it."

Mr. Ogden smiled. "We'd like to talk to you."

Daddy gave Olan a look that told him he was going to get it for pulling a stunt like this.

We all sat down to talk as if Olan actually posed some threat to the Mouseketeers. "Tell us exactly what your complaint is," Mr. Ogden said. Olan cleared his throat, adjusted his glasses, then in a shaky voice laid out the silliness of the *Mouse* show and the virtues of the Stooges. I was impressed at his honesty in the presence of Daddy's simmer and the unknown retribution of a lawyer and movie theatre owner, and I nodded along until Daddy gave me a look too. The two men listened without much expression until Olan finished. They exchanged smirks.

Mr. Ogden leaned forward. "Olan, we think *The Mickey Mouse Club* is a fine show. We believe the Mouseketeers are exactly the sort of wholesome young people America needs as examples. The reason we're here is that we hope you'll give the show a chance."

"We admire your get-up-and-go," the lawyer said, "though we're disappointed that it seems you faked some of the names on the petition." He paused. Olan didn't look at Daddy, but we could all feel the heat coming off of him, could anticipate the skinny belt coming out of its loops. "That said, we would like you to work for us at the theatre this summer. Until then, we're willing to pay you to watch the Mouseketeers and write a brief summary of the show and the commercials. All you have to do is send it to us on these stamped envelopes we'll give you."

Mr. Ogden smiled. "We think you'll see what a fine organization the Disney family is."

Daddy glared at Olan. "Yes, sir," Olan said, and took the envelopes from the lawyer.

Everyone stood. "Do you like *The Mickey Mouse Club*?" he asked me. Daddy cleared his throat.

"Yes, sir." The lawyer reached into his brief case, brought out some large red, blue, and yellow pieces of plastic. "We'd like you to have these," he said, and handed them to me. Stencils of Donald Duck, Goofy, and the hated Mouse himself. Mr. Ogden and the lawyer shook everybody's hand, including mine, told us he'd be in touch about the job, and left.

"You do anything like that again," Daddy said to Olan, "I'll tan your hide." He pointed at me. "Yours too." We nodded and went to our room.

Olan plopped onto his bottom bunk, the envelopes still in his grip. I looked at the stencils. "These are crummy," I said, and threw them across the room

Olan didn't speak. I sat next to him on his bunk, but he didn't look at me.

"You think you'll get free popcorn?" I asked.

"Daddy would've like it if Alan did it," he said. Expressions of sadness, anguish, then anger scrolled across his face. His eyes snapped onto the envelopes as if he'd just realized they were there. He tossed them to the floor.

Like Alan, Olan didn't excel at school sports, but he was determined that I was going to be a great player like LSU's Heisman Trophy winner, Billy Cannon, who had gone to our high school and whom I worshipped. Olan and I loved football, but I suspect that beyond football he wanted to somehow make me strong and impervious to criticism by making me into an athlete. By the time I was three, he was tossing me the football in the backyard. By the time I was seven, I was running patterns and making difficult catches, ducking beneath the lopsided, circular clothesline and button-hooking just as the ball hit my stomach. The most difficult route was from one end of the yard to the other. I would run hard on a line and cut behind the pin oak just as he hurled the ball toward the corner where I was heading. Behind the tree I would lose sight of the ball, but because Olan was accurate, I always knew where it would be in the air. He taught me to never take my eyes off the ball and I would keep going full blast toward the corner choked with snapped bamboo saplings and torn vines, would jump and flatten out, the ball dropping into my outstretched hands as I landed and rolled through the foliage and up against the chain-link fence. I'd toss the ball back to him and we'd do it over and over for hours, me in my Houston Oilers Billy Cannon helmet, he in his Johnny Unitas Baltimore Colts helmet. He always encouraged and taught me as he molded me. He gave me a confidence and arrogance as a ball player that most kids around me didn't have, as well as a toughness that later kept me going half a season with a badly swollen knee and all the way through a championship game the day after I'd literally split my nose down its center and blackened both my eyes running into the edge of a brick wall. I thought of myself as special, nearly invincible, and ironically I think that belief made my fall even harder when I became fully afraid.

But church would be the main engine of, first, our bonding, and then our anxiety and dread. We didn't talk about it, but we loved Jesus and his promise of protection, salvation, and acceptance. I saw the seriousness Olan carried into church, saw him publicly rededicate his life to Christ several times when he felt he'd sinned or, I suppose, felt lost and unappreciated. No matter what we did or how we thought we'd failed, Christ was there to forgive without criticism. We saw him as pure and unchanging. We saw baptism as a way of literally washing away our sins and restoring perfection. Olan believed so strongly that he asked to be baptized a second time when he thought he'd failed Jesus. And when he thought he'd failed Daddy.

The darker messages haunted me, and Olan too, I think. Sunday school highlighted Jesus's benevolence, but the main services painted horrifying visions of hell, with its agony of eternal thirst so intense that a person would beg for a single drop of water and only receive reminders of their sins on Earth, sins that were equally bad whether committed or simply considered. Olan and I weren't sophisticated enough to mock this vision, had no way to distance ourselves from its hatefulness and sadism, and so it saturated us. I also believed that in order to have Jesus's protection and forgiveness, I had to accept the possibility of his Father's wrath.

Deepening my anxiety, our pastor pounded the message that until people turned eight (the youngest age at which one was allowed to join the church), they were safe from hell. Nonetheless, I lay awake at night as young as five and worried the pastor was wrong. I wondered if I might be allowed to be baptized early. I literally shook when the invitation to accept Jesus Christ as my personal savior came at the end of services and I wasn't allowed to go. On top of that, our church's favorite text was the book of Revelation, and even though I loved Godzilla, Mothra, Rhodan, giant tarantulas, and the other fare of B-monster movies, the horror-show images of horses with breastplates of fire, the heads of lions, and the tails of serpents killing a third of humankind permeated my nightmares. These things weren't fantasy; they were the inevitable.

Even worse was the perversion of Christ, whom I understood would become a warrior in a battle in which blood rose as high as a horse's bridle, a battle that seemed to loom closer and closer with the war growing in Vietnam, with the bear in Revelation representing the Soviet Union, and with unrest in the Middle East. Our church seemed to revel in the prospect of the apocalypse, and for me, and Olan too, I now know, the only way to avoid damnation and resist the fear seemed to be to fight against the unholy intruders—Communists and Muslims, and eventually blacks.

On April 2, 1966, Olan and I thumped the paper football back and forth across the kitchen table, Olan keeping score on a wrinkled piece of paper. An explosion in the distance vibrated our windows. We froze. Alan's feet clomped down the short hall, then Olan and I sprang up and joined him and Momma in a circle in the living room. "Esso?" Momma asked. Daddy was at work thirty miles away at Wyandotte Chemicals, but any plant explosion sent panic through us because we knew men at all of them. The three of them gave each other concerned glances, but I felt mostly excitement. Alan pushed through the front door and we clustered in the yard. We peered toward the river and the plants, where the sky was no brighter with fire than usual.

"The Russians?" Olan asked.

Alan sneered. "You see a mushroom cloud, stupid?"

"It's nighttime."

"You can see a nuclear bomb at night."

"How would you know?"

"I know, dummy."

"Shut up," Olan said.

"You shut up," Alan said.

"Boys," Momma said, still staring, her knuckles pressed to her lips.

Next door, Mr. and Mrs. Goudeau and their five daughters spread out onto the driveway.

"What y'all think it is?" Momma asked them.

"Got to be a plant," Mr. Goudeau said in his thick Cajun accent.

"Times, Tunes, and Cartoons will say," Olan said, disgust at Alan still in his voice. Olan spun, stomped to the house and slammed the door behind him. I thought of joining him in a show of solidarity, but there was too much going on outside.

"It wouldn't be Cuba, would it?" Momma asked.

"There's *no mushroom cloud!*" Alan said. He crossed his arms, adjusted his glasses and looked straight up between the canopies of trees in our front yard. The night hung quiet except for police sirens now whooping. I thought of walking the few steps over and talking to Sherry and the other Goudeau girls but stayed next to Momma. I wished Daddy were there, pointing out satellites like he sometimes did, stars that moved across the sky and didn't twinkle like real stars.

The air and ground jolted. We crouched. The sound rolled around on us before traveling along and dying like thunder. Olan crashed through the door and back outside to join us. We peered away from the river now. "Howell Park," Momma said. I pictured the old jet fighter we climbed on near the pool and wondered if it had somehow blown up. Our other next-door neighbor tore from his house in his police uniform, still buckling his gun belt. Momma called to him what was going on, but he jumped into his car and screeched off without answering.

"The windows almost busted out," Olan said.

"They musta blown up the pool," Alan said, his lips a dazed half-smile. "I heard Mr. Bowman say they might." Mr. Bowman was the local Boy Scout leader, and, although I didn't know it yet, the head of the local Klan.

"He did?" Momma said.

"Yep."

"The swimming pool?" I asked. Nobody said anything.

The next morning Daddy came from work wearing a bemused smirk, newspaper in hand. He kissed Momma and sat at the kitchen table with her and me. Alan and Olan walked in, Alan buttoning his shirt, Olan holding a toothbrush. "They blew up the building at Howell and tried to blow up Webb," Daddy said. "I figured it'd happen once they let the niggers in. I heard some of them Klan fools at the Boy Scout meeting say something last week."

"I told y'all," Alan said.

Daddy frowned and pointed. "Don't nobody say a word about that to nobody. Y'all go on get ready for school."

"I wanta go see," Olan said.

"Y'all get dressed," Momma said.

Alan and Olan slumped and trudged off. Momma poured Daddy a cup of coffee and went over to scramble eggs and fry patty sausage.

The Baton Rouge Recreation and Park Commission had closed the city pools two years before, right around the time the federal government had ordered them to be integrated. The previous week, BREC had voted to reopen them, but I hadn't gotten excited about returning. Daddy had made it clear that none of us would be going.

"Was it loud?" Daddy asked, glancing at Momma and me.

"We heard both of them," Momma said. "We were in the yard when we heard Howell Park."

"What'd you think, Timmy?"

"I thought that jet blew up."

Daddy chuckled and sipped his coffee. "I know a old boy who

works over there. Maybe we'll go look at it after school. You wanta go, Momma?"

"I don't think so." She and I had often gone to the pool together during summers, and she had been sad when it closed, not outraged like Daddy over the reason it had to be closed. She came over and scooped eggs onto his plate. He set the newspaper at her place and tapped the article on the front page. She sat down and stared at the words with her hands in her lap.

"They ought not even fix it," Daddy said. "Federal government'll probably come in here and charge us extra."

Daddy may have known an old boy, but the police cordoned off the entire park for two days. Howell was a half-mile from our house, but when we finally were able to go, the drive seemed as far away as Mississippi, where most of our relatives lived. We turned onto the lane that ran between the oak-shaded playground and the public golf course clubhouse. The red brick dressing room for the pool lay a ways from us, but the damage was obvious, half of the building collapsed to a pile. For the past two days I had imagined the pool itself having had all of its water blown out like cartoon water and not the destruction of the pool house. I had trouble comprehending it.

"They *used* some dynamite," Daddy said. We parked with a handful of other cars and stepped out to join the several oglers. A policeman stood talking to some people and I followed Daddy over to him while my brothers went up close to the rope that kept people away from the scene. Daddy walked up to the big cop, who stood on the other side of the rope. "Y'all making sure nobody sneaks in for a dip?" Daddy asked. The cop harrumphed. "They done a number on it, didn't they."

"Looks like it," the cop said.

"They shoulda known it'd happen when they let 'em in."

"I 'spose." He looked Daddy up and down. "Didn't catch you by surprise?"

Daddy's expression went flat. "I was out working." He turned and strode away. "Smart aleck," he said.

We went over next to Alan, Olan, and some others who were

gawking. "Pickaninnies won't be swimming here a while," a woman said to us.

"Too bad they did it at night," the man with her said.

Daddy shook his head and whistled. "Maybe this'll put a stop to some of this integration nonsense. Better off this way."

Alan pointed at the exposed lockers, benches, and bricks heaped and scattered before us, explaining to a disinterested Olan how the dynamite had worked. I tried to put it all back together in my mind. Many a time I had changed into my bathing suit and showered off the chlorine water here. The shallow foot wash at the exit to the building always had colder water than the pool, and I enjoyed the tingle it gave my feet before and after I swam. I wondered if it had survived.

I strolled a little ways from my daddy and brothers so I could see past the debris to the pool. I'd missed swimming there. I'd liked not only the chilly water but the energy of so many people and how my mother relaxed when she sunned in a lounge chair. The pool was still blue, but drained of water. I remembered doing cannonballs off the low board, dunking my friends, screaming without a thought. I missed it. Something I loved was gone. Taken by the niggers, I thought, blown apart because of the niggers.

1969: Pyrrhic Victories

Our pastor Brother Toms dabbed at his glistening, pink forehead and bald dome with a white handkerchief. Flanked by the American and Southern Baptist flags at the front of our small, unadorned church, he had just finished the invitation to accept Christ after a rousing sermon that invoked everlasting torment and ended with a prayer to protect our boys in Vietnam as they battled the enemies of God. Brother Toms was mild compared to our previous preacher, Brother Lamb, an older man with a shock of white hair straight out of a movie version of God, a man whose fervor for hell's torments had carried a fetishistic, almost sexual dimension. Not that I had thought that way three years earlier when I answered the call, went down front, and was baptized two weeks later. At eight, I had been the youngest person ever to join our church. Now I sat awaiting Brother Toms's unusual post-sermon announcement.

He gripped the sides of the pulpit and leaned toward the congregation of eighty or so. "Next Sunday after the service, there will be a special meeting of church members to vote on whether Negroes will be allowed to attend should they ever come here." He mopped at his forehead again. "Some may wonder why we as Christians would hold such a vote. We hold it because many members have expressed concern that Negroes may come, and even though I am told that there was a similar vote that carried unanimously against their attending before I came here, some members insist we revisit the matter."

In the tiny choir loft behind Brother Toms, Daddy scowled. I knew how he would vote. He was my guide in all things racial, but at ten going on eleven, I squirmed, the Sunday school lyrics to "Jesus Loves the Little Children" alive in me. I glanced at Momma's pale profile and high blonde bouffant, and she turned and smiled, her eyes bright blue. Then I looked to Olan on my other side, a high school senior, his arms sullenly crossed as they had been the entire service because Daddy had made him sit with us as punishment. Alan I couldn't check because he was at his girlfriend's Methodist church.

Brother Toms said another prayer seeking God's guidance in the vote and dismissed us. As we shuffled down the aisle, Momma put her hands on my shoulders. Olan strode through the crowd to catch up with the Dumas girls before Daddy could shed his choir robe and pile us all into the Ford Galaxie 500. By this time I would usually be chattering to Momma or my friends, but as we moved along the covered walkway, I studied the younger men with high pompadours and cheap black suits already lighting cigarettes—something Daddy said was sinful—and grumbling about integration. Some of the older ladies, with blue hair piled high, strolled in a cluster. One of them talked about how she'd heard of "Nigras coming to churches just to agitate," her voice as strident as her off-key caterwauling during hymns. Ahead, Olan talked to the beautiful sisters in their short skirts, his hands gesticulating until Momma touched him on the arm, he snorted, and we headed to the back lot where our car was parked on the grass. He refused to take the front seat when Momma offered it. In a minute Daddy flopped in behind the wheel.

"That preacher ain't got no sense," he said as he cranked the car. "Ain't no need to vote on that again. He's only voting 'cause he thinks he can get his say in." Daddy had said before that he thought Brother Toms was a liberal and had even wondered if the pastor was an atheist.

"I'm voting to let 'em in," Olan said, slumped and looking out the window. A tremor went through me.

"You what?" Daddy said.

"Niggers don't even live around here."

"They living in Glen Oaks. They coming in there just like they coming toward our street."

"That's miles from here. Anyway, they got a right to go to church, just like you. Doesn't Jesus say to accept everybody?" Olan winked at me to let me know he was needling Daddy.

"This ain't about Jesus," Daddy said. "They come to white churches just to start trouble."

"You don't know why they come. They ain't started any trouble at my school. They're the ones get beat up."

"'Cause they's just a few. You wait till there's a swarm."

"Y'all stop," Momma said.

Daddy pointed at Olan in the rearview. "Your big brother wouldn't vote to let 'em in."

"Another good reason *to* let 'em in."

"I said enough," Momma said. "Let's have a nice ride home."

"Yeah, nice," Olan said.

Olan was in his last several months of high school and hadn't taken well to Daddy's punishment of having to ride to church with us instead of with his friends and fellow sinners. His crime had occurred two weeks earlier during Brother Toms's Wednesday night Training Union sermon. Daddy was working the three-till-eleven shift and wasn't there, and Olan and his friends, Amodee and the preacher's son, hadn't shown up for the service either. I was sitting midway back in the church when I heard the outside door to the choir room slam and then giggling and shushing. The door through which the choir entered was at the front near the pulpit and baptismal tank, the door's bottom half made of louvered metal slats for ventilation. The giggling died down, and after a moment, three faces appeared close together through the vent, snickering and pointing, evidently drunk and under the impression that they could not be seen or heard in the auditorium. I covered my mouth to keep from laughing. In the front row, the preacher's wife waited a minute, probably hoping they would leave, before she stood and stalked out the back. I held my breath until I heard the outside door to the choir room open again. The trio's heads turned and disappeared from the vent. There was terse whispering and the closing of the heavy door once more. Through the closed side window of the church came scolding. I'd thought Olan would get the belt once we got home, but he didn't. Instead, he was grounded for three weeks.

He was angry at Daddy's punishment, of course, as he had been at Daddy's constant criticism of his hair and his running around and his grades and his lack of planning for college, but he also seemed stricken by what he'd done. His moods went back and forth. Olan napped and zoned out, seemed at times almost not to notice Momma or me, then seemed ready to ignite around Daddy and Alan. Over the past two years, tension had been building as Olan physically changed. He had grown to six-two, gotten his silky auburn hair cut in a mop top, exchanged his thick glasses for contacts that highlighted the same blue eyes Momma had, and started lifting weights in the garage. His arms and shoulders thickened and broadened above his thin waist, his outward confidence swelled, and girls flocked. He'd taken an edge with Daddy and Alan when they pushed him on what he was going to do after graduation, and he sniped at Alan about why he didn't move to a dorm room at LSU and give him his room so Olan could move out of the room he and I shared. Something momentous and contentious was also happening between him and his identity, and between him and the church. The contradictions between Jesus's message and the message of our church were clear and maddening.

And yet his punishment brought him closer to me than he'd been in a long while. Afternoons, nights, and weekends when he was home and not burning up the roads with his friends, we played paper football, threw the football in the yard, and played electric football. If we'd known other types of football, we would have played those, too. Olan reminisced. "You remember that electric football set we had that was all dented in the middle? That's 'cause you sat your ass on it when me and Alan were playing, just like you sat on that cool, metal, toy car garage we had. You sat on everything. That garage had three stories and a lift. When you did it I told Momma I wanted to throw you in the river and she went, 'Okay, load him up and let's go.' I went, 'Weeell, I guess we could keep him around for a while.'" For a few weeks he was mine again.

Still, having him around didn't keep me from fretting about the upcoming church vote. He'd said in the car he would vote to let blacks in, but I doubted it was true and was scared to ask him because his answer might confuse me more. Daddy grumbled about Brother Toms, and I steered clear of the topic with him, too. I believed, like Daddy, that blacks would come to cause trouble and take what was ours, believed that a vote to let blacks in would disappoint Daddy, even betray him. But I also believed that Christ would want me to vote to let them in. My vote seemed something I had to work through with prayer, so I prayed hard. No answer came.

Finally, I gave in and asked Momma what she was going to do as she sat watching *The Dean Martin Show*. "I don't know yet, sugar," she said.

"Jesus says to love everybody."

"That's right, but I think Negroes should worship in their own place and have their own part of Heaven."

"You think niggers might try to start a fight at church?"

She laughed and patted my arm. "I don't think so. But you have to decide what you're gone do. You have to do what you think is right." I stared at her as she focused again on her heartthrob. Momma had been the one who accidentally let me know there was something about race going on inside our house that shouldn't be let out. When I was four, she and I had been in line at a department store and I tugged on her arm and said, "Look, Momma, there's a little jigaboo," meaning the black kid directly behind us. Momma's cheeks went red as she met the kid's mother's angry eyes. Momma glanced at the child and said she was sorry, then pulled me out of the store, knelt in front of me on the sidewalk, and gripped my arms. "I know you didn't know better, Timmy, but you don't say things like that outside the house. When we're out, you only say 'Negroes.'"

I got up from the chair and went to my room. Olan was already asleep, and I thought of slapping the soles of his feet or jumping on him to start a wrestling match. Instead, I climbed into my bunk and tried to read a book on former NFL stars. It was no use. Jesus's words warred in my head with Daddy's commentary about black protestors on TV. I imagined my lone raised hand in church and the disapproval from almost everyone around me. I stared at the plastic LSU tiger head on our wall, its marble eyes glinting green with light, then looked out the window at the flames tearing away into the sky by the river.

The church was barbed with emotions throughout the service the following Sunday. I barely listened to the sermon, except to know that it was again the book of Revelation, and a rehashing of the belief that the previous year's Six Day War between Israel and Egypt was the start of the End Time. I knew which way I was going to vote and had been ramping up my courage while trying not to look at Daddy in the choir loft. When the invitation to join Christ came, Olan stood and walked down the aisle, whispered to Brother Toms, and faced us as we finished singing. I was shocked. He had been baptized a second time just two years ago. When the hymn ended and the preacher said that Olan had come forward to rededicate his life to Christ, the expression on Olan's face was a mixture of sadness and determination that I hadn't seen before. Then Olan took a seat in the front pew and the discussion began.

Most of the talk was a repeat of people's worries that blacks would be coming simply to start trouble and force integration, some of the voices brimming with anger. When the discussion ended, the preacher asked for those in favor of allowing blacks to raise their hands. I looked straight ahead at the back of the pew in front of me. I raised my hand, perhaps the most ethical thing I would do for a long time, maybe ever, and something that would soon seem completely alien. Pain knifed through my stomach. Afterward, I lowered my head more so I wouldn't have to see the others vote, but I heard the rustle of arms shooting upward. As church let out, Momma told me she was proud of me. Some people glared and shook their heads. Nothing more was said.

Back at home, the whole family sat at the kitchen table for dinner. I was still nauseous as we served up Momma's roast beef, mashed potatoes, gravy, field peas, and cornbread. Daddy told Olan he had done the right thing to rededicate his life and he hoped that Olan was serious about it. Olan didn't answer. He also didn't begin eating with the competitive ferocity he usually did. After everyone else took several bites, he said, "I'm joining the army." Momma's fork clinked as she lowered it hard to her plate. "Do what?" she asked.

"I talked to the recruiters and y'all have to sign 'cause I'm still seventeen. I'll go in when I turn eighteen."

"You know there's a war going on," Daddy said, his voice flat in a way I couldn't read.

"I'm gonna get drafted anyway, and I ain't going to college."

"Think you can cut it?" Alan asked.

"I can cut it more than you and your little college books."

"You're gonna be a soldier?" I asked, barely able to keep myself in my seat.

He smiled. "Military police."

"They signed you for that?" Momma asked.

"Yes, ma'am. I said that's what I wanted to do, and they said I'd go to Germany or Korea 'cause they need MPs there."

"Son," Daddy said, "they'll send you where they want."

"You don't know that."

Alan said, "I've been thinking of the army reserve when I get out of school."

"Why don't we think about it?" Momma asked, glancing at Daddy.

"I already thought about it," Olan said. "I ain't going to college and I wanta be a cop. I'll be twenty-two when I get out and I'll go straight onto the force."

Everybody sat quietly. I looked between Olan and Daddy, who looked at each other. "Well," Daddy said, "might be good for you.

You ain't got no plans and you barely doing anything in school." He cut his roast, took a bite and focused strangely on his plate as he chewed.

Olan stared at him as if he were waiting for something more, then he leaned in and shoveled potatoes into his mouth.

1970: Shifting Ground

Olan was assigned to Vietnam in the spring, the prelude to the destabilization of almost everything I knew. He'd left for boot camp the previous October, but before then life had been the best for me it had ever been. I had hummed with excitement that my brother was going to be a soldier and that I was someone special in school and sports. That fall, all of Olan's tutoring in the backyard and Daddy's teaching as we watched other games came together. In a league where passing was rare, people called our team the "aerial circus." Most games I threw for touchdowns, sometimes two or three, and I radiated with confidence from running the huddle, telling bigger boys what to do, and passing the ball better than opposing quarterbacks. No matter how tiny the stage, the spotlight puffed me up with Daddy's and my brothers' appreciation, wrapping me in a false sense of invincibility. Then Olan left, and a heaviness settled in the house, especially on Momma, but on Daddy too.

During boot camp, Olan clung to the belief that he was going to be an MP, although his couple of phone calls sounded desperate and miserable. Midway through boot, Momma and I, plus a girl Olan had been briefly seeing before he went in, were allowed to visit him at Fort Polk, a hot, dry camp several hours from Baton Rouge. Olan was buzz cut, thinner and more drawn than when he'd left, his stomach suffering, he told us, from nerves, bad food, and the fifteen minutes they had to eat every meal. He fell like a starved dog on the fried chicken and biscuits Momma brought.

After lunch, he and the girl began making out on the pine needle-covered ground. Olan rolled on top of her, felt her up, and dry-humped her. I was fascinated and disturbed until Momma took me by the hand and we went for a long walk that took us past bayonet dummies and obstacle courses. Her high color and nervous chatter told she was shaken, and I joked and acted silly to try and make her feel better and to clear my own confusion. Eventually, we returned to where Robert and the girl reclined, disheveled, against a tree. We stayed a while longer, then hugged Olan before we left. Momma held his face as though she wouldn't ever let go, until finally he lowered her hands, kissed her and told her, "I'll be all right, Momma." For the first time it struck me that he was going to be gone for a long time. And also that he had already changed.

A few weeks later he was sent to medics' training in San Antonio. He joked on the phone that they must have found out he hated the sight of blood before they assigned him. He struggled with the training, broke his nose in a night drill when he ran into someone, then in late spring called to tell us he was going to Vietnam. Not long after his call, someone dynamited the Louisiana Senate Chamber and part of the Baton Rouge Country Club, setting Daddy off on blacks and Communists. I was proud Olan was going to fight Communists, was relieved that someone was.

He came home before deploying overseas. His first night back, he stood next to the console stereo my parents had stretched their budget to buy. "Sit down. Y'all will get a kick out of this," he said, his grin too wide as he put a record on the turntable. I smiled, eager to take in whatever he gave, despite my parents' tense silence. The needle hit with a thunk and a hiss, and then a man's voice said, "Give me an 'F.' Give me an 'I.'" I grinned as the man spelled out FISH, then launched into the song's circus lead-in. It was the studio version of Country Joe and the Fish's "We're All Gonna Die," so the chant wasn't obscene. Olan smiled at us and sang along about Uncle Sam's needing the help of young men to get him out of a jam. Olan swung his arms and sang how he didn't give a damn what we were fighting for because it was going to be fun. I smiled and tried to sing with him, but his agitation and Momma and Daddy's obvious discomfort were churning in my stomach. Daddy shook his head and glared, and Olan sang more loudly about coming home in a pine box. Daddy stood and said, "That's enough." He went over and turned off the stereo. Olan narrowed his eyes at him and for a second I thought he was going to put the record back on. Daddy

1970: Shifting Ground

dropped into his chair again. "Your Momma and your brother don't need to hear this." Olan glanced furiously back and forth at all of us. "It's a joke," he said, and walked out of the room. He left with his friends a half-hour later. "That boy," Daddy said, and went to the garage.

I woke up with Olan shaking me. "Hey," he said when I came awake, his breath sharp with beer. "Don't you worry. I'm gonna send you some boots for those big feet to match that helmet liner I got you." He grabbed my stomach and started tickling me hard until I was thrashing and we were both laughing. "Shh," he said. "I don't want anymore of the old man tonight, or Alan either." He patted my chest and ducked down into his bunk. I listened to him toss and turn for a long time.

On the first cassette tape he sent home from Chu Lai, he told us about smoke rising from near the airfield as they landed and how he and the other new guys rushed from the plane thinking it was an attack. "Turned out they were just burning a pile of shit," he said. The tape was hilarious and crafted to sound both as if Olan was isolated from combat and that his job unloading wounded from choppers onto his bus to drive them to triage and the hospital was no more serious than driving a city bus. He told us about cleaning latrines and bad army rations, including a brownie that he and his friends threw against the side of a truck hundreds of times before it broke. Momma recorded "beeeeps" over parts to take out some "potty mouth," as she called it, and my teacher let me play the tape for my class. I gloated as my classmates listened to him. He had landed in a safe place, or so I believed, and no one said differently even as my parents and I watched the bodies, the wounded, and the firefights on TV at supper time. Then his letters came in heavily censored by black Marks-A-Lot, the words that survived written in a kind of vague code about an increase in casualties and a different front. We would soon find out that his hospital was taking in wounded from the invasion of Cambodia.

The tapes we sent him back were chatty documents of the everydayness of home, which must have been both comforting and depressing. Momma brought the tape recorder in the car so that she and I could report our progress down local streets ("We're going by Holsum Bread and it smells so good"). She enlisted neighbors like "Papa Goudeau" and "Mama Goudeau," who had two future son-in-laws in 'Nam, and friends to tell what was going on. Alan talked about his excellent grades in college and asked whether Olan could get certain items through the PX. Daddy talked about LSU and Istrouma High football and goings-on at church, avoiding any of the serious matters like his worsening back pain or the looming strike at work. My friends and I sent lots of silliness—skits, reports of school ("This kid got hit in the head with a baseball bat somebody slung, but he's okay"), updates on our pet dog and guinea pig, and our favorite teams' football exploits. Mostly, though, I just chattered in my high-pitched drawl because I couldn't chatter to him in person. To comfort myself, I taped to my walls the prints of Cobra helicopters and other war scenes he sent. To try and connect, I had Momma take a photo of me dressed in army gear as I pretended to charge the camera with a toy M-16 and plastic machete.

Every day had a hole in it, and yet I hung on to a kid's version of war, a war in which death and injury and damage remained abstract and sterile. It was a version doomed, of course, to collapse, and events at home were already nudging its supports. The situation between labor and management at Daddy's plant had plummeted, and with it the condition of Daddy's back. His Toluene-Di-Isocyanate Unit at Wyandotte Chemicals was a noxious volatile forest, a claustrophobic tangle of hissing, dripping pipes, massive iron tanks, cylindrical towers, and a concrete floor slick with moisture and sticky with brown TDI, as I would find out when I briefly worked there many years later. Daddy worked both inside the control room, running the technical aspects of production through the operating board, and outside in the unit, twisting monkey wrenches and climbing towers. Chlorine and phosgene were abundant in Daddy's unit, and he had told horror stories of men dosed by clouds of escaping gas and of a man dying from fumes when he left his work clothes in his car for several days. He loved the job, though, and knew everything about the operation of his unit, even though his rancorousness toward bosses had evidently kept him from being promoted to supervisor. Now he gave us resentful reports on the impasse between management and the union. He thought management wanted to take advantage of the workers, but he didn't seem to like the union either, because they were asking for too much.

Then one night he came home from work and inhaled sharply as he sat in his chair, a lumbar pillow stuffed behind him. "We going out on strike," he said to Momma and me. "Nobody's budging." He didn't pat my shoulder or reassure me, didn't say anything more about it, but the look he exchanged with Momma reminded me of the one they had exchanged the day Olan had told them he was going to the war. The next morning he could barely get out of bed and when he finally made it to the kitchen table, his face ashen, he didn't speak. "Hollis," Momma said, "you got to go to the doctor." She had been on him for weeks, and he had deflected her. Now he nodded and closed his eyes. I wanted him to tell me he was all right. Instead, he scratched at his brow and rose with a grunt. After work he could barely walk.

Two weeks later, on the day the strike began, the doctors removed a disc from his back.

"Don't rub the skin off, Rachel," Daddy said as he lay on his stomach. He was home again and Momma was cleaning the scar on his back, a cut held closed by bristly stitches. He smiled at me. "You wanta touch it," he said, and grabbed at my arm. I jumped back, but then eased up and stretched a fingertip toward it. "Ouch!" he said, and I started. All of us broke into laughter. When Momma had rebandaged him, he swung his legs off the bed with a grunt. "Guess I'm gone get out in the yard and do some work."

"You not doing anything until the doctor says so," Momma said. The doorbell rang, and Momma went to answer it.

"You ain't gone tell on me if I cut the grass while she's off at work, are you?" he asked.

"I will tell," I said.

"Reckon I oughta be good then."

Men's voices came to us from the living room, and Momma reentered. "Two men from the union are here. Said they wanted to check on how you're doing. I heard their names before, but I don't know them." Daddy's expression darkened.

"Get my bath robe," he said to me.

"You don't need to get worked up," Momma said. "I'll tell them to come back later."

"Fetch me that robe, Timmy," he said, using the voice I didn't refuse. Momma and I helped him stand, and he took a deep breath, nodded and went to the living room. He shook hands with the men, told them to have a seat, and asked Momma to make some coffee. "Timmy, why don't you go outside for a spell," he said. I looked at Momma's hard-set expression, and she motioned for me to go on.

I shot baskets on the driveway until the men came out a half-hour later. Daddy shook hands with them, but he didn't do it hardily, and he didn't wait for them to drive away before he shut the door. I rolled the ball into the garage and went into the living room where he stood with his hands on the back of his recliner, Momma in the kitchen door. Daddy's dark brown eyes had a hard sheen. "They said they wanted to check if I was all right, but they come by to check if I really had surgery," he said. "They know I ain't keen on walking that picket line 'cause I think they shoulda settled, so they gone come check on me. Sonsabitches. They brand new to running the union and they irritated 'cause a lot of folks don't like how they wanting to be like Teamsters and shut down everything at the plant gate carrying pipes and clubs." He exhaled through his nose. "Hardly ever missed a day of work in my life and never took no bull from no white hat supervisor and them sonsabitches gone come check on me."

"Well, you're not going anywhere for a while," Momma said. She went into the kitchen to get her purse, came back in pushing up her hair and fussing with her pink dress before she left for work at J. C. Penney's. She had always taken care of us with good cheer. When my lung collapsed from pneumonia in fifth grade, she brought chocolate eclairs into the hospital and slept on the couch next to me. When Alan missed fifty days of his senior year with mononucleosis, she nearly tied him down to keep him from school and painted jocular skulls and crossbones in pink fingernail polish on the glasses he drank from to warn us from using them.

She did inventory in her purse, then smiled and pointed at me. "Timmy, you make sure he doesn't go out of this house, and you tell me if he does." She kissed us both and left. I waited for Daddy to continue the joke about telling on him, but he ran his fingers through his deep black hair and snorted.

"Me and your momma don't want you to worry Olan with this mess, you hear me?"

I nodded. I hadn't thought of worrying him. Now the thought that it could worry him chilled me.

Fall 1970: Invasion of the Others

"How many nigger teachers you got?" Daddy asked after my first day of seventh grade, my first day in an integrated school. The strike had lasted through the summer and was still going on. Olan had been in Vietnam for three months.

"Only one. There's niggers in all my classes, but not many."

"Timmy," Momma said. "You ought not say that. Don't you say that at school."

"I know."

Daddy slowly chewed and shook his head. "All downhill now," he muttered. I watched him for a while, his uncertainty percolating in my chest. I saw the country as he saw it, as being at war here as much as in Vietnam; the riots, sniper shootings, and violence among antiwar demonstrators and desegregationists all caused by black insurrection and Communist subversion. The murder of Black Panthers in Chicago and Oakland, the killing of students at South Carolina State, Jackson State, and Kent State, the police attacks on other black campuses—these were all justified and necessary to save America.

Nonetheless, at school I quickly became confused. There I was unable to see blacks in a monolithic way. Some confirmed Daddy's view of them as "uncivilized," like Don Landry, who pulled his dick out in the back of math class and showed it to two girls, or clusters of blacks on the playground, who seemed to laugh too loudly and be too boisterous. And yet I liked some black kids, like Jason Stanley, a fellow athlete and good student who was shy and dressed conservatively. I sympathized with Lon Harris, the only black kid in Louisiana History, whose face screwed into a pained expression every time our ancient teacher referred to "Nigras."

The most unsettling person, though, was my Social Studies teacher, Miss Monget, who stirred intellectual curiosity, empathy, and sexual stimulation. She dressed flamboyantly in bright dresses and bold necklaces that hung down into her significant brown cleavage. Her lessons veered away from rote depictions of society as white-centered and into praising the Civil Rights Movement and criticizing the war, although not the soldiers. She liked the boys with long hair and hippie clothes and tended to the badly outnumbered black kids. She taught with passion, her voice charged as she moved up and down the aisles. When she found out that Olan was in Vietnam, she regularly asked how he was doing, and when I brought a photo of him in his army fatigues, she said he was a "beautiful young man." Once she touched my shoulder and my pubescent dick hardened, filling me with shame.

Then one day we heard there had been a large race fight at Istrouma High, where my brothers had gone, where we were all going, and where Miss Monget had taught the year before. She told us about a similar fight that had erupted while she was there, whites attacking some of the few black kids who attended. In the hall she had pulled white boys off a black boy they were beating and tugged him away toward her classroom. The white boys called her names but none of them touched her. She said, "I pulled him down the hall and into my room where I thought he'd be safe, but in there they were going after this sweet black girl." Miss Monget smiled, her eyes shiny with tears and focused above us. "She was standing up on a desk chair and swinging another to keep them off until I could get to her." I had been allied with the white kids until that moment, had already imagined the white kids taking the black girl down and pummeling her. It was abstract to me, of course, but Miss Monget's fervor set me spinning. I both cared for her and prickled at her betrayal of her role to take care of me by aligning herself with the way Daddy and I believed. Then my thoughts spun back to the black girl, suddenly a real person, the attack on her perplexing. Shouldn't I, as a Christian, have sympathy for her? And yet if I did, wasn't I a betrayer of my own kind? I tried to shrink. I knew I couldn't tell Daddy what Miss Monget had said or what I'd thought. I wanted to scream at her.

However, it wasn't only blacks who disturbed me. A new breed of transients had infiltrated our seeming one-street sanctuary. My friends and I were minor delinquents, setting junked furniture afire in the middle of the road, shooting bottle rockets at cars, knocking over garbage cans, throwing large acorns that could take out each others' eyes. We had always fought one another, kid fights with wrestling, a couple of roundhouse punches, and endings, if not always resolutions. But these new, broken-home kids were harder and more troubled, signaling something ominous. A kid actually named Jesse James broke into my friend Little Johnny's house, drank a bottle of cooking wine, vandalized the house, vomited all over, and fell asleep on the couch, where they found him when they came home. Another kid, Vic, moved into the first rental property on our street with his single mother, the first of those we had ever known too. He had a manic energy and crazy temper that flared unexpectedly.

And yet he was nothing compared to Lassiter, a truant who hung around with the hoods outside the convenience store we passed on the way to school. He showed up on our street to hang out with Vic, chain-smoking and coughing with what sounded like an older smoker's cough, even though he was around my age. His eyes would lock on me and he would say smart-ass things about my being a pussy brainiac or a momma's boy, although never seeming to say it to start a fight, but to impress Vic and my friends. His skin was ravaged with acne and his oily hair hung past his shoulders, all of it indicative of a dissoluteness I'd never experienced in a kid. He seemed not to have a home. I had to force myself not to stare at the cylindrical scars on his forearms, marks I would later decide were cigarette burns. Lassiter stood out as the embodiment of the increasing instability around me. And the more I saw him, the more I knew that soon he would come after me.

I watched over Daddy's shoulder as he muttered at the kitchen table, index cards with tiny scribbled columns spread before him. Earlier, I'd asked him if he wanted to go for a walk, and he'd said he was too busy, but I was hoping proximity might get him to change his mind. He wasn't prone to curse, but he was mumbling "shit" under his breath with enough regularity to qualify as a chant. For a while, after his back had healed and as the strike stretched into months, he'd walked the picket line. He and my momma discussed bills more and more, something I had never noticed before, and fretted to find cheaper ways to get food. He pushed to do carpenter work, but she had taken a stand against it, so he had gotten a job as an insurance salesman, a job that entailed monthly visits to all his clients' homes, the strategy at that time being that if the agent made house calls on people to personally collect their premiums, he would have the opportunity to update their coverage or sell them more. Daddy had proven good at it, would in fact be the top salesmen in the state at selling new policies, but being good at it didn't stop him from hating it. He wanted to work with his body and his mind, and the archaic bookkeeping system of tallying the incremental premiums constipated his brain. Even I felt unbalanced as I surveyed card after card marked with his quivery handwriting.

I glanced up to see Momma in the living room, the TV off even though it was evening news time. She had tried to help him tally and organize, but the more she tried to help the tighter his face had drawn, the more stubborn and pessimistic his resistance to being helped, until she said, "Fine, do it yourself," and left the room. I decided I would join her before the pine walls blew out in the kitchen. She smiled at me and perked up her eyebrows when I came in and sat beside her. I smiled back, knowing the code to share her amusement at Daddy's crankiness and frustration. It was a way of staving off the seriousness of things without mentioning them.

"After I finish this, why don't you and me play some Chinese checkers," Momma said, pausing in writing her daily letter to Olan.

"All right," I said.

During Daddy's normal shift schedule, my mother and I were often kids together, going to Frank's Drive-In for chocolate milkshakes and cheeseburgers, going to movies, recounting our days. But since Daddy had been home every night, we hadn't been able to do as much together, his presence heavy. She seemed different anyway, less cheerful and more distracted.

Fall 1970: Invasion of the Others

I looked back into the kitchen where Daddy held his forehead in one hand while he tapped a pencil on a card with the other hand.

"Can I write and tell Olan about our campout this weekend?" I asked. "We're gonna tape a skit for him."

"Uh-huh," she said. Daddy pulled a group of cards from one of the little plastic boxes and thumbed through them, his expression scrunched as though the cards had farted.

"Where's Alan?" I asked.

"You know he's studying at school or over at Vicky's."

"I didn't know tonight," I chattered. "I thought he might be doing something stupid. He wants me to wash his car and shine his shoes again this weekend before he goes out on his big date. The big dummy always says I don't make everything shine right or I don't use enough polish 'cause he doesn't care about his loafers shining, he just wants to keep the rain from soaking them."

She chuckled at something she wrote as she read over it again. I wanted to reach over and shake her arm so she would listen to my motor mouth, but I looked past her once more. Daddy scratched furiously at the back of his neck and shook his head. "I know I put that durn card back in there," he said. He flipped through a few cards in the box, plopped the box down on the table, and leaned forward, running his eyes over the spread cards, his breathing audible. Momma put her pen to paper again.

"I let the guinea pig eat some monkey grass from the garden today," I said.

"Timmy, I'll be finished with this in a little while," Momma said. "Why don't you go do something in your room till I'm finished, or go help your daddy."

"Ain't no helping with this shittin' mess," he said. "Two dollar and twenty cent, one dollar and forty-one cent, four dollar and three cent. Make anybody crazy trying to figure all this."

"Then why don't you put it down a minute?" Momma said.

"'Cause it ain't going nowhere till I finish it."

Momma inhaled and focused on her letter. I squirmed in my chair.

"Trying to sell people this stuff they don't even want," Daddy said and shuffled another stack of cards. "Got to keep up with these durn cards." He dropped his stack on the table and started scooping the rows into a pile. "If all them work sonsabitches wasn't so greedy we could be back at the plant." Momma looked up from the letter toward him. He picked the cards up the best he could, a rogue sticking out here and there, a couple slipping from his grip and crazily slicing downward. His dark complexion went red. "Durn this shit!" he said and tossed the cards into the air. They snowed around him onto the floor and the table. He slapped the table and scowled. Momma covered her mouth, holding in her laughter. I did the same. "Y'all go on and laugh," Daddy said. He shoved his chair out and stormed toward the door that led to the garage. When the door slammed, Momma's laughter disappeared.

Mostly my routine stayed the same, overachieving at school and sending letters and tapes to Olan, but something was happening to me as I grew taller. The small trench where the plates of my breast bone connected was becoming lopsided as one side of my chest grew higher and the other side seemed not to rise at all. Whenever I could, I stole peeks at other boys' chests in the locker room and saw that, although their chests weren't all the same, the sides didn't seem to be growing at different rates. When I could, I saw the scar on Daddy's back as it changed from bright red to pink. In the encyclopedia, I examined the human spine and discs between the vertebrae, became more aware of bone and cartilage, studied the encyclopedia without success to understand what had happened to Alan's knees those six weeks during his junior high growth spurt when both of his legs were placed in casts to slow his rapid sprouting and calm the pain of his Osgood Schlater's disease. I had been very young, but I remembered him screaming in his sleep and my mother's footsteps padding from her room to his to soothe him. I didn't say anything to my parents about my chest. So much was changing that the oddness of it almost seemed fitting.

With Olan away, Alan tried to spend more time with me, even taking me to LSU's campus one day. He proudly wore his "Win the War in Vietnam" button as we strolled the beautiful grounds, graced with live oaks and Spanish architecture, and peopled with college students (some with long hair and hippie clothes that Daddy and

Alan despised) who intimidated me and seemed a planet away from our neighborhood across town. I had only been to LSU's campus for ball games and to see the caged tiger, and when Alan took me to the engineering building and showed me the water-control model he was working on, talked about turbidity currents and other things I didn't really grasp, I had my first inkling that the university wasn't there only to support football.

Finally, Alan took me to the student union for lunch, the day bright but late-fall cool as we passed the bare crepe myrtles lining the parade ground. Near the concrete union building, a man in a brown uniform talked loudly from the steps. Nearer, I saw that his red armband was emblazoned with a swastika. Even at twelve I knew that this was wrong and bizarre, wondered why nobody was stopping him or really paying him mind as we went on past. "What was he doing?" I asked Alan as we walked up the long steps. "Don't worry about him," he said. "He's just some nut named David Duke." I would see him up close again, after he became the local Klan's Grand Wizard and long before he ran for governor.

Despite the saturation of war images on TV, I still never envisioned Olan as being in danger. Then one evening the news said that twelve marines had been killed when a firebase was over run. I said, "That's not so many." "That's twelve sons and brothers," Daddy snapped. "Don't you forget that." He popped up and strode into the kitchen. I remained still, the air warping around me. After that the war looked different. When we heard that fifty-four Americans in Chu Lai had been killed in a rocket attack, I walked in a haze of confusion until my mother, after hours of trying, managed unbelievably to reach Olan by phone in Vietnam to confirm that he was all right.

On his cassettes, Olan told us more about his job of handling maimed, dying, and dead young men, and about the mortars that hit the base. Then in late December he sent us a tape in which his voice was matter-of-fact flat. He told us how he missed Christmas back at home: Momma's green jello pudding and the lighted, plastic angel with the burnt stomach, which Momma couldn't stand to replace atop our tree. He said it was even hotter in Vietnam at Christmas than it could be in Louisiana, and that he'd like some Christmas music. Then, without segue, he said, "I've been sort of upset. Griff, one of my best friends, got killed a couple of weeks ago. He was going through this ville with his German Shepherd and kicked in a door and a bunch of VC opened up on him with AK-47s. Griff and the dog took off to a ditch. They made it back to the ditch all right, but the gooks tossed a grenade in and Griff threw the dog out and got blown up himself. Nobody knows why he didn't get out. His dog is pretty pissed off about it and we don't know what to do with him. He's got eleven confirmed kills." He went right on with other mundane news, his voice unchanging.

Early Spring 1971: "A World of Hurt"

On a warm afternoon, I strolled out of school with a mind full of Jacqueline Bisset. Through every class I'd struggled to push aside thoughts of her sexy toughness and vulnerability, willed my nascent boner not to rise. The night before, Momma and I had gone to a drive-in movie to see Dean Martin in *Airport*, an illicit pleasure she'd told me not to tell Daddy about. Now, as my neighbor Richard and I strolled across the school ground, I was Dean Martin heroically caring for Bisset as she lay unconscious with a splinter of metal blasted into her eye.

"Hey, smarty pants," came the voice from behind, "eat me!" I turned, already knowing it was Pogue, an eighth-grader I barely knew and a friend of my future sister-in-law's cousin, Skye.

"Why don't you shut up," I said. Several weeks earlier, Pogue had started calling me names. He was larger and more muscular than I was, yet also nerdy-seeming with his black-rimmed glasses and dorkiness in gym. I couldn't fully understand why he had picked me, the quarterback and honor student, naively not yet considering that maybe he'd picked me *because* I was quarterback and an honor student. What I did consider was that it had something to do with my chest. Boys in gym had started to make fun of it as I became taller and scrawnier and the lopsidedness began to show through T-shirts. "Make me shut up," he said. "Cornholer."

"Come on, Pogue," Skye said.

"Chickenshit, chickenshit." He flipped me off with both hands.

"Let's go," I said to Richard. He delayed a second watching Pogue, and my cheeks flushed at the thought Richard believed I was a chickenshit, especially since it seemed true. "I hate that shitass," I said as we walked away.

"What's his problem?"

"He's a dick. I don't even know him except for Skye."

We silently walked the several blocks home. As we passed the convenience store where the hoods hung out, Lassiter barely nodded his chin when Richard waved. I didn't respond at all. At my house, I peeled off as Richard kept going toward his. I figured he would go over to Vic the renter kid's house or the kid would come over to his and they would talk about motorcycles, something I didn't care about at all. Worse, Lassiter might show up. I wished Vic and his single mother would move, then I felt ashamed as a Christian for wishing that. Christians were supposed to like and forgive everyone, but I'd continued more and more to doubt I was a good Christian. The un-Christian things my friend and I did, silly as they were, gnawed at me: worshipping the several *Playboy* magazines we'd dug out of someone's trash; constantly whoofing about wanting pussy (even though we had only a vague notion what it was); telling each other to suck donkey dicks; rarely turning the other cheek with each other.

"Timmy?" came Momma's voice from the back of the house as I stepped inside.

"Yes, ma'am?" I said, surprised that she wasn't at work and trying to recall if I had seen the car in the driveway.

"Could you come help me?" Her voice was husky, and my steps down the hall felt spongy. The bedroom was dark from the drawn, lined curtains designed to allow Daddy to sleep days when he had worked the dog shift. I could see her shape in bed, and I stopped at the door to let my eyes adjust, my heart speeding.

"Momma?"

"Something's wrong, sugar. I'm sick." She was lying on her back, I now saw, the covers pulled up to her chin. A mop bucket sat by the bed. The room smelled like sweat and vomit. I stepped up close

to her. Her face wasn't right, her eyelids puffed as if they'd been in-
jected with fluid, her skin blotched red, her hair damp and swept
back from her forehead. "I'm having a hard time getting up. Could
you get the thermometer out of the bathroom cabinet?"

I retrieved the thermometer and shook it, although I wasn't sure
if I had shaken it enough. She was shivering and I placed the thermometer under her tongue, then stood sentinel-straight next to her.
She groaned from deep inside, something I had never heard, not
even from Daddy with his back problems. I touched her forehead,
which burned beneath my palm. Daddy was at work until late, and
I tried to think of how I could get him, tried to remember Alan's
schedule and how I could reach him too.

"Okay," she said, and I removed the thermometer. I wanted to
turn on the bedside lamp and let her read it, but she said, "The light
hurts my eyes too much. Go to the bathroom and see what it says.
Remember you have to turn it just right to see the silver part next to
the numbers."

Back in the bathroom I turned the slender stick back and forth,
the silver of the numbers playing dodge with the silver band of mer-
cury. Whenever the band focused, the numbers were on the curved
side, and then there were only even numbers and gradated strokes,
which made it tricky to exactly locate. A splinter of panic moved
through me at the prospect of failing at something so crucial, a shot
of anger at my ineptitude too, until I decided the band seemed to
reach up between 103 and 104. I went back in and told her.

"Bring me a cold wet wash rag and go see if Mr. or Miz Goudeau
are home."

I wet the small towel and spread it on her forehead, then rushed
next door. I was already going down the list of other adults, Mrs.
Slaton and Mrs. Clark, in case Mrs. Goudeau was still at their store.
Luckily, she answered. When she saw my expression, she put her
hand on my arm and hurried back over with me. She was a small
woman with black hair and a quiet, sweet voice, almost my second
mother, one of her five daughters born just two hours after me. She
sat on the edge of the bed. "What is it, Rachel?"

"I don't know, Gladys. I felt fine till this morning. Hollis went in early to work and I started feeling hot and itchy and my head started killing me. I been throwing up and I think I'm broke out. Maybe it's the bug repellant I used last night."

"I'm going to move the covers down and take a look." Mrs. Goudeau clicked on the bedside lamp, and Momma turned her head away from the light. Carefully, Mrs. Goudeau pulled the covers lower, Momma hissing through her teeth as if she were being scalded. On her neck, arms, and hands, red hives humped up like hornet stings. Mrs. Goudeau pulled the covers up again and touched Momma's face. "We going to swab you in a little alcohol. I think we ought to get you to the doctor's. When's Hollis going to be back?"

"I don't want to worry him. They're just back to work and he carpooled today."

"When's Alan coming home?" Mrs. Goudeau asked.

"I ain't sure," Momma said.

"We could call Vicky's," I said.

"You do that," Mrs. Goudeau said. A fit of shivering took Momma, and she moaned and leaned over the side of the bed. Mrs. Goudeau held Momma's head as she dry heaved into the bucket. "Timmy," Mrs. Goudeau said, "do you know where the rubbing alcohol is?" I nodded. "Let's get that and another rag, and you try and call your brother." I kept staring at Momma. "Timmy?" Mrs. Goudeau said, "You can do that?"

When I came back from calling Alan, Momma's teeth were chattering. Mrs. Goudeau and I sponged her with alcohol while she muttered delirious nonsense. Alan arrived and not long after that Daddy screeched up outside in a co-worker's car that he'd borrowed and used to travel the thirty miles from Geismar. The house swirled as we helped Momma get dressed. Then Daddy and Alan nearly carried her to the car to head to the hospital, leaving Mrs. Goudeau and me behind.

The next day at school I rubbed my forehead as if I could massage away the image of Momma's splotched body. When the final bell rang, I ran to the pick-up area, hoping somebody would already be there, maybe even her, but I had to wait and endure Pogue asking me if I wanted to suck his dick. My skin burned to do something to him, although he still spooked me because he was older and bigger. Alan pulled up in his Fairlane, his dirty blonde hair combed straight back and high in front like Cookie's on the TV show *77 Sunset Strip*. He smiled behind his black-rimmed glasses, his expression cheerful, and pushed the passenger door open for me. "She's a lot better, sport," he said. "They got her fever way down. I'm gonna take you to see her."

"You seen her?"

"No, Daddy's been there the whole time. I called him. I've been at school. Got back a test I made a hundred on." We pulled away from the school. "The doctor says he thinks it's a reaction to the bug spray y'all used at the movie."

"Can she open her eyes up?" I asked.

"She can see better. They've been having her rest. Miz Goudeau and Miz Slaton and the preacher have all been by, Daddy says." Out the window, I watched the white clouds billowing upward from the plants by the river. I wiped at my stinging nose.

"Things are gonna be fine, Chief," Alan said.

The antiseptic hospital smell combined with a sour odor to form a clog in my throat. Alan led me toward Momma's room, my body going leaden. "Don't upset her," Alan said, just outside her door. I pulled myself up into my chest and shoulders and pushed through into the near darkness. Momma came clear beneath the dim light above the head of her bed. Her face was monstrously swollen and blotched raspberry.

"Come on in," Daddy's drawl whispered, and I flinched, not having seen him in the chair in the corner. He got up, pushed his palm against the stiffness in his lower back, grimaced and came over to me. He draped his arm around my shoulders. "She's doing a world better. The doctors and nurses done got her fever down, but be real easy with her." I walked over and rested my hands on the cold railing of her bed. An IV tube snaked along her forearm to the top of her hand where the needle went in. Her arm and hand were so puffy I wondered whether they were pumping too much of something into her.

"Hey, Timmy," she said, her voice thin, her eyelids still shut. "You can kiss me." I put my lips to her cheek, hot and dry. She winced.

"Alan got me from school," I said.

"I know."

"Is your fever gone down?"

"I'm doing better. You can hold my hand, just not too tight."

I slid my hand beneath her fingers to avoid the tape and tubes. Daddy laid his hand on my neck. "When are you coming back to the house?" I asked.

"Soon. I got to let the doctors say. You know how they do." Her mouth stayed open, but her eyes closed and she breathed heavily.

"They got her all drugged up to make her feel better," Daddy said. "She's give out from that fever." He dropped his hand from my neck. "You can pet her hair a little," he said. He went back to his chair and grunted as he sat. I reached and stroked the strands that had been disheveled by sweat and wet towels, knowing she wouldn't like it that her hair wasn't just right.

The days and nights passed like a dream of being lost, the only constant being Pogue's daily taunts and my visits to the hospital. My parents told me not to write Olan what was happening, but I knew he would wonder why Momma missed even one day of sending a letter. I prayed more, even beyond the prayers with the preacher and our Mississippi relatives who drove over to see about us. Every adult tried to comfort me, and I tried to act as if the darkness I sensed from where Olan was wasn't creeping over us as well. From bed I kept watching the flames tear away and curl into the sky like dragons.

Her fever went away, the swelling began to drop, and the rash receded, yet sleep still ruled her so completely that she dozed off as I was talking to her. Sometimes she snored so loudly that I laughed just to purge whatever was rising in my throat. In the afternoon and evening, I sat with Daddy in her room, and he told me stories about growing up on the farm in Mississippi, singing in a gospel quartet on the radio, striking out to Mobile shipyards in search of work, leaving home for World War II, and about knowing an ancient black woman in Mississippi who actually remembered being captured in Africa and shipped to America in slavery. The woman, a tiny girl at the time of her capture, had been attracted to bright cloths strung in trees and the cloths had turned out to be a lure. Daddy's voice, deep and calm, unspooled at the normal slow pace, but I could still sense his distraction without grasping that it was possible for him to be afraid. The doctors kept insisting that Momma's sickness was a reaction to the insect repellant, though later they would talk about it being rheumatic fever, the first sign of her lupus.

The day she was to be released from the hospital, neighbors and relatives surrounded her. She was wheeled to the hospital's exit, where Daddy and Alan helped her stand, her face pinching as they lifted her. The sky shone bright blue, and she smiled and hugged the nurses who had also come down with us. We helped her walk to the car, her steps slow and careful, and eased her into the backseat. "Say goodbye to my bedpan," she said to a nurse. I sat next to her and blathered as Alan drove. Daddy glanced back and told me to let her rest. It was hard to close my mouth, the words like frantic birds trying to escape. She patted my arm. In a minute, she was asleep, slumped against her door.

"Fucking queer," Pogue said. "'Sposed to be the big tough quarterback. I bet you cry when you get a answer wrong. You cry, you big baby? Why don't you cry right now?"

Pogue followed me to the edge of the school ground, the mania in his voice scraping along my spine. I took quick looks at his crinkled face as it leered each insult and the words curdled in me. Still, I did nothing, and he peeled off and headed his own way. I was walking by myself that day and Pogue's insults scrolled through my head and twisted in my solar plexus. He was right, after all. I *was* a pussy. Neither of my brothers would have been intimidated by what he said. Certainly Daddy wouldn't have taken it. So why did I? I'd never backed down from fights in the neighborhood.

When I reached my street, I kept walking past, went on to Skye's house and knocked on his door. He was surprised to see me since I had never visited him before and only knew where he lived because Vicky had shown me. "Where's Pogue live?" I asked.

He stared. "You gonna fight him?"

"Probly." He nodded.

"He'll be on Winbourne playground in about a half-hour for soft-ball practice."

I turned and walked toward home, my vision blurry from the pressure building. When I reached the house, I knew I should go in and see about Momma, but I sat in our dark, oily-smelling garage and waited. After what I thought was a half-hour, I hopped on my bicycle and headed out. The school ground was close enough to reach on foot in five minutes, much closer than the junior high, but I wanted to get there fast. I strangled the handlebars and stood as I pedaled. I leaned forward and sliced the air with my head, filled with angry clarity, the anodyne, at least briefly, for my fear. I remembered how Olan had taught me to punch a stomach when my next-door neighbor kept antagonizing me into fights. "You punch him good in the belly a couple of times, that'll cool the little bastard out," Olan had said. My neighbor hadn't stopped completely, but he had backed off some. I'd enjoyed punching him.

I jumped the curve to the school ground and pumped furiously, my tires bumping through the ruts and pocks dug by kids and the rain. I saw him a hundred yards away, sitting like a mirage alone on the roots of a huge oak tree. Rage coursed through me as pure as sweet Jesus had the day I walked the church aisle. I pumped harder. Pogue held a pint carton in his hand, took a sip, glanced at me, and strangely looked down again. I coasted up, skidded to a stop and swung off. He gripped the carton with both hands and didn't rise as I strode toward him. "I'm sick of you calling me names," I said, and struck him in the side of the head with a roundhouse punch. It stung my fist and sent him down on his side, where he curled. I'd never landed a head punch that effective, and its strong medicine powered a viciousness in me. I straddled him and slugged his back and shoulders over and over as he covered his head. He didn't resist at all and I kept on, aggression spilling out of me until I hyperventilated and stood. "Never call me another name," I said. I noticed the carton of chocolate milk that had miraculously fallen upright. I picked it up, held it poised a moment, then slowly drenched him as he remained in a ball.

My bike wheels barely touched the ground as I rode home.

Momma was up and cooking in the kitchen, but I only said hi and went straight to my room. That night guilt nagged me and I prayed to God to be forgiven, but I also wondered why God had allowed Pogue to antagonize me, why my mother had been taken sick, why my brother had been gone so long, why Daddy had been tortured by his work. I pushed the guilt and doubt away and slept better than I had in a long time.

At school the next morning, Skye walked up without Pogue. My anger hadn't completely left me, and I almost asked him why he was friends with such an asshole, why he had never said anything to Pogue about hassling me, but his serious expression kept me from speaking. "Pogue ain't coming to school," he said. "He ain't hurt, he just ain't coming." He paused and wrinkled his nose. "He deserved to get his ass beat, but you shouldn't have poured the chocolate milk on him."

It's possible to laugh about it now, but I just stood there as Skye walked off. The joy and power of seconds before bled away. All I felt was cruel.

"At least I lost weight so I can fit in my dress for Alan's wedding," she said as she stepped off the bathroom scale. I laughed, even though her weight loss from her sickness a month ago still scared me, her face gaunt despite her high round cheeks and bright eyes. The rash had disappeared, but patches of tiny blood clots remained beneath her fair skin and made her look as if she'd been scraped along her limbs. For a while, the stiffness in her joints had showed not only in her movement but also in her winces and flinches. She had tried after she returned home to act as if nothing had happened, even to start back to work, but it was evident that the least thing tired her out. At night, I dreaded that her fever would begin to boil again.

I stepped onto the scale and nodded at my gain of ten pounds over the past several months, the result of lifting weights and drinking protein shakes that I hoped would ready me for football the following year and somehow cover my chest in muscle. Momma was gazing at herself in the mirror with a displeased expression. She wanted to look healthy in a month when Olan arrived home. He was supposed to already be home, but he'd volunteered to stay an extra month in Vietnam, so that his tour and service would end simultaneously. We hadn't liked that at all.

A knock came from the front door, and we heard Daddy answer it. "Preacher's here," he called to us.

Brother Toms stood just inside the door in his black slacks, white shirt, and plain tie. "I brought a tape I thought y'all oughta hear," he said. Daddy glared at him, but Momma told him to sit and asked if he wanted some coffee. "No thank you, Rachel. Olan sent this to me, and I thought y'all oughta hear it."

"He tell you to play it for us?" Daddy asked.

"No, but I thought it best you hear it."

"If he didn't mean it for us, I don't think we oughta listen."

"I wanta listen," Momma said. "Brother Toms came all the way in town."

I thought Daddy was going to say more, but he stared at Momma until he sighed and sat back in his chair with a gloomy expression. Momma asked me to retrieve the tape player and I hustled and brought it back. Brother Toms leaned forward, put the cassette in the player on the coffee table, and shut it. "There's strong material on here," he said, looking at me and then at my parents.

"I wanta hear," I said. My parents exchanged looks and Momma motioned to play the tape.

Brother Toms pushed the play button. Olan's voice began, halting and deadened, worse than when he'd told us about his friend Griff getting killed. He talked about how tired and depressed he was. He told in detail about the agony of the young men he loaded onto his bus almost every day and how hard it was to want to save them and not be able to. He went on about how he helped work on the wounded as they waited to get into surgery at the hospital, and how it was his and his companions' job to bag amputated limbs as well as the dead. He told about the nightmare of going on patrols in the jungle, of terrible firefights they'd had. Daddy frowned, his hands gripping his thighs as he stared straight ahead. Momma sat forward, her hands covering her mouth, eyes fixed on the floor. I'd never seen them quite like this, and I looked away to study the ornately framed print above the couch, a painting of a mountain stream lined by deer growing smaller and smaller the farther away they were. I recalled our trips to the Smokey Mountains, vacations my mother planned like military operations, remembered Daddy goading Alan, Olan, and me to follow him into the icy mountain creeks, his laugh big and unrestrained as he stood unaffected while we thrashed and hooted.

"I was doing all right until something happened a week ago," Olan said. "There was this sergeant I was really close to, kind of like a second daddy to me, and he was standing in front of this chopper, a Cobra, on the ground. Nobody knew there was missiles in it and some dude in the cockpit accidentally pushed a button and fired 'em. Took the sergeant's head right off. The rockets kept on going and one hit a hootch and split off into several chunks. It was a friend of mine's last day in country and he had slept late and right when he was coming outside, a sheered off piece of rocket popped him right in the arm. I came up on him and two guys were putting the fire out on him. I couldn't even help. They had to amputate his arm, but he was all right about it. He said that'd teach him better than to sleep late." Olan chuckled on the tape and inhaled deeply. "Brother Toms, it's hard to believe in anything over here. We don't know what we're fighting for and we don't believe what Tricky Dick and the generals say. I don't even know if I believe in God anymore. He put us in a world of hurt."

Daddy pushed himself out of his chair, ejected the tape, and put it in his pocket. He stood in the middle of the room and glared at the preacher. "Why you wanta upset Olan's momma like that?"

The preacher looked up at Daddy from the couch. "I just thought y'all should hear."

"That's what you thought, but he asked you to keep it to yourself. If he'd wanted Rachel to hear that he would of sent it to her."

"I wanted to hear it," Momma said, but Daddy kept his eyes on Brother Toms.

"Now I'll ask you kindly to leave."

Brother Toms glanced at my father's pocket, nodded to Momma and me, and went out the front door. We all stayed quiet until we heard his car drive off, then Momma stood. "He was trying to help, Hollis," she said.

"He ain't never helped nothing."

Daddy walked past her, through the kitchen, and out the door into the garage. "Leave your daddy alone for a little while," she said. She laid a hand on my shoulder. "Olan's all right, sugar," she said, her voice unsteady, then she turned and went to their bedroom. I waited for a minute, picturing a headless and armless man and trying to connect the voice I'd heard with the joking, laughing voice of my brother. I stared at the cassette player door, open like a thing ready to launch or purge.

Mid-1971: Trying to Get Right

I braced, waiting for Olan to come home. I could feel the tension in my parents, too, but nobody mentioned our worry that he would be killed during his last days. Momma put on a cheerful face as she talked about the meals she would cook when he got home and as she helped to plan Alan's wedding. Daddy seemed more and more freighted by the war and rebellion against it, watching the evening news as if the anchors were responsible for everything going wrong. His talk veered more and more toward the End Time and the approaching apocalypse and blacks undermining the country, as if all these things were related. I focused on school the best I could and tried to ignore my increasingly lopsided chest and the mocking and freakish attention it was getting in the gym locker room. More than that, I struggled with Olan's voice and his statement that he didn't know if he believed in God anymore. I prayed that Olan would be okay and believed that when he returned things would be the same as they had been when we were much younger.

Then finally came the day he would arrive, straight from Vietnam to Seattle to California to us, home from the war and in his own bed in forty-eight hours. We seldom went to New Orleans, the city too exotic and alien for my parents, and the eighty-mile drive seemed like forever. The twilit swamp stretched away from both sides of the road as I gripped bottles of six ounce Coca Cola between my feet and held in my lap a loaf of Holsum white bread, the two items Olan had requested. "Can't wait to get back to the World," he'd written, and I had pictured it literally, a globe on whose top we waited while his plane navigated toward us.

There must have been twenty of us there. Olan came off the plane in a dress uniform, grinning, his hair long in front, bleached from the sun and swept to the side. He was even thinner than when he'd left. He dropped his duffle and we swarmed him, hugging and kissing him. He smelled different, cigarettes and pungent body odor, but I hung on as long as I could in the crowd. Amodee handed him a Coke and I pressed the loaf of bread into his hands. He swigged a whole bottle then tore into the plastic and stuffed a piece of bread in his mouth. We all cheered. In the parking lot he lit a cigarette, pulled the smoke deep and spewed it out, something I'd never seen him do. Daddy said, "You not smoking in the house." Olan laughed. Then we guided him to the car, surrounding him as if we could keep him from any harm forever.

That night he glanced off home before going out with friends, came home in the dark early hours and was still asleep on his back, sprawled and snoring in the bottom bunk, when I returned home from school. "Let's get him up," Momma said, grinning. She touched his shoulder and said his name. He flailed awake, throwing punches as he sprang from the bed. Momma staggered backwards, holding her shoulder. Olan froze, arms out, fingers spread wide, and took in the room, squinting. He found his glasses, dropped his arms and looked at Momma holding herself where he'd hit her. "Oh, Momma, I'm sorry, I'm so sorry."

"It's okay, sweetie," she said, but she didn't move toward him. He dropped onto his bed and put his face in his hands, looking as though he wanted to disappear.

Olan reminded us to call him Robert as he scarfed down Momma's fried chicken, fried okra, rice and gravy, and cornbread. I asked him questions about the war, but he just laughed and gave jokey answers. Then his expression darkened beyond what I'd ever seen. "Some idiots mouthed off to us about killing babies when we got off the plane in Seattle. Some other ones said some shit in the airport and me and this dude I was walking with said, 'I'll get the two on my side and you get the one on yours,' and we knocked 'em on their asses with our duffles." He laughed. "These cops ran up and told us they'd take care it."

"They were hippies?" Alan asked. He was still living at home until he was married in a couple of weeks, when he would move to married student housing.

"I didn't look at their hips," Robert said.

"Smart aleck. You know what I mean. Long-haired and dirty."

"I didn't sniff 'em either."

Daddy snorted. "President's trying to put a stop to all that. Ain't nothing but a bunch of Communist agitators."

"They even started protesting on campus," Alan said. "It hurts the war effort." I nodded in agreement.

Robert laughed and chugged his iced tea. "War effort. Tricky Dick ain't made an effort except to get us killed."

"We'd be winning if it wasn't for all this bull back here," Daddy said.

"That's right," Alan said.

"Who cares?" Robert said. "You care, Timmy?" He tousled my hair.

"You going out again tonight, Olan?" Momma asked, trying to change the subject.

"Call me Robert, Momma." He shoveled in some food. "Amodee and them got something planned."

"You oughta let yourself get some rest," she said.

"I'll have plenty of time to rest."

"You thought about what kind of job you gone look for?" Daddy asked.

"I been home two days, Daddy."

"You gone have to think about it."

"Or the G.I. bill if you think you're ready for college," Alan said.

"It ain't good to have nothing to do," Daddy said.

"I got plenty to do."

"I don't mean gallivanting around with Amodee and George and them girls."

"Well, that's too bad."

"And that hair looks like you a damn Communist."

Robert's expression registered shock, then narrowed into an expression worse than the one I'd seen a few minutes earlier. "You ain't serious. I been off killing Communists for thirteen months and you're gonna say that."

"You know what I mean. Ain't no need to get all mad."

"Fine, I won't get mad." Robert shoved away from the table, dabbed at his mouth with a napkin, and stomped out of the room.

"Hollis, he's just back," Momma said.

Daddy scowled at the table as if he hadn't heard her. "It ain't good to be like that," he said.

Robert kept partying and keeping odd hours. He was jittery and his hands had acquired a slight shake, his fingers brown on the tips from nicotine. His sleep was chaotic, and nearly every night I awakened to his loud mumblings from the bottom bunk, shouts that jolted him awake, his tortured snoring and his dreams about battle, complete with the sounds of explosions and jets. Sometimes when he spoke to me, I felt as if he were behind a hard, crazy mask. Momma kept after him to go to church, but he waited until the second Sunday home when Daddy was at work. Momma's elation made her glide through the house as we dressed, and as I watched Robert struggle with the tie to his dress uniform, she came in. "Thank you for wearing that and going to church," she said.

Robert loosely knotted the tie for the third time, gagged, loosened and tightened the tie, and gagged again. "I hate these things."

"Just loosen it more," she said. "Here, I'll do it." She let the knot out some, then tightened the tie away from his Adam's apple. I was already dressed for church and happy to see the wide smile she wore. I was also mesmerized by the ribbons and medals on Robert's chest, all of which I had made him explain to me. She stepped back and patted his chest. "You're so handsome. I'm so proud of you."

"This is the only time, Momma."

"Everybody will be glad to see you."

"Everybody I want to see from there I've already seen except Brother Toms."

She nodded and patted me too as she walked past. Robert gagged once more and wrestled with the knot. His eyes bulged and watered. "I'm strangling."

"Your uniform is cool," I said.

"Well, you can have it after today. Every time I wear this god-damn tie I think about a dude putting a tourniquet on a guy with a neck wound. Don't ever put a tourniquet on a dude's neck." He pantomimed a noose pulling him up. "Gak!"

"You saw that?" I asked.

"I saw everything."

He walked outside onto our little porch and I followed. The late May sun weighed hot on my black sport coat, so I took it off. Robert leaned against the ironwork and lit a cigarette, inhaled, and blew out. "That's bad for you," I said.

He leaned his head back. "So is sticking your nose in." He took another deep drag.

"Why you do it?"

"I like it. I'm doing better, though. I was up to three packs a day over there."

"I don't like it."

"Oh, so now it's Daddy, Alan, *and* you giving me grief?" He shoved my head and smiled. "I ain't gonna make it through church without it."

"We already missed Sunday school."

"You can thank me for that later." He flicked his cigarette and smirked.

"I remember when you and Amodee and David got caught laughing through that door."

"Yeah, that was pretty stupid."

"Is that why you don't like church?" I asked.

He looked at me as if he was thinking about his answer, then he brushed his nose. "I just don't like it, okay?"

Momma came out the front door in a blue, knee-length dress. Her tall blonde hair threw a cloud of hairspray odor that mixed with her perfume. She frowned slightly at his cigarette, then kissed both of us on the cheeks. "Y'all ready?" she asked and held the keys out to Robert.

"Why ain't the college boy joining us?" he asked.

"He says he has wedding stuff to get done today," she said.

"I bet. Well, I say we hit Krispy Kreme on the way back."

Momma touched her middle. "I'll just have coffee. And maybe one donut."

"Chocolate covered," I said.

Robert laughed. We piled into our car, Momma in the passenger seat and me in the back. Robert cranked the car, revved it in a way that would've upset Daddy, and grinned at me. Momma touched his arm again.

"They'll be so glad to see you," she said.

He put it in reverse and strained his stiff neck to look backwards. "I swear, Momma, I ain't going back after this."

"We'll see."

"No, we won't," he said.

The day Alan married Vicky, Robert moved out of our room into Alan's. For a month he didn't work, and Daddy rode him every day. Most likely Daddy's guilt roiled over Robert's having gone to the war Daddy supported, a war that was clearly not going well no matter how much Nixon and Kissinger bombed North Vietnam. And Robert's apolitical tirades vexed Daddy even more, rants and rough jokes about *gooks* dying and Tricky Dick being an asshole. I'm sure Daddy didn't know where to put Robert. Robert wasn't for the war and he wasn't a righteous Christian warrior who abstracted and sterilized the reality of hating the enemy as they did at church. Neither of them had a way to work through it, and both of them seethed with an undercurrent I tried to joke around but could already feel tugging at me. Besides, Robert wasn't all that was twisting our father. Blacks had moved toward us across Plank Road, the symbolic dividing line between the mostly black neighborhood called Dixie and us. For Sale signs were popping up like mushrooms in formerly all-white neighborhoods, and Daddy fretted over how crime would simultaneously rise as property values dropped. When somebody stole my bike from the yard, it was like Mongol hordes had breached the wall.

In June, Robert began to look for a job. He told us how people studied him as if he'd just gotten out of prison or the crazy house when he told them where he'd been. Finally, he landed a job washing separator tanks in plants, came home caked in dirt and chemical residue, and drained from the summer heat. His routine was to arrive home, shower, eat, fall asleep, go partying, and get up early for work. Even though his skin browned, his color seemed paled a shade as his edge grew sharper. His original plan to come home after he'd turned twenty-one had been thrown off by leaving the army early, and he groused about the bullshit of having to bide his time until he could become a cop.

Toward August, he quit and took a job working at a convenience store on North Acadian, between us and Plank Road. Store robberies were rampant in town, and the shoplifting and mau-mauing by groups of black teenagers rattled Robert so much that he recruited Amodee and even Daddy to sit next to the Icee machine with a shotgun when he worked the late-night shift. Sometimes he alternated working at a store closer to the high school; on a night when he had been asked to work there and refused, the clerk was shot in the arm. The next week Robert came home early from working a shift that no one typically rode shotgun on, stormed straight to the kitchen, and drank three glasses of water. Momma, Daddy and I all followed him in and waited until he turned, his lips tight. "I'm done with that goddamn job."

"Watch that language," Daddy said.

"It's a *goddamn* job and you know it. Nigger kids coming in a pack after school and shoplifting the shelves bare. 'Hey, white boy this, hey, white boy that.' Bastards." Robert wiped his lips with the back of his hand. "You know last week the manager wanted me to work that other store on the night the counter guy got shot."

"You can't keep flying off the handle and quittin' jobs," Daddy said.

"*He got shot,* Daddy. I ain't gonna get shot to sell orange drinks and cigarettes." Robert and Daddy looked away from each other.

"Robert," Momma said, "did something happen tonight?"

With his thumb and forefinger, he cleared the cottony spittle collected at the corners of his mouth. "I got robbed."

"For Heaven's sake," Daddy said, and shook his head. Momma touched Robert's forearm.

He shoved away from the counter and paced. "Deborah, y'all know I've been seeing her, she stopped by and she was hanging out when this dude comes in. He's all shaky and he's wearing a green trench coat and it sure ain't cold. I'd seen him before looking strung out, so I send Deborah on. Soon as her car pulls off, the dude pulls a revolver and points it in my face. I could count the frickin' bullets." Robert lifted his cigarettes out of his pocket, remembered he was inside and jammed them back in. "I tell him to be cool while I get the money out the register, but the register dings and he jerks and starts poking the gun at me, so I give him the money and he tells me to turn around and walk to the storeroom. Well, I ain't turning around, so I start backing up and the dude comes around the counter and I dive into the storeroom and cut the light off and break a broom for a stick and hide behind some boxes. I chunk some bundles of bags at some liquor bottles on the shelves and break them to make a racket. After that I don't hear nothin', so finally I peek out and the dude is gone. That's it. I quit."

We all stood silently for a while, until Daddy exhaled through his nose, his sign for general disgust, and left the room. Robert, Momma and I still didn't move. "Daddy thinks I'm 'sposed to hold the line against the niggers coming across Plank," Robert said. "I ain't holding no line till I'm a cop."

Come fall, Robert went to LSU and I went to eighth grade back at Prescott Junior High. Just as he'd become Robert, I became Tim instead of Timmy. Early in the term, I heard of racial violence for the first time at our school. The story was that a group of black girls was shutting off the lights in the bathroom and cutting white girls' hair. Nobody could figure out who the attackers were until Pat B., who had black friends in a group called the Oreos, was jumped and punched one of the girls, making all of them run. When the girl's black eye appeared, other black girls took justice into their own hands and the hair-cutting stopped. I was only semi-aware of all this. My focus was on having won the starting job at quarterback, beating out my only actual black acquaintance, Jason Stanley.

At the same time, Robert was failing. I could see how hard it was for him to settle down and read. I'd study in his room with him, and I'd see him knitting his forehead, mumbling, writing and furiously erasing in his notebook, sometimes nodding off to sleep on his desk.

Mid-1971: Trying to Get Right

He exhibited textbook PTSD, but there was no textbook yet. He told me the crowds at school made him anxious and antsy, and the classes taught on remote TV brought back medic training at Fort Sam Houston. He stared out the window to fight claustrophobia and rage at other students, who seemed carefree about everything. Plus, he said, the women were nearly naked "with their boobs falling out of their halter tops all over the place" and "how could anybody concentrate with that?" Daddy and Alan told him that he just needed to "get over" the war, that soldiers from World War II and Korea had shaken off much worse experiences, that Robert's experiences hadn't actually been so bad.

Robert also seemed cursed with bad luck and untimely provocation. One day, he came home and told us as he'd been heading toward the parking lot, he had seen smoke rising and began to laugh because it looked like somebody's car was on fire. As he moved closer and closer, though, he saw that the smoke was coming from his section. "I turn a corner and I see it's on the row where my car is and sure enough when I get close the smoke is coming out of my trunk and the whole inside is filled up. I run up and open the door and see the backseat is all smoldering 'cause the wind must've took a cigarette I flicked and blew it back in. The smoke airs out some, but the fire starts jumping up in the backseat, so I get in and drive like hell down to a Texaco station with flames going all up behind me. I hosed it down and waited till the smoke cleared. The backseat is all melted plastic and scorched up springs. Y'all come see."

"That oughta be a lesson not to smoke," Daddy said.

Another day, he came home and told me that two campus police had approached him about driving down a restricted street. He'd asked what they were talking about and they pointed to a sign obscured by a low tree limb. "You can't even see that sign from the road," he said.

"You got to move your car and we have to ticket you."

"I'm late for class."

"Too bad." They stepped closer. Robert stomped the closest one's foot with the heel of his boot. "I heard a crunch," he said to me, "and the cop just dropped, so I booked. The other cop booked in the other direction, so I hopped in my car and got the hell away."

The last straw was an incident as he was strolling to class. He thought he heard yelling as he passed the hissing campus power plant, and when he glanced across the street, he saw a uniformed army officer next to the gold-painted Civil War cannon in front of the ROTC building. "Yeah, you!" the officer said. "Pick up that litter." He thrust his finger to the ground where Robert had tossed a cigarette butt. "No litter." Robert ignored the butt and crossed the street. "I said you dropped litter," the officer said. "No littering my campus."

Robert studied the dress uniform. "You're a lieutenant colonel."

"That's right. Are you going to pick it up?"

"You been in 'Nam? I been in 'Nam."

"I don't care where you've been, you're littering my house."

"I hate lieutenant colonels." Robert shoved him backwards over the cannon.

"Fucker landed on his back and didn't say nothing," he told me. "His shit looked shocked. I just went on to my car." He told these things smiling, but his eyes simmered and his voice quavered in ways that unsettled me. Still, I managed to partly convert his rage into a kid's idea of conflict, the images cartoonish and completely justified in favor of Robert, even though Daddy told him he was wrong.

Then, just before he dropped out of school, something happened that truly spooked me. Momma and several ladies from church sat in our living room and listened to Robert spin funny war stories. Two ladies relaxed on our long brown couch, tittering at Robert and sipping coffee. Once in a while, thunder rumbled as a storm brought the sky alive. Robert flinched every time. Then a boom shook the house, rattling the decorative cups on the table by the picture window and the picture window itself. Robert dove toward the sofa, lifted its end several feet in the air, and started scrambling under it. The lady on the high end tumbled down the slope, spilling her coffee and screaming. "Olan!" Momma yelled, and sprang toward him. He went still, panting, scanned the room, his skin white. "Olan . . . Robert, it's okay," Momma said. He froze, eyes wide, took us all in and slowly lowered the heavy couch.

"I'm sorry," he said, his hands shaking, his eyes watering. "I'm really sorry." He moved toward the ladies he'd covered in coffee, but hesitated, then stopped. The ladies sat bunched together, still in shock. "It's all right," one finally said, and the rest chimed in. There was a flurry to sop the spilled coffee, then thunder cracked near us again and Robert crouched. Everyone went silent. Robert wheeled and left the room. I wanted to follow, but for the first time in my life I was unsure around him.

Late 1971, Early 1972: Blood and Bone

"What the fuck you doin'?" came Lassiter's voice like a slap to the back of my neck. I started from scrubbing the mildew on our ironwork, stood and spun. Water dripped from the soapy rag in my hand. I felt naked in the wet shirt glued to my chest. I crossed my arms. Now that football season was over, I could barely wait the several weeks until surgery to level out my breastplate by removing a large piece of bone. To, as the surgeon had said, "fix the deformity so it won't affect his equilibrium."

"I'm washing this," I said.

"I can see that, dildo. Why?"

"My daddy told me to."

"*My daddy told me to.*"

Heat then cold traveled through me. I hadn't seen him on our street in a while, only at the convenience store, and he'd never been in my yard. My urge was to hit him in the face, but his appearance froze me. Red veins and rust colored the whites of his eyes. His hair hung past his shoulders as heavy as if coated in motor oil. I imagined how hot he must be in his army jacket, jeans, and square-toed boots on this warm late November day. He pulled a cigarette from his pocket and lit it. "Ain't nobody at Vic's house," he said.

"He moved," I said, knowing somehow that saying this was inflammatory.

"He moved? When?"

"About a month ago."

"He just fucking moved?" His arms hung at his sides.

"Him and his momma moved."

"I figured that, dumb fuck." Sadness flitted over Lassiter's face, and this expression rattled me more than his anger. He saw me seeing him and his cheeks twitched. He took a drag and blew it at me. "They move around here?"

I shrugged. "They just went."

He shifted his feet and his body odor came to me. When he focused on me again, I tried not to show any emotion.

"He was fucking queer anyway," Lassiter said. "Screw him."

"Yeah, he *was* a queer."

"Eat shit. You're a fucking queer."

I wanted worse than before to punch him, but his voice was flat and detached, more like slightly warmed sheet metal than hot iron. He didn't adjust his posture or stance as if we were going to fight. In fact, he seemed to want to keep talking even though I had nothing else to say.

"So what's been happening?" I said.

"What?"

"What you been up to?"

"What's it to you?"

I didn't know what to say. I glanced at my bucket of soap and water, then at the picture window, half hoping Momma would come out and tell him he couldn't smoke in our yard. I had the urge to tell him about the hood kids in my French class who seemed to accept me and to ask him if he knew them. My words calcified inside me. Anything I said could betray me. I tugged at the hem of my damp shirt and hunched a little to make sure my chest didn't show. He took a long, last drag and flicked the butt into the yard. "Tell them other pussies I said to suck a dick." He laughed and walked off.

Three weeks later the doctor removed the four-by-one-inch piece of bone. The last several months had become nearly unbearable with humiliation from taunts and stares in the locker room and from the constant neck-to-sternum bruise my shoulder pads pinched on me. I was glad to be rolled into surgery, even though I could barely stand to look at Daddy's worried face. He had resisted the surgery, but Momma had listened to my urging and used her insurance from J. C. Penney's to pay for it.

The day after surgery the doctor removed tubes from my ribs

and stomach, my body twice feeling like a deflating balloon. Then he stitched up the holes. The nurse rolled me over and a jelly of pain slid through my chest, intense yet unfocussed. Later a nurse and Momma woke me again. Daddy was there, too, arms crossed, expression pulled back. "Help us sit up, Tim," Momma said. She and the nurse lifted me behind my shoulder blades. I experienced collapsing, literally, as if my breastplate had been completely removed. My chin dropped forward and I saw down my gown for the first time, the stitching along the center of my chest six inches long and smeared with mercurochrome like war paint. Frankensteinian, but flat. My chest flat. Fixed. They eased me upright and helped me swing my legs off the bed. The nurse moved the IV stand to get closer to me. She and Momma lifted while Daddy stationed himself close in front, and Alan and Robert stood off to the side. Gravity took my feet to the floor. Everything blurred. "Hold your shoulders back," the nurse said. I strained to stand straight, but I sagged. Momma clutched my arm, while Daddy held his arms out toward me. "You doing fine," he said.

The next day, I sat up and examined myself with a handheld mirror. Stitches stood above the cut line like spider hairs. My entire chest quivered with every heartbeat. Hideous, but level. The day after that, they took away the morphine and the doctor's saw work came alive. Two days later, the surgeon strolled in and examined me once more. "He'll have to stay out of school at least a month," he said to my parents. "When he goes back, he can't be bumped or the whole thing could collapse. He'll need to arrive at school and to each class early; he'll need to leave each class early and leave school early. His chest should be completely solid again in three months, but we'll want to be safe." He shook my hand. "I'll see you before then." A few minutes later, they wheeled me to the hospital door. I was new, but no longer quite me. Not the cocky quarterback. Not the kid who had beaten Pogue's ass. Not even a kid who could be jostled.

Several weeks later, Larry, Robert's closest friend from Vietnam, arrived from Wisconsin, and his presence unleashed a desperate camaraderie and harshness I hadn't seen in Robert before. They had been in touch long-distance since they'd both come home, and although I didn't know it, Larry had come to Louisiana after temporarily kicking a heroin addiction that would evidently later help lead to his suicide. He had gentle, deep blue eyes, shaggy blonde hair, a thick droopy mustache, and a booming laugh that was a surprise, coming from his thin frame. He lived with us only a week, sleeping in the bunk below me before finding his own place, but because he visited so often he seemed to live with us longer. Momma took him in almost as another son, while Daddy distanced or went into tirades over Robert and Larry smoking on the front stoop and staying out late drinking. Larry infected Robert with exuberance to tell stories about the war, using their strange vocabulary—LZ, frag, CO, zap, grease, short-timer, dee-deed, Cobras, Hueys, Puff, claymores, fifty cals, dinks—which is so familiar now. Their exotic language kept me so off balance that one afternoon when Robert said, "That was a shitty J-O-B," I asked, "What's a J-O-B?" He and Larry laughed. "A job, dumbshit," Robert said.

They careened from the excitability of boys telling anecdotes of defiance, pranks, and practical jokes, to the bitterness and callousness of men who had seen and caused death. My bedroom connected to the kitchen and when they came home late, I heard them talk about how much they'd drunk, the women they'd fucked, and finally what life over there had been like. "You remember the day that Chinook flew over carrying that big net filled with dead gooks and dumped 'em in the sea?" Larry asked. "Looked like a big insect, all those arms and legs sticking out."

"Yeah, nobody went to the beach for like two weeks," Robert said.

"I remember the first time I saw 'em shove a dink out of a chopper to get another one to talk."

"Right. Then they shoved the other one's ass out when they got what they wanted."

"Fuckin' A, Geronimo."

"Day I got there," Robert said, "they took me to triage and this dude who'd stepped on a mine came in with his foot still in his boot and just hanging on to his leg. Nurse takes a scalpel and snips the meat holding it on and hands me the foot to bag. I go to puking and when I come up she goes, 'I'm sorry, honey, is this your first day?'"

Late 1971, Early 1972: Blood and Bone

They talked about their nightmares, Robert's recurring one of snow falling in the jungle and his dropping bullets into it where he couldn't find them, then having his M16 melt in his grip. They talked about battles, like the one where Robert's squad wandered into the middle of a North Vietnamese regiment and had to literally run while setting off claymores, firing backwards, and calling in napalm yards behind them. They talked about dead person after dead person they had known and seen, and they talked about some things that I couldn't quite process or that my mind pushed away, even though I would find later that it had all stayed with me.

"Amodee and them ain't bad," Robert said. "They care, I 'spose, they just don't get it."

"They *can't* fucking get it," Larry said.

"I wouldn't tell 'em some shit anyway. Like that day we had that crazy firefight in that ville and we were all scattered out shooting and that kid ran out and got wasted."

"We did what we had to do, brother."

"Motherfucking Christ, he was about Timmy's age. Everybody was shooting. How they gonna understand that shit?"

When Daddy wasn't home, they sometimes sang dirty army songs. Once they sang all of "Closer to Home," by Grand Funk, about being lost for days uncounted. They stayed quiet for a long time after that.

I would lie flat on my back in the dim light from beneath the kitchen door, my hands resting on my chest. Even though Robert was in the next room, he was somehow no longer in my world, and his and Larry's talk of war seeped into my bones and made them feel even more fragile.

Six weeks after my surgery, Robert started a new job as an orderly at a local hospital. He had been working at a department store dressed as the Disney character, Pluto the dog, and kids kept sticking him with straight pins taken from folded dress shirts. One twelve-year-old had finally stretched him too thin. He told Larry and me, "I told his mother that if he stuck me one more time I was gonna shove him in a basket and roll his ass out the door. Bitch just laughed." He chuckled. "Little motherfucker stuck me again and I flipped him upside down and jammed him head first in a basket. Rolled that shit to the front door and shoved the basket in the parking lot with his old lady screaming at me and all the other kids waving their arms and going 'Pluto's gone crazy! Pluto's gone crazy!' Security guards took me upstairs to the boss and I sat there with my big Pluto head in my lap telling him what happened. He goes, 'They're sticking you with pins?' like he didn't believe shit I was saying. So I took my costume down and showed him the bloody pin marks and told him to ask Minnie Mouse and she'd tell him I was telling the truth. He brought her in and she said, 'Yeah, they do that all the time.' He told me to take the rest of the day off. I went over to Chris's bar and got drunk. I ain't gonna be Pluto much fucking longer." He had quit soon thereafter and started his new job as an orderly, which at least had the familiar setting of a hospital.

On his second day, though, reports of trouble near downtown began coming in as snippets and then full reports on TV and the radio: first, of a rally led by Black Muslims from out of town blocking North Boulevard; then of a local television reporter being beaten almost to death; and later of a shoot-out. Three Muslims and two policemen would ultimately die from gunshots, all the confirmed bullets from police weapons, and dozens would go to the hospital.

Momma, Daddy and I were all home, and there was hysteria in the air as we waited for Robert to come home. Daddy cursed the TV and predicted violence would spread across town, as it had in other cities after Martin Luther King's assassination. I was still several weeks from returning to school, and I took it all in with a mix of excitement and dread. We knew from reports that wounded were being taken to the hospital where Robert was working, and Momma called unsuccessfully to make sure he was all right, also checked to see if the two policemen we knew (our next-door neighbor and a man who went to our church) were okay. We knew Robert would have more information for us when he came home.

He burst through the front door late that afternoon, and my parents and I popped up from watching the TV. Robert wore a wild smile that told us the news was grim. "Shoulda guessed," he said. "Second day on the job."

"They brought 'em there?" Daddy asked, dressed in his work khakis.

"A bunch of 'em. Reporter with his brains hanging out. Cops and niggers shot and beat up." He paced between the back of the living room chairs and the console stereo. Momma squeezed the cushiony back of her chair and held her other hand over her mouth. Robert squinted in the direction of the TV, then went outside. We followed. He stepped off the stoop into the rain, pulled out a smoke, shaking so much that he struggled to light it. He kept it cupped in his hand to keep it dry.

"Are you all right?" Momma asked him from the covered porch where we all stood.

"That wasn't nothing. What'd they say on television?"

"Muslims shot several po-lice," Daddy said. "Po-lice shot a bunch of them. They don't know if that reporter's gone live or not."

Robert sucked deeply on his cigarette, then spoke thickly through the smoke. "At least two cops dead and I think two Muslims. I carried one in with a red hole in his chest that matched his red bow tie. I told him he looked nice. Good sucking chest wound." He laughed and flicked, inhaled a third of his Marlboro.

"It's cold and raining, sugar. You sure you're okay?" Momma asked.

"Fine." He pointed his cigarette. "Talked to a couple of cops graduated Istrouma and they said it's a cinch I'll make the force. That means I'm a short-timer. No more shitty jobs after August 25." He field-stripped his cigarette, dropped the filter back into his pack, and lit another one. I waited for Daddy to say something about the smoking and cursing, but he was scowling toward the distance and tapping his fingers on the sides of his legs. Robert was wearing a thin, reddish T-shirt he'd worn all through high school, the shoulders growing deeper red the wetter they became. I asked him where the nice white shirt he'd left the house with was. "Threw it away. Got blood on it. I ain't going back to changing bedpans and stripping sheets anyway." He picked tobacco from one of his front teeth and nodded. "Now if they let me do what I did today, I'm there."

"What'd you do today?" I asked.

"Got to carry 'em off the ambulance and do triage just like old times."

"No telling now," Daddy said, still looking off. "They might go shooting up the whole town."

"Shit," Robert said, "they better have a assload of ammo and some big-go-gettin' guns 'cause the cops are pissed. They ready to pop every black face they see."

Daddy pointed at Momma and me. "Nobody goes nowhere for a while."

My mind swirled with images, the black man with a red dot slurping air, rifles bristling from a car filled with black men, the reporter with a cracked skull. I hoped the police would pour into the streets and mow down the blacks.

"Anyway," Robert said, "I'm going to Chris's bar as soon as Larry gets here."

"There's a curfew," Momma said.

"It's nothing but cops there and they know me."

Daddy shook his head. "Niggers'll be burning things like after King died."

"Let 'em," Robert said.

Momma and Daddy turned and went back inside, as if a string had tugged them simultaneously. Robert smiled almost through me. He put his arm around my shoulder and squeezed it. "You ain't got to worry." I nodded.

Larry's car pulled up in front of the house, and he and Robert shot each other the bird. "Had to bring the shit home with you, eh?" Larry said through the open window before he stepped out.

"I thought *you* brought it, motherfucker. Shit was fine till your ass showed up."

Larry nodded as he crossed the St. Augustine grass in our front yard and stopped in the rain with Robert. "They all come visit your new job?"

"Oh, yeah. Some motherfuckers got zapped today. Cops were freaking out."

Late 1971, Early 1972: Blood and Bone

85

"They didn't have our little vacation to get used to it."

"You right about that," Robert said. "Got their cherries popped, Jack. Let's go get drunk."

"Isn't there a curfew?"

"Fuck a curfew. That curfew ain't for white people. Let me change my shirt."

Robert left Larry and me. Larry moved onto the porch, brushed his mustache on both sides with a knuckle and slung the water. "Exciting day, huh?"

"Yeah," I said.

"You weren't scared, were you?"

"Nah. We got that .22 we used to shoot cans with."

"You miss me in your room?"

"No. You snore worse than Robert."

He laughed. "How you feeling?" He touched his chest.

"I get to go back to school pretty soon. I can't play basketball or football for a while, though."

"You'll be back tearing 'em up in no time."

Robert blew through the front door, tersely saying something behind him. "Bullshit never ends," he said to Larry. "Let's book." He tousled my hair. Larry waved to me and they took off in Robert's car.

Our street was quiet. I thought of going to see what my pals had to say about what had happened, but I wasn't allowed to leave the yard yet. Daddy came to the door and told me to come inside. By the time I went in, he was standing and muttering before the TV again, his hands balled in his back pockets. In the kitchen, my mother sat at the table with her head lowered against her fingertips. I couldn't tell if she was thinking or praying. I hoped she wasn't sick.

1972: Getting Scared

When I returned to school in early February, Momma or Daddy drove me there and back every day, escorted me to my locker and to class before the other kids poured in. Five minutes before each bell, I left and entered the next class before the hallway stampede began. Kids pestered me to explain what had happened and to show them the scar. During gym and recess, I sat in the library near the librarian. I wasn't allowed to go to assemblies. At night, I examined my chest in the mirror, proud of its evenness, yet repulsed by the pink scar, the extra belly button where a tube had been, and by my skinniness and gauntness. I began to think of myself in a new way, as vulnerable, although I didn't yet have that word.

By late February, I was allowed to walk to school again. And by late March, I was beginning to feel comfortable in my new body, although simply walking tested my stamina and my heartbeat still moved my whole chest. Being able to walk with my friends again began to give me back myself, and I was burning to play ball and ride bikes and join in Hot Tail, where the person who found the hidden belt could whip everybody until they reached base. And yet I was more nervous than I'd been before surgery, especially when passing the cheap new apartments populated by transients. The nervousness was worst in the parking lot of the convenience store and biker bar, in front of which hoods like Lassiter and the sexy girls in tube tops and hiphugger bell-bottoms smoked cigarettes and sometimes smarted off. The blast and blat of Harleys jangled me as we passed next to the bar's sidewall and hit the short cut that took a half-block off our walk. When I walked past these places, the possibility that more could crumble arose in me.

Then one day in early April, as we walked by the store, Lassiter called out, "Hey, dude." He thudded toward me in his boots, his mouth set in an unsettling smile. He tossed his long hair, flicked his cigarette and shifted his shoulders inside his army jacket. "Hey, man," I said to him as he came close. I didn't see the swing before it crashed into my jaw. I staggered back a step. My brain caught hold enough to see his fists raised, his feet dancing, then I bolted through the cluster of limbs and vines in the shortcut and hurdled the rail that stopped cars from taking it. My sight narrowed and my lungs burned as I sprinted for one of the few times since my surgery. A block away, I slowed to a stride, breath heaving, my stomach sick. I glanced over my shoulder, expecting Lassiter to be trailing with a pack on onlookers. Only my friends followed. I thought of going back to fight, then a fright like I'd never had stabbed through me. My legs quivered. My friends came closer. I thought of myself as their leader—the tallest, the oldest, the best student, the quarterback—and somehow I had let them down. I wanted to turn and walk fast from them, but I waited, my breath ragged, my pulse wild in my chest.

"You chickenshit," said Freddy, the youngest of them, a small, unstable kid who'd provoked me into several fights by calling me names and spitting on me on our street.

"Shut up," I said.

"He laughed," Chaney said, a wide fire hydrant of a kid who'd tutored us in cursing. "He said he's gonna catch you and whip your ass."

"You pussy," Freddy said.

"Fuck you. I'll beat your ass if you don't shut up," I said, but my breath was running out by the time I finished. I turned and walked.

"You gonna fight him?" Richard asked, the only one who wasn't younger than I was. I didn't say anything.

No one was home when I got there, so I went to my room and lay on my bed. My jaw ached, and I replayed the punch and yelled at myself for not punching back. Why hadn't I? I'd fought before when I was scared, the only difference being that those times I was also mad. But Lassiter had shaken me, not angered me. His punch had come from outside the established order, even though I'd expected it almost from the moment I'd met him. When I calmed down some, I prayed to Jesus about what I should do. Forgive Lassiter? Turn the other cheek? No. That may have been all right for Christ, who had died for others without complaint, but for me and the men I knew, only pussies did that. I stayed in bed until Momma got home from work, then avoided her as much as possible. I didn't say a word about the punch.

That night, when I stepped from the tub, the sink mirror showed me waist up: scrawny arms, dark eye sockets, a shrunken chest bisected by a reddish worm. I could see why Lassiter would attack.

The next morning, I paused at the turn that took us through the shortcut and past the convenience store. My pals watched me, then went along as I took the extra half-block that would avoid Lassiter. When I reached the four-lane at which the store sat within view, I lowered my head, stepped fast across the street, and paced the final block to school. That afternoon, I took the longer route again, dread filling me as it would every morning and afternoon I went this way. I was scared of the beating Lassiter might give me and how a punch might collapse my chest, but more than that, Lassiter's punch had reverberated as a loss of safety and as a physical manifestation of all the things that had gone wrong—my mother's illness, my father's anger, the way Robert had come home. Of course, none of this was conscious, and yet it was there sleepless night after sleepless night, fear and confusion pressing me until humiliation began to outweigh them both. I could barely eat, barely concentrate, barely look at myself in the mirror. I told none of my family about the punch, but I still imagined that they could see the cowardice inside me. I decided that anything was better than the shame I suffered day after day.

On the morning I couldn't stand to avoid Lassiter anymore, I put on the green polyester bell-bottoms and mod puffy-sleeved shirt Momma had laid out. It was only after I was dressed that I realized what a sissy I looked like. Still, I left them on. She'd bought them and loved them and if I changed she'd question me, something I was afraid might make me blurt out what I was going to do. I didn't speak as my friends and I walked to school. When we reached the shortcut that I had been avoiding, I headed into it with the others. Little Johnny asked if I was going to fight. I nodded. Sausage and eggs rose in my throat; a bungee cord stretched tight between my sternum and my intestines. I walked with my eyes forward. My heartbeat spread across me as I entered the convenience store parking lot.

"Hey, fucker!" Lassiter yelled. I turned. His long, dirty blonde hair lifted from his shoulders as he strode toward me. His arms swung wide, his boots clomped on the concrete parking lot. I dropped my book sack and handed my glasses to Richard. Lassiter and the backdrop of boys and girls by the convenience store blurred. All feeling went away, except for the nerves scurrying along the cut-line of my chest. I briefly recalled how it had been as soft as an overripe peach.

The noise of my schoolmates bunching to watch and the traffic on the four-lane next to me faded, leaving only the cadence of Lassiter's boots. When I thought he was within reach, I threw a roundhouse right, missed, and spun off balance. His arm locked around my neck, my head facing the same direction he was. His fist met my cheek, then my nose, then my chin with a sound like gravel crunching between my teeth. My braces cut the inside of my lips and sent coppery blood into my throat. Fear rifled through me, but at least the source was tangible, the pain immediate.

I jerked my head against his looped arm and pushed his back with one hand while trying to block his punches with my other. He was cursing me, and beyond that and the jarring of the punches rang the yelling of my friends and the other spectators, my awareness of audience keen despite what was happening. Each jerk of my head threw him slightly off balance and I was managing to deflect some of the punches, yet it seemed sickeningly clear that I wasn't going to escape. I stretched my arm up and clawed at his eyes. Skin peeled from his cheek beneath my fingernails. He shrieked and I clutched his hair, tugged downward, shoving his back at the same time. "Cocksucker," he yelled, and I tugged and jerked again, broke free, and staggered backward. He spun to face me and this time my roundhouse caught him in the jaw. He stumbled and I punched him again. I charged, pushed him to the cement and jumped on him. We tangled, slugging and wrestling, both his smell and the stink of tobacco surrounding me. Then, somehow, he was on his feet, and I was on my knees. His square-toed boot came at me and I ducked my head and covered my chest. The kick landed on the crown of my skull—that crunch again. I rolled and hoisted to my feet and we were locked, grappling.

We careened across yards of parking lot, trying to hold the other's arms, to keep the other close to avoid long-armed punches, and to land or block punches when we separated the least bit. Every muscle strained as if I were suspending my weight between two rock faces that were constantly shifting. My mind had never processed so much information—how to stay balanced as our legs intertwined; how he would try to hurt me next; how to protect my chest; how best to hurt him; how much I could stand to hurt him; whether hurting him would worsen the fight; what my friends were thinking about my scratching and pulling hair; whether some adult would break us up; how badly I was already hurt; whether I might die; whether I might lose. At the same time, I was trying to block the pain and the fright.

We spun and spun. Lassiter grabbed my hair and huffed, "See how it feels." We stumbled over a slight drop, then the blaring of car horns and the crossing guard's yells told me we were in the middle of the road. For a second, I thought she might stop us, but we kept clutching. Already I was tireder than any football practice had ever made me. A massive ringing like feedback cluttered my head. We broke apart for a flurry of punches that took us back into the parking lot, then we tangled again. We tripped and went down hard, me diagonally on top of him, my back on his stomach. I held his arms as darkness flitted at the edge of my consciousness and black mist rose before my eyes. His breathing was the only thing I could hear outside the noise in my own head. "I'll kill you," he wheezed. I turned my head and saw scratches down his cheek, felt a twinge of shame before fatigue heavied me again. I wondered how I would find energy to fight anymore, knew that the magic kid words, "I give," would not apply here, knew that neither of us would consider saying them anyway. Lassiter's arm squirmed beneath me, not trying to escape, but doing something I couldn't decipher. Then suddenly he was sliding away. I staggered to my feet and saw Jarreau, a notorious sixteen-year-old criminal, drag Lassiter a few feet off before Lassiter made it to his feet. I thought they would both attack me, but Jarreau pulled him to his ragged-out Ford, tossed him in, flipped me off and laughed as he went around to the driver's side. They peeled out.

My breakfast came fully into my throat and I swallowed it again. I bent at the waist and touched the ridge of my chest. My heartbeats shook the bone. My shoulders and neck spasmed like whiplash. The scene around me pulsed, the light dimming and brightening.

"He pulled a knife," Richard said through the fog. I straightened and he handed me my glasses. I slipped them on and brought into focus the kids already moving toward school again, some giggling, some jeering, some staring and pointing, some oblivious. I touched the top of my head, found a Ping-Pong ball knot and checked my fingertips for blood. I spat pink.

"What?"

"He got a knife out his pocket and was trying to open it and Jarreau grabbed him."

"You pulled his hair, you sissy," Freddy said.

"Shut up," Chaney said.

I tried to process the knife and Jarreau, who was rumored to have killed two black kids with a rifle and was known around our neighborhood for his run-ins with police. My exhaustion and shaking chest kept me from grasping any of it.

"You oughta go home," Richard said, looking at my clothes. My collar was ripped, a button was torn, dirt was ground into the knees and elbows. Dust coated me. Richard handed me my book sack. Its small heft tweaked my bicep.

"Y'all fought for like ten minutes," Chaney said. "You stopped traffic."

"You going home, sissy?" Freddy said.

Streamers of smoke rose on the horizon from the refinery stacks off by the Mississippi. The long angle of the morning sun struck me as impossibly normal. I shook my head.

"We better get to school," Little Johnny said.

We moved toward the crossing lady, who stood with her fists on her hips. From the convenience store, some of the hoods hooted and cussed me. The crossing lady scowled. The guard stepped to the middle of the road where I had been just a few minutes before. She held out her arm. "I thought you were a nice boy," she said. A picture of Lassiter slipping a knife from his pocket drifted to mind. I had no idea what was supposed to happen next.

All day at school, I clenched against the building stiffness in my neck, shoulders and legs, the ache in my hands, the throb in my skull and face, and the strain across my chest. Classes passed in a slow blur, my head drooping toward sleep, while at the same time my mind skittered. I waited for the principal to call me in, for some teacher to say something, but no one did. None of them even knew, I'm sure, but my brain couldn't fathom that. When recess finally came, I went into the bathroom and sponged at the dust and dirt on my clothes, checked the friction rash on my neck from tugging against Lassiter's headlock, tested the knot on my head, then sat on the closed toilet and dozed before going out into the large school-yard. Outside, I braced against accusations that I had fought like a girl. A few kids said they had seen me fight, made light of it or commented on who had won, but mostly people stayed quiet. A few of the glances seemed to say they were as unable as I was to process why the good kid had been in a brawl against a hardcore juvenile delinquent, but most acted as they always did, probably because they had no idea it had happened or didn't care if they did.

Finally, the Hughes brothers came over. Rangy, wide-shouldered, scraggly haired boys, both were older than they were supposed to be for the grades they were in, and everybody suspected they sold pot, even though my friends and I didn't know much about that world yet. We'd gotten to know each other a little because the younger had been a tight end on the football team, and I'd passed him the ball when there wasn't a play for that.

"Lassiter pulled a blade on you?" he drawled.

The question seemed so foreign that I had to work to get an answer. "They said he did."

"Jarreau took him off?" the older Hughes asked. I nodded. They looked at each other. "Why you think Jarreau to keep him from using that knife?"

"I don't know," Thomas answered. "Maybe Lassiter's carrying for him."

"Might could be. He maybe thought Lassiter might spill something if the cops got him," the older Hughes said. He spat. "They both sorry shits." The brothers focused on me as if I could confirm this. The bell rang. I flinched. They nodded and walked off, but I didn't move.

That afternoon, my friends and I took the longer route again, another concession to cowardice, I believed, as they rehashed the fight and speculated on what would happen next with Jarreau and Lassiter. Finally, I told them I didn't want to hear it anymore. I walked down the scruffy, asphalt streets next to grassy drainage ditches, waiting for Lassiter to appear, my whole body protesting with soreness and exhaustion not quite like any I'd ever experienced, not even when my lung had collapsed. When we turned the last corner and

I saw that Lassiter wasn't there, I breathed fully at the safety of my street. I almost smiled, too, until a second later it struck me that my problem with him was going to continue, an ellipsis of fights, even if I won one here and there. I remembered he had a knife. For the first time in my life, futility struck me.

I peeled off from my pals without a word. I had decided not to tell my parents or brothers. Daddy wouldn't be home from the plant until around midnight, and Momma would be at J. C. Penney's until about nine. I would tell her my pants were dirty and my shirt ripped from playing football at recess and take my scolding. In the house, I slammed the door behind me, and the tears I'd been holding burned out of my eyes. "Tim?" came Momma's voice from the back, then the creak of her bed and the pad of her footsteps down the hall. I wanted to bolt, but she came into the living room wearing a work dress wrinkled from lying down, her pouf of blonde hair crushed on one side. "What's wrong?" she asked. Her face was flushed, eyes bleary from napping, and I knew she was home because she wasn't feeling well. "You all right, sugar?" she asked and stepped forward to touch me. I moved back. Something dropped from my throat through my chest. I wanted to tell her what had happened, and I would within the hour, except for the knife, which I thought would worry her too much. But right then, admitting how scared I was and how weak I'd been, first in avoiding and then in not winning the fight, seemed a sure way to bring pity that would only multiply my shame.

I was in bed when I heard Daddy come in from work and the murmur of Momma's voice, punctuated by the deep rumble of his replies. I had asked her not to tell him, but I knew that was what she was doing. I stared at the dim glint of the plastic tiger's eyes and grinded my teeth. I didn't know what Daddy would say or do. After kid fights on my street, I'd sometimes gotten whippings and punishments, sometimes praise for sticking up for myself. But those were neighborhood scraps. I didn't know if he'd be proud that I had defended myself, angry that I hadn't avoided the fight like a good Christian, or disappointed that I hadn't beaten Lassiter's ass. When they were finally quiet, I traced the spongy seam on my breastbone over and over. Some time during the night I dozed off, but I was awake again earlier than usual. Daddy was up early, too, and at the breakfast table drinking coffee when I walked stiffly in and sat, forcing myself not to wince. My entire body felt as though I had been racked. I was thankful that Robert hadn't gotten up yet, most likely having stayed out late with Deborah, his steady girlfriend now.

"Heard you got in a scrape," he said. His heavy whiskers were shaved, his black receding hair slicked back from his dark features, telling me he'd been up even earlier than I thought. "Who'd you tussle with?" I didn't look at Momma, who was setting a skillet of her buttermilk biscuits on the table. They were as large as bagels and as light on the inside as cotton candy, but I couldn't stand the thought of tasting one. Daddy put a large daub of butter on his plate, poured cane syrup over it, and mixed them. I wondered if he was awake of his own accord or if Momma had urged him to get up.

"He's a kid hangs around that store. He doesn't go to school."

"How come you to fight him?" Daddy asked. He reached for a biscuit and then speared two patty sausages. Neither Momma or I moved for the food.

"He's one of them kids that just likes to fight," I said. "He hung around here some last summer, before that kid Vic moved."

"Vic's the one was in that rental house?"

"Yes, sir."

"And y'all ain't had words or nothing?"

The thought of Lassiter's original punch and my running flushed through me. "No, sir."

"Eat," my mother said, and I picked up a hot biscuit and dropped it on my plate, my stomach greening.

"Well," Daddy said, chewing his biscuit, "your momma and me think you oughta ride in the car to school for a little while. I want you to stay away from scrapping too." His voice sounded casual, but for a second the concern flashed across his eyes. Was he scared? He couldn't be. I nodded, my ears hot, my chest cold. I was certain he saw me as a coward, although his reaction didn't say that. Maybe Momma had told him to say what he said, told him how the night before I'd squinted against a headache as I moved around the house

1972: Getting Scared

95

like an arthritis patient. I took a bite of biscuit and chewed, the biscuit expanding as mush.

When Momma asked my friends if they wanted to ride to school with us, they glanced around at each other before piling in. At school, after they'd gotten out, I leaned back inside the car. "You shouldn't of told him. Don't tell Robert." I slammed the door.

Micro Terrorism

At school, some of the hoods who thought I was okay told me that Lassiter was mouthing off about me, and a couple of older holdbacks even told me they hoped I would beat his sorry ass. One said to look out for Jarreau. "Why?" I asked. "Fucker's crazy," he said. A chill went through me. Even so, a week after the fight I convinced my parents to let me walk again, and again I took the longer route. My friends sometimes took it with me and sometimes they didn't. On the way home several days in, we safely passed both the intersection from which I could see the convenience store and then the shortcut we'd avoided. Relief lifted me when I got past this point, and I was still feeling it as I neared the last turn onto my street.

"Hey, you," somebody called from behind. I glanced back and saw three people twenty yards away. The one in the lead, who had obviously called out, was a tenth-grader with long bright red hair, black-rimmed glasses, bell-bottom jeans, and a tight T-shirt. I knew him only by sight, but I knew he was the older brother of a kid I knew from school. A couple of steps behind him was a beautiful black-haired girl in tight jeans and flowing hippie blouse. Next to her strode Jarreau, his body as squat and muscular as a boxer's, his face, I imagined, scrunched beneath his outdated crew cut hair, his eyes agleam with unsteady light. I figured he was siccing Chandler on me for entertainment.

"I said *hey*, you little sonofabitch," Chandler yelled. I picked up my pace and made the turn onto my street.

"He's talking to you," Freddy said.

"I know he's talking to me."

"You chickening out again?"

"Shut up, prick."

"You better stop!" Chandler yelled. "I want to talk to you!" The laughter from Jarreau and the girl reached me, but I kept walking. When I reached the street in front of my house, Chandler said, "You better talk to me," and I stopped because I didn't want him to see which house was mine. He closed the gap between us fast with long strides, while Jarreau and the girl watched from the end of the street, four houses away. I hoped that some adult would look out, hoped that Robert would miraculously show, that my friends would help me. And I also hoped that none of that would happen since it would just heap more evidence that I was defenseless. Chandler pulled up a foot away.

"Heard you been calling me names, motherfucker," he said, pointing close to my nose.

"I don't even know you, *man.*"

"You calling me a liar?"

"Man, I ain't calling you a liar, man." The word "man" crowded my head as if it might offer me some coolness as protection. My voice trembled, my desire strong to claim that I was friends with his little brother.

"Jarreau said you were. You calling Jarreau a liar?"

"I don't even know Jarreau. I didn't say nothing."

"Don't call me a liar, you little shit."

In my head a voice said, *Hit me and get it over with.* Sweat wetted my palms and a shiver erupted from my core. My arm tensed with the notion of hitting him first and getting my beating over with. The possibility of pain scared me, but it wasn't the pain that terrorized me most. My house was thirty feet away, my friends were standing there next to me, and yet I was the most unsafe and hopeless I had ever been. I broke and sprinted across the street to the house of an old lady who sometimes tried to get us to dance to Hank Williams when she drank too much. I still didn't want Chandler to know where I lived, and I also figured the old lady wouldn't see me, or, even if she did, wouldn't judge because she wouldn't understand how cowardly I was. I jumped up on her porch and looked back, but Chandler hadn't followed. He just laughed hard as he headed back toward Jarreau and the girl, his derision worse than any punch. I wanted both to die and to kill, and not in the abstract way of a kid. I barely heard my friends as I recrossed the street on the way back to my own house, which I hoped again was empty.

The two detectives distorted our living room, and I kept glancing through our picture window, praying that none of my friends would see the detective car and figure out what it was. They were there because my mother had read my intensifying fright and pressed me until I told her about Jarreau and Chandler. Then, despite my begging her not to, she contacted the juvenile detectives through a policeman who attended our church and asked them to our house. Telling them about Jarreau and Chandler in front of Momma was like regurgitating venom, but I was glad, at least, that Robert and Daddy weren't there. She hadn't told Robert about the fight because I had pleaded with her not to and, I guess, because she was afraid of what he might do. Likewise, I suppose, she hadn't told Daddy about Jarreau or calling the detectives because he would feel like he needed to handle it himself or be ashamed that there really was no way he could handle it.

I told the detectives the story with as few words as possible, metal bands forming across my shoulders and neck. But I didn't mention the knife. I thought if I did, Lassiter would be arrested and I would have given in. I also thought that the situation might escalate to every day stalking by Jarreau and Chandler. When I finished, I glared at the floor.

"So Jarreau and Chandler didn't hit you," said the detective who was drinking coffee and staring at me while the other took notes.

"No, sir."

He sipped and focused on Momma. "We know Jarreau. He's a troublemaker; been in and out of juvey detention. We can go talk to him and this Chandler character, but we can't really do anything until they lay a hand on the boy."

"Would that do any good?" she asked.

"We could see." He looked at me. "We could haul in this Lassiter too and book him with battery."

Spit filled my mouth. It was true that Jarreau and Chandler hadn't touched me. I sensed, whether it was real or not, how weak these detectives thought I was, believed that what was happening to me was nothing compared to the crimes they usually dealt with. "I ain't scared of Lassiter," I said. The coffee drinker uh- huhed.

"You're telling me," Momma said, "that you can't do anything about these older boys coming to our house and threatening our son?" Her complexion was pink, as if her fever had spiked, and I looked past her through the picture window to the street where Chandler and I had been.

"Not really, ma'am," the note-taker said. "I think if we talk to Jarreau, it might just add fuel to the fire."

"Then I'd like you to arrest this Lassiter boy and maybe show the others."

"No!" I said and popped up.

"They need to talk to somebody, Tim," Momma said.

"No," I said again. "It'll make it worse."

The three sat silently. I had never seen adults appear so helpless, ashamed, whatever they were, and it was my fault. I wanted to scream at all of them and vanish.

The detectives stood and shook Momma's hand, told her if the older boys touched me, to let them know. When they were gone, Momma and I just stood there. I knew she wanted to protect me, but I was furious at her that she couldn't, that I couldn't, that no one could, and that two strangers now knew it. She reached to touch me and I moved away. "You have to let them do something, honey." I brushed past her and went out the back door. In the garage, I grabbed a baseball bat, went to the backyard, and beat a pine until my hands couldn't grip anymore.

Fear Itself

I faced it over and over without facing it, until one morning I again walked with my friends through the shortcut brambled with saplings and vines, the stench of the low canal thick, walked past the rear of the biker bar, its cinder block back mottled with mildew and graffiti, and into the convenience store parking lot. I inhaled as we headed to the spot where Lassiter and I had begun to fight. My legs and arms tingled. My friends fell quiet. What logic was there in not going the extra half-block, except that all logic had been pulverized. I flexed my fingers, tensed my shoulders and fixed my eyes straight ahead. In my peripheral vision, I could see the kids by the convenience store, the girls and boys who already knew sex and were already doing drugs that I would soon do, some of these kids suffering humiliations like the dark cylindrical scars I'd seen on Lassiter's arms. "There's that fucking pussy," Lassiter yelled. My muscles tensed. "You fight like a girl, bitch." I looked at him next to the store, his face sneering, cigarette in the corner of his mouth. The fight came back to me as slush in my bowels, a crash of boot to skull, exhaustion that had quaked my legs. I would have given anything not to fight again, but nothing could pay off the little dying every time I strode that extra half-block. I kept moving, my eyes locked with his, and so did Lassiter's mouth. But Lassiter didn't move. He cursed and laughed and took a drag off his smoke. I turned my head. The crossing guard stopped traffic, and my friends and I passed between the stopped cars, or so I suppose. My perception had blitzed white. I didn't consider that Lassiter may not have wanted anything more to do with me either. All I thought was I hadn't changed anything by taking the shorter route, because next time Lassiter might decide to attack or Jarreau might be there in his place.

Finally, summer came like a gift. I didn't sleep well, but I could forget the trouble when I was shooting basketball or playing RISK or visiting the Goudeau or Sims girls. My friends and I went back to our dirty-talking, roughhousing selves. Our newest activity was to jump off our bikes while they were moving and see who could get theirs to travel riderless the farthest (the bikes often crashing into neighbors' cars parked on the narrow street). A kid turned us on to Black Sabbath, Chaney beat the kid up for being a smart-ass, Little Johnny's dog fought mine, Freddy called us names, and Richard's dad bought him an Elsinore dirt bike. Richard and I talked about ninth grade, our last year of junior high, talked about being so close to tenth grade and high school, and about getting our drivers' licenses.

During a campout in our garage, Robert, Larry and Amodee showed up drunk and found me reading H. P. Lovecraft out loud to my friends. They mocked us, then grossed us out by saying that pussy tasted like peanut butter, onions, and tuna fish. After that, they gave us two cigarettes to share. "Make sure you don't smoke 'em in the garage next to that gasoline," Robert said. Late that night, we threw matches into the storm drain at the end of the street, setting off an explosion of accumulated methane gas that set us running to hide in the backyard until we were sure no one had called the police. Still later, we tore through the quiet neighborhood on our bicycles, knocking over garbage cans and an abandoned washing machine that boomed when it toppled onto the asphalt.

Sometimes I forgot about Jarreau and Lassiter, again experiencing joy like a kid, but whenever I left the street on my bike to go to work at a snowball stand not far from Jarreau's house, my bones thrummed with anxiety. Jarreau and Lassiter were always there like specters, and so I also prayed hard. I asked God to protect me, asked how I had failed as a Christian, even as I counted the commandments I regularly failed and asked for forgiveness. I wanted Jesus's love, but I had begun to doubt its power and importance. In church, I was still pounded by the threat of Arabs and Communists and blacks, and by our need to be stalwart Christian soldiers. Services seemed more and more to be preparation for the impending apocalypse than a call to be loving and tolerant. I wondered what I was, then, not to welcome personal combat against my enemies.

August came with a blow. Robert announced that he and Deborah had gotten married and had already rented an apartment. He would begin receiving pay as a policeman in a couple of weeks, so they could afford it. Momma, Daddy and I sat in shock. Momma finally hugged him and said she was proud. Daddy shook his hand. Then the conversation flared over why they'd eloped and not included anybody. Robert said they just didn't want the hassle of a big wedding and eventually stormed out. Momma and Daddy stood silently. I went to my room. I wanted to be happy for him, but he'd shut us all out and was leaving the house without having talked to me first. I had never told him about what had happened, but his being at home had somehow protected me nonetheless. His leaving felt like betrayal.

◆　◆　◆

As school neared, dread slithered in, but I had been cleared to play football and that was a balm to the corrosiveness of constant wariness. A week before classes, my pal Mike Coats called to say that the ninth-grade coach had asked him to round up a couple of people to throw and catch the ball in order to simulate penalties for a training session for new referees. It thrilled me to be going to play ball, but as soon as I hung up, I pictured the route to school hotly lit and unpopulated by my schoolmates, thought of the route to school impending every coming day. The next morning, I hopped on my bike and pedaled, my throat tight until I bumped onto the football field, its grass slightly browned and patchy from the summer sun. Mike and his pal, Hebert, were already there tossing the football as Coach talked to a group of about fifteen men in their twenties and thirties. I had worried all summer about whether I could make it as quarterback, because Coach liked the wishbone, which featured a running quarterback instead of a passing quarterback, and Jason Stanley was a faster, better ball carrier than I was. I also worried about whether my body would serve me, not only because of the surgery and the lack of physical activity, but also because I was surging taller without putting on much weight and feeling clumsy for the first time in my life. Plus, my knees ached from growing too fast. I saw this day as a tryout for quarterback, or at least for split end. If I couldn't start in football, that would be final proof I was weak.

Coach put some of the young referee wannabes on defense and Mike, Hebert and I took turns being center, quarterback, and receiver. A few minutes into the session, Coach whispered to the ref playing defense (and then to us) that he wanted to simulate pass interference. We weren't wearing pads or helmets, and the penalties simulated so far had been light contact. I split out wide and the man in his twenties crouched and eyed me as if he and I were in an actual game. My blood rose. I wanted to beat him, even though I knew he knew my route and was going to interfere before the pass reached me, so the other refs could make the call. Hebert snapped the ball to Mike, and I sprinted off the line toward the defender. Just in front of him, I cut hard toward the middle. Mike threw the ball high. I leaped and extended as far as I could, determined to hold on even with interference. At the peak of my jump, just before the ball reached my hands, the ref cut my legs at the ankles from behind. I saw the sky, then the world going upside down as I flipped backwards. I kept my arms out to break my fall and caught my full weight on my left wrist. Pain fired through my arm. I smacked down on my chest. I heard the future refs making the call and Coach's gruff voice saying, "This ain't full contact, boy," to the ref who had hit me. I stood and gripped my wrist. "How 'bout that?" the ref whispered.

I jogged back to Mike, Hebert, and Coach. "You okay, Parrish?" Coach asked. I let go of my wrist and nodded. "Good, shake it off," he said.

The next round of plays, I was quarterback, and I took snaps that jammed the ball into my hands and shot red through my wrist. But I stayed until the finish, my passes accurate from my uninjured arm. On the ride home, I struggled to grip the left handlebar, my fingers numb, and finally rode the straight-aways with no hands, turned corners with just my right.

I hid the injury from my parents at supper, and all evening wriggled my fingers against the pain. The thought of another doctor made me clench. I couldn't lose football.

During the night, the throb in my wrist awakened me. The next morning, I studied my swollen, purpled wrist and fingers. At breakfast, I tried to hide it, but Momma caught a wince and told me to show her. A disproportionate panic rushed through me. I held my arm behind my back. "Tim," Daddy said as he walked into the kitchen, "you stop that foolishness."

"It's just sprained."

"Hush," Momma said. She took my hand in hers. "Goodness gracious," she said. My wrist was twice its normal size.

"I ain't going to the doctor," I said.

"What happened?" Daddy asked. "You fight that boy again? You best tell me this second." I exhaled and did tell him. "I'll be goddogged," Daddy said. "I oughta whip their sorry asses. I'm going to see that durn coach."

"Please, Daddy, don't." Inside me almost everything I could call a self was spiraling.

"We're going to the doctor," Momma said.

I didn't bother to argue. I knew this was it. My last chance to be a man taken away. My ability to care for myself in the least of ways stripped down. To my mind, the cast I wore by noon was akin to a little tomb for who I'd been.

When school began again, so did the movie from the previous spring. I avoided the convenience store, but even on the longer route I saw Lassiter within the first two weeks. He didn't say anything, his expression distracted and tired. Jarreau, though, was seeing a girl from our school, and I had seen him a number of times driving to drop her off. Somehow, my reaction to him had multiplied exponentially, a spring in my core twisting and then stretching to the point of fragmenting. I lowered my head to avoid being seen, gripped my cast as if that would hide my vulnerability, but one day he caught sight of me just as I crossed the street onto the school ground. He pulled into the parking lot along the road, his girlfriend close to him, and stuck his head out the window. "Little cocksucker!" he yelled. He flipped me off and cackled. I kept moving, glad I was safe on the school ground, although every ounce of terror, doubt, shame, and confusion concentrated in my veins like toxin. My vision tunneled. Jarreau's laugh faded as I strode toward the beige brick building and around its side, leaving my friends behind. Out of Jarreau's sight, I leaned against the wall and breathed, the schoolyard rippling before me, tears pressing the backs of my eyeballs.

My cast came off a week later, exposing my wrist, white, thin, and atrophied, symbolic of my general condition. Without football or even the confidence that I could safely walk to school, I didn't really know who I was anymore. Disgust at myself constantly percolated. My only respite was to shoot basketball in our driveway. I tried to lose myself in the roll of the ball off my fingertips and the simplicity of jumping, hoped to strengthen the wrist and regain my body before basketball season. That's what I was doing when Robert drove up in his white Fairlane.

He stepped out in his brand new police uniform, Confederate gray with red epaulets and red piping. The force was so short on personnel that they had put him on the street without sending him to the academy, and he bristled with a manic happiness that gave the stories he told about his new job an edgy fervor that even his 'Nam stories sometimes didn't have. He adjusted his gun belt and strolled toward me. He wiped the corners of his mouth, the sign that he was keyed up. I dribbled, staring at his wood-handled .38, at his belted copper-headed bullets, and at his blackjack and mace—so many things that could erase Jarreau. He lit a cigarette.

"Why didn't you tell me?" he asked.

I caught the ball. "About what?"

"Jarreau."

I hadn't told Momma about Jarreau cursing me at school, but maybe she had noticed that I was leaving earlier in the morning, noticed, like before, other things that I didn't even know I showed.

"Momma told you?"

"What you think?"

"I told her not to."

"Well, she did." He flicked his smoke. "Can't believe this shit's been going on since spring." We stared at each other, shame, betrayal and something close to relief colliding in me. "Well, you ain't gonna have anymore problems," he said, his blue eyes alive with sunburst wildness. "I went to Jarreau's house."

"You did?"

"Goddamn right I did." He grinned. "His old man answered the door. Just let me in and told me Jarreau was taking a nap in his room. I figure his old man's let the cops in before." Jarreau lived two houses down from one of Robert's old friends, so Robert knew Jarreau and the criminal decline he'd been on for years. He flicked his smoke, waiting. "You wanta know what happened?"

"Yeah."

Robert laughed and nodded. "I went down this little hall till I heard that fucker snoring and I eased the door open. Piece of shit was laying there on his back on this bed about a foot off the floor. Looked like he was stoned 'cause his mouth was wide open and he was out. I took my nightstick"—Robert mimed the gesture—"and got up next to him. Then I just shoved it between that fucker's teeth and pushed my foot on his throat. You should've seen that sonofabitch choke awake with his eyes all bugging out and his mouth fulla wood." Robert took a deep drag. "His arms flew up there to grab the stick, and I went, 'Try something, Jarreau, please try something.' He looks at me like he'd done shit his pants and he kinda laid back. I asked him if he knew who I was and he nodded a little, his teeth all pried open." Robert leaned toward me, poking the air with his cigarette, making me want to take a step back. "I told him, 'You fuck with my brother again and you're a dead asshole.'" He straightened. "I gave him a stomp on the throat and took my club back and just stood there looking at him." Robert's eyes gleamed. He wiped several times at the spittle collecting at the corners of his mouth.

He took a last drag and spoke through a cloud of smoke, but not directly to me this time. "Piece of shit. He was holding his windpipe and still choking when I left." Robert shifted his feet and hooked his free hand in his gun belt while he rolled the last fire and tobacco out of the cigarette butt, then put the filter in his shirt pocket. He leaned back against the ironwork that lined our short walkway from the driveway to the front steps. "You happy?" he asked me.

"You think he'll let me alone?"

"He will if he wants to stay alive."

"That'll be cool." I stood there looking at Robert smile. "Thanks."

"Uh-huh." He kept nodding. "You shoulda told me, though. You shouldn't make Momma figure this shit out and have to worry."

I nodded back because I didn't really know what to say. I wanted to be happy, but already the fleeting relief I'd felt was passing. Anger was roiling off Robert like smoke from a heavy smolder, and even though I knew that he had fought in Vietnam and heard him tell brutal stories, heard his nightmares, I understood for the first time that he could actually kill someone.

He shoved off the ironwork and **grabbed** my shoulder. "If some older dude messes with you, you better tell me, all right?"

I watched him drive off, the smell of his cigarette lingering. He was still my brother, but the sense that he wasn't quite the brother I'd had before was more intense than ever.

The next afternoon, I stayed late after school for a meeting about running for class president. The world felt different. All the previous night, I had reveled in the images Robert had given me of roughing up Jarreau. I put myself in Robert's place and stomped Jarreau more than once, hit him with the club, even pulled the trigger with the pistol at his temple. I should've known this fantasy would have a dark cost. Two blocks from home, I saw him. He leaned against a street sign smoking a cigarette, no Chandler or girl this time. I thought of turning and running, but running would only bring me to the next day. He squinted as I approached, maybe unsure it was me, then shoved off with his shoulder when I came close. My head did a slow spin inside. He flicked a cigarette in my direction. I looked at the ground and braced for something so bad I couldn't even imagine it.

"You sorry cunt," he said as I passed him. He stepped behind me so close his words touched my shoulder. "Little fucking dickless wimp, send your brother to fuck with me. I'm gonna take care of you and that pig." His words were the edge of a blade raked along my spine. White spots exploded like tiny fireworks in front of me. In my head I could see his fist swinging at my skull, or his hand reaching to turn me and stab me, but he didn't touch me. Instead, he kept following close, spewing insults that almost washed my legs from under me, every syllable spoken with animal conviction, my consciousness thinning to paper until I walked in a haze.

At the end of my street, he stopped, but I didn't believe he stopped because he was scared of Robert or of anything. "You remember I'm waiting, motherfucker," he yelled. "I'll kill you and your brother." I kept my eyes on the grain of the street's cement so that I wouldn't collapse. It didn't register that even though he'd threatened me, he still had never touched me, and it wouldn't register for a long time, his words alone a splinter deep in me. When I entered my house, I collapsed on the couch and didn't cry, didn't move for an hour or so. I gathered whatever I had in me so I wouldn't say a thing to Robert or my parents, so that this time they wouldn't see what was inside.

Book Two: What Follows

Spring 1974: Looking for Salvation

All of ninth grade I avoided the convenience store, and after a while a semblance of normalcy returned. In the seeming other world of school, I was elected student council president, earned the highest GPA in my class and played second-string on the basketball team. In that world, Jarreau and Lassiter sometimes shrank to only presences in my spine. Outside of school, though, I still understood that part of what had marked me was being the goody-goody overachiever. I dreaded more humiliation and looked forward to tenth grade and JV football to prove myself strong. But at the start of summer, my parents told me my football days were over, a wise move considering how spindly I was, but no less crushing. I ranted and argued, and when they wouldn't give, I signed up to attend basketball camp in the mornings before I went to work as a stock boy at TG&Y afternoons and nights. By the time basketball season began, I'd earned a starting position, but as the season progressed, the constant criticism of coaches eroded my flimsy confidence and raw skills. I quit three-quarters through. Another defeat. Another flight from challenge and a fight. Near the end of tenth grade, I felt transported back to when I'd felt least secure and most helpless. And the fear I had suppressed waited like both a land mine and a trapdoor.

My equation of self was both simple and complex. The simple was obvious: I'd lost my sense of safety, and with it a clear sense of self. The complex equation was the convoluted way I thought I might reclaim myself from fear and confusion. Deep down I still loved Jesus's teachings and hated the church's hypocrisy. And yet I wanted the security of belonging to the implied army of angry people who professed a need to stand against the threat of intruders; I wanted the clarity of a clear enemy. When I switched to the church near my house and the congregation there also chose to vote on whether or not to allow integration, the enemy became clearer than ever. The vote offered the opportunity for me to join them in their anger; however, rather than join with them and *belong* in the way I wanted, I didn't vote at all. I began to skip church, disgusted by the contradiction between their professed Christianity and their lack of tolerance, disgusted at myself. My ambivalence created double binds in every direction. Every day brought alienation and the expectation of humiliation, and those brought desire for the armor of rage I saw around me. I couldn't make sense of it all. I wanted a simple solution. Naturally, the illusion of one—of protection, masculinity, power, approval, and purpose—showed up right on time.

He appeared out of the darkness at the mouth of our garage. His shiny auburn hair hung past his huge rounded shoulders. His narrow face and thin, angled eyebrows radiated intensity. His thick forearms pulsed as he opened and closed his hands. "Mind if I lift?" he asked, his voice a rumble. My friend Stem and I paused from putting more weights on the barbell, momentarily speechless. "Come on in," I said. He stood loose and smiling, charging the scene like a movie gunfighter. My nerves sizzled in my ridiculously thin, six-four, hundred-forty-pound body. His six-two, two-hundred-plus pounds of muscle thinned me even more. "Kurt Dyer," he said, and shook our hands, his grip a crank too strong for a simple friendly gesture. We already knew who he was. Only in eleventh grade, he was already a legend in our school of 1,200—a fierce brawler rumored to have beaten up fifteen black guys at once, as well as a cool dude respected by fighters for his toughness and desired by some of the best-looking girls. I knew he'd moved onto my street a month ago because I'd seen him cruising past in his older black Firebird, cigarette dangling, rock 'n' roll blaring, but I never imagined him speaking to me there at the end of my unworthy first year of high school.

Stem slid up the bench on his back and gripped the barbell above him. I helped lift it off its support, and he began bench-pressing. Stem was Robert's drawling, sawed-off brother-in-law. We were in the same grade, and he and I had become pals after Robert and Deborah's hurried, secret marriage, better pals than Robert and Deborah from what we could see. Stem finished his reps and stood, his bare chest deep brown, his wavy blonde hair combed to the side.

"You done?" Dyer asked Stem.

"Done enough."

"Y'all spot me on some reps?"

"Sure," I said.

"Hold it steady." I held the middle of the barbell as Dyer slid two more twenty-five-pound plates onto each end. Stem and I raised our eyebrows at each other. Dyer slipped beneath the bar. We struggled it off to him and he bounced the weight off his chest, expelling ferocious breaths as if he had a grudge against the bar. After twenty reps, we cradled the bar back into the brackets. "That felt good," Dyer said as he sat up. He rubbed his breastbone. "I shouldn't bounce that shit off me. Year ago, I separated the cartilage doing that." I touched my own chest.

Stem, Dyer and I did some curls and military presses, mine the lightest weight of all, then Dyer did dead lifts with all the weight I had. "That's it for me," I said, soaking wet in the hot garage, which smelled like chemicals and gasoline. Stem and I stacked the weights while Dyer stood off to the side. When we finished, Stem slipped his shirt on. "I gotta get home," he said to me.

"Stem can't see over the wheel to drive, so I'm his taxi," I said.

"You just my bitch," Stem said.

"Mind if I ride?" Dyer asked.

Dyer took shotgun and Stem sat in the backseat as we took off in the Dodge Dart that Daddy bought as a second car. I cranked Deep Purple's *Machine Head* in the 8-track as the humid breeze brushed the sweat from me. Dyer looked over his shoulder.

"Why they call you 'Stem'?" he asked. "You bad at cleaning weed?"

"I ain't never touched weed. *Yet.*"

"We call him that 'cause he's a midget," I said. "We're gonna call him 'Branch' when he grows some."

Dyer looked at me. "You got a dumbass nickname too?"

"A b-ball buddy calls me 'Bean.' Gave it to me 'cause I needed a fake name to play in a basketball tournament under another dude's name."

"What?"

"This church basketball tournament. They wanted me to play, so they put me on the roster under this other kid's name, and they had to call me something I'd know."

He laughed. "You faked a name in a church tournament?"

"It was Methodists."

"So you ain't done with basketball."

"What do you mean?"

"You quit JV, didn't you?"

My stomach flipped. "How you know that?"

He shrugged. "Word gets around."

"Better not talk about that or Parrish might throw a hissy," Stem said.

"Eat me," I said, my face heating.

"See?" Stem said.

"That nigger, Johnson, coaches it, right?" Dyer said.

"Acts like he coaches it."

"Fuck him. Fuck all them coaches. I woulda played football, but I ain't putting up with all that bullshit." I met Dyer's eyes, which didn't seem to hold any judgment. When I'd quit, my teammates seemed to have bought Johnson's words that I'd be a quitter all my life and acted as if I would contaminate them. The only one who'd appeared to treat me the same was our center, a black kid named Virgil.

We crossed Prescott Drive, the road on which I'd fought Lassiter two springs ago, passed through the undeveloped block of brushy land that divided Stem's part of North Baton Rouge from mine and entered a neighborhood where the asbestos-tiled houses were even smaller than those on my street. I pulled up in front of Stem's. He stepped out of the backseat and came up to my window. "Later, Dyer," he said. He slugged my arm and walked off laughing.

Dyer pulled a pack of Kools from his pocket. "You want one?"

"Uh-huh. Just blow it out the window so my old man doesn't freak out."

He flicked open a silver Zippo like Robert had, pulled hard, and exhaled into the wind, the aroma of menthol drifting to me. "You run into anybody else on the street?" I asked.

"Nah. Just seen you shooting ball in your driveway and you dudes in there tonight."

I named the old crew, most of whom I rarely hung with anymore because they were still in junior high or we'd drifted toward different interests.

"Your brother's a cop, ain't he?"

"Yeah." I almost said, "He likes to fuck with people and shoot his mouth off about it," but I held it in.

"You got some time to cruise? I ain't ready to go home and hear my old lady bitch. She's pissed I been over at my girlfriend's too much and my girlfriend bitches I ain't over enough." He tilted his head slightly out the window so that his hair lifted behind him. I looked forward, trying not to stare at him as if he were a celebrity in my car.

"I will take one," I said. He thumped the pack and I pulled one out. He lit it and I inhaled my first menthol cigarette, the smoke both cooling and burning my lungs like a hot peppermint. "Why'd y'all move to our street?"

"Niggers took over our old neighborhood."

"Where's that?"

"Over on Houma, coupla blocks from school. My old man wanted to split before the property value went to nothing. Over twenty years they lived there. I didn't even know nobody anymore when we left. Five years ago there wasn't a black face in the neighborhood, now you can't walk the street without thinking you might get jumped."

"You got jumped?"

"Me? Hell no. Didn't like leaving my momma and sister in the house though."

I took a shallow drag and thought of Daddy's nearly constant worry over losing our house. I gripped the wheel harder and glanced at him again.

"Man, is it true you beat up fifteen dudes at once?"

"That JV game? Probly more like eight," he said matter-of-factly. "Mighta been fifteen around me. Bunch of 'em surrounded me in the parking lot. Dumbshits woulda all come at once, they woulda got me, but they came in one or two at a time. I just wrapped my belt short around my left hand and swung my buckle to throw 'em off and took 'em out with my right."

"Jesus."

"Stupid fucks." Dyer thumped his cigarette out the window. He leaned his head back to take in the rush of air as we drove down Evangeline. "Guess I oughta get back and take my bitching."

I worked my hands on the wheel, a sense of importance rising against my too-common sense of powerlessness. Since quitting the JV team, I had won all-tournament team in the state church tourney and Most Valuable Player in a small independent one, but those awards mostly convinced me I was playing against second- or third-rate competition. When a former teammate told me he'd told Coach Johnson about my MVP, Johnson told him I was a good ballplayer. That, after Johnson had helped dismantle my confidence. I wanted to spit in his face, but I knew I would do nothing.

Now here was Dyer, the perfect engine of seduction. I believed he might *have* spit in Johnson's face. I glanced again, then looked straight ahead, his image so clear in my head that I didn't need to look anymore. He radiated confidence, power, and virility. His body held stillness without calm; an inscrutable energy emanated from him. Already I was prepared to consider anything he wanted.

"He ain't coming to this house and that's the last I'm gone say about it." Daddy stood, arms crossed, in our front yard, studying several loose shingles as if they were deliberately spiting him. Fresh from work, he still wore his khakis. I fidgeted, steaming after he'd just told me that my black friend Virgil would not be allowed to join a slew of white kids to film my Super 8 spoof of *Julius Caesar* for English.

"He's the only one stuck up for me, Daddy."

"I don't care. I ain't having the neighbors worrying over him at our house."

"What neighbors? The Goudeauxs had their maid and she was black."

"That ain't the same."

"No, it ain't. He's my friend."

"Your friend?" He looked at me as if I'd said Virgil came from Neptune. "You might think that, Tim, but you're wrong."

"What if I bring him anyway?"

"You might as well bring him to the woodshed 'cause that's where you'll be. Now go on get me that ladder so I can check this roof."

I fetched the metal ladder from the side of the house and slammed it against the gutter. "You better calm down, son. Hold that while I go up." As he climbed I thought of jerking it to give him a start. I wanted more than anything for him to be proud of me, but more and more I had no clue how to please him. And he confused me even in matters where I shouldn't have been confused. Earlier in the basketball season, he and I had gone to an LSU game in which Collis Temple, LSU's first black player, was playing. When a fight erupted between the Tigers and Vanderbilt, Temple leaped into the air and kicked an opponent in the back. "That goddamn black son of a bitch!" Daddy had screamed. The outburst shocked me. I'd never heard him say "goddamn." But more than that, I couldn't believe he was siding against our team. It should have been obvious by then but, unbelievably, only now was it sinking in that race trumped everything. I wasn't quite ready to fully embrace racism, but the thought was knocking around that that was the only way I could win his approval, the only way I could fit in, no matter how mad I was at him or how repulsed I was by myself.

"It's cool," Virgil said the next morning after I'd told him he couldn't come. He clanged shut his locker and we headed toward class. "My daddy probably wouldn't want you at my house either."

"No shit?"

"Who knows? I never asked nobody white over." He and I towered above almost everyone in the hall, Virgil's 'fro and wide shoulders making him impossible not to identify even from a distance. Almost the only time blacks and whites walked together was when they were teammates, and I was rancorously aware that we weren't teammates anymore.

Virgil pulled up outside his classroom door. "Don't sweat it, man. We'll get drunk sometime."

We slapped hands, and I headed down the hall again, oblivious to the close stream of students and the din of class change. I could never explain to Daddy how Virgil had helped me retrieve my confidence the previous summer. I'd only played competitive basketball one season and had never really been coached. I didn't have the arrogance I'd carried in football and was worried I wouldn't even make the team. Still, when I arrived for summer camp, I had faith in my work ethic and my past success at football. The new varsity coach rattled on in a stream of consciousness that there would be access to weights all day and scrimmages two mornings a week and he would be there much of the time to help with conditioning drills and we were going to make basketball as important as football at Istrouma. Like the coach's speech, the camp was disorganized. It was also sporadically attended, but Virgil and I showed up every day.

He and I met at eye level, very different from the previous year when our ninth-grade team had gone to his all-black junior high and lost by sixty points. Virgil had already been bearded and man-sized, and he dunked on us several times, since none of us could even touch the rim. Each of his thighs was the size of both of mine together, his big Afro made him look fierce, but his easy laugh was as goofy as mine.

Outside, in a grotto formed by three oven-hot brick walls, stood the free weights. We did leg presses, bench presses, and squats beneath the vicious sun. In the super-heated gym, we ran up and down bleachers and jump-roped wearing canvas vests with lead bars sewn into them, the vests so loose they slapped against my ribs, stomach, chest, and back like heavy paddles. We snatched the ball over and over from the rebounding machine, Virgil setting it higher and higher for me until it rose above the height of the rim. He pushed me on the weights, encouraged me during drills, and told me we were going to dominate as the tallest center/forward tandem in district junior varsity ball. When I dunked for the first time, Virgil gave me double dap hand slaps.

I knew I had a long way to go to be anywhere as good in basketball as I'd been in small-time football, and this coach wasn't much of a teacher. Stud, yes, a hairy, six-two white guy who had played two years for the ABA's Memphis Tams and could dunk two balls at once, his giant hands throwing them down from opposite sides of the rim one after the other. Enthusiasm boiled off him, but so did his lack of intelligence. His teaching consisted almost entirely of strengthening and toughening us up on rebounds, and when he thought Virgil and I were slacking, he would make us try and stop him from scoring. He plowed over us, elbowed us, jammed the ball on us, left our cheeks, jaws, and bodies even sorer. Whenever we missed too many free throws, he would recount how he'd stepped to the line in college and hit two to beat the University of Houston.

"Two free throws, two free throws, I had to hit two free throws."
He would always hit them again. His talent awed us, but behind his
back we mocked him. "I'm Coach Dumbshit, I'm Coach Dumbshit,
I'll tell you twice, I'll tell you twice."

During breaks, Virgil and I talked about normal things—sports,
school, girls—which was revelatory to me. Virgil and his family lived
in a neighborhood that Daddy considered taken over, and their living there confirmed what Daddy had once disparagingly said: that
"they just wanted what we had"—I guessed meaning our jobs and
homes. But Virgil also confirmed some of Daddy's stereotypes. He
told stories of times when he and his friends had come through my
neighborhood stealing bikes, one guy pedaling, the other riding the
handlebars so he could jump off and snag one. "My bike was stolen,"
I said.

"What'd it look like?" he asked. I described it. "Oh, yeah," he said,
"that was a nice bike." I shoved him and laughed.

In increments, the confidence torn down by Jarreau, surgery, and
the other changes began to come back. I believed my body would
serve me. I didn't even grieve football too much, especially when
the JV season began with Virgil and me as starters. The junior varsity coach was a defensive line coach for the football team, a wide,
thickly muscled black man with limited basketball scope, and our
offense had no plays for us big men, only the ever-pressed demand
to rebound, get garbage buckets, and play defense. Like the varsity
coach, Coach Johnson taught us little and did bizarre things like
perform football grass drills on the wooden court, drills in which we
ran in place until the coach's hand signals told us to hit the floor on
our bellies and our nuts, roll, and pop back up. Nonetheless, because
I paid attention to Virgil and to what was happening around me, the
complexity of the game emerged—cuts, anticipation and position,
communication—which allowed me to play more naturally, something I had always done in football. I fell in love with the sensation
of the ball rolling off my fingertips on a turnaround jump shot, the
contact and method of boxing out, with elevating and clutching a
rebound, swatting away shots, setting solid picks, rolling to the basket for a pass, and with the angles of movement and spacing away
from the ball as well as toward it. And being able to rise over the rim

and slam the ball gave me back my body even more. Then Coach Dumbshit complained publicly that basketball didn't receive equal treatment to football and was fired by our sixty-something, former All-American, football player, and army colonel principal. At least we thought it was because of insubordination, although the administration spread the rumor he was sleeping with a student, something at least two football coaches were suspected of doing without reprisal. Whatever the reason, he was gone.

His replacement was a slump-shouldered, thin-faced, older assistant football coach, known mainly for being a smart-ass and a drinker. JV and varsity ran conditioning drills and often even practiced together, and Coach Redick seemed to fixate on me, maybe because he and Alan hadn't gotten along years before. He rode me constantly, criticizing and mocking almost everything I did in a way I believe he thought was amusing but which seemed to infect the younger Coach Johnson because he also started calling me "Grandma," the nickname the varsity coach had given me because I was slow running suicides and had limited stamina. Every mistake I made was met with hollering, a time-honored approach to coaching, but corrosive to me. No criticism was simply a criticism, but rather an assault that included Jarreau, Lassiter, Chandler, and all of my physical shortcomings. I was weak-minded and weak-bodied. I lacked mental toughness. I was defenseless. Half the season I had started, but my confidence thinned and tore as another kid on the team rapidly improved and received the encouragement I'd gotten earlier. In football, criticism had never rattled my game, but here my play quickly deteriorated, making me unable to play without thinking and worrying, turning my hands to wood, slowing my reactions. My movements lost what fluidity I'd gained. Just after mid-season, I lost my spot as a starter. Three-quarters through, I was riding the bench.

In football, I had always started and was the leader of the offense. I had almost always had fun. When I asked Coach Johnson what I needed to do to get back on first team, he said, "Get better," and smiled. He and the varsity coach kept up their derision. During the worst times with Jarreau and Lassiter, shooting basketball alone had been the least complicated thing I had. The hours alone in my driveway, fantasizing and laboring, were my respite from anxiety. Now the fun was gone. Virgil tried to buck me up, but Daddy's irritation that the black coach had replaced me with a black kid stoked my resentment and sense of failure.

Late in the season, Coach Johnson put me in with twenty seconds left in a half. He was trying to save someone from getting a foul, but I took it as an act of humiliation. As I lagged behind the team toward the locker room, I looked up at Daddy in the bleachers. He came down. "You wanta go?" he asked, furious at Johnson.

"Yes, sir."

"Then tell that sorry coach we're going."

In the locker room, I put on my street clothes. The team glanced at me but said nothing. Coach Johnson came over, his shoulders as wide as two of me. "What's going on, Parrish?" he asked, puzzlement flitting over his face.

"I quit," I said.

"You what?"

"I quit."

"Boy, you quit now, you'll always be a quitter," he said. I pulled up like I'd been uppercut. Behind the coach, Virgil stroked his chin. Daddy stepped just inside the door and glared. My father was a wiry man, but I would've bet on him in a fight. I didn't want that though. Burning with both shame and relief, I went past Johnson and Daddy. Daddy followed me out. This situation was a no-win for him. He'd supported me and protected me, but I resented him. I believed Coach Johnson was right about me—I had taken the longer route; never fought Jarreau; never fought Chandler; fought Lassiter only once; had quit basketball like a baby and only when my daddy gave me permission. Plus, I wondered if the permission had more to do with Johnson's being black than with me, even though I knew my father had always done his best to take care of me.

The next day in the halls, some of the black players on the team laughed at me, while the whites seemed to have cooled. Virgil, though, acted the same. He told me, as he had before, that he was sorry Johnson and Redick had treated me like shit, and said he would miss my being on the team. Only Virgil knew how I'd regained something of myself that previous summer and it seemed only Virgil knew I was losing it. What he didn't know was how close I was to becoming Brutus.

1974, Summer: Seeing Black and White

"Let's get on it, girls," Dyer said. He opened the trunk of his car, hoisted my heavy, six-man, canvas tent, and slung it across his shoulder as Stem, an old friend of Dyer's named J. J., and I lifted out the ice chest of beer, bundle of tent poles, and bags of junk food. "Y'all fixing to get your cherries popped," Dyer said and grinned. "I know Stem's scared. You scared, Parrish?"

"Scared of sleeping in a tent with you," I said.

"Fuck sleeping." He led on.

The early summer sun filtered through the scraggly pines as we humped across pitted dirt to find a campsite. A thunderstorm had left the air palpable, but the ground was already dry from the June sun. I didn't wonder why Dyer would go to this trouble for two guys he'd met only a couple of months ago, was too flattered with having been chosen to consider anything except that I was his neighbor. And I hadn't hung out with him enough yet to notice that he didn't really have any close friends besides his girlfriend's little brother, Skeeter, or notice that his friends at school were all tough guys and troublemakers who treated him with a respect that didn't seem to leave much room for connection. When my daddy had questioned why a bunch of boys would want to start the summer with a camping trip not far out of town, Dyer had charmed him by saying he was going to get Stem and me out to chop some wood and cook on an open fire and swim in the river to make us stop being city wimps. I'm sure Daddy knew this was bullshit, but Dyer's self-assurance and presence swayed him. He ended up laughing along with Dyer and agreeing, even though he grumbled almost as soon as Dyer was gone.

J. J. pointed. "River's a hundred yards that way over a drop. Don't go charging out there when you get wasted tonight." He cackled. After we'd picked him up, he'd led us to this undeveloped cul-de-sac near the Comite River. He was short, tough-looking, jittery, and nearly bald. He and Dyer had known each other a long time, but I didn't know specifics except that J. J.'s family had moved outside of town, blazing the white flight trail. He seemed skittish of Dyer, a nervousness I could at times already relate to in Dyer's presence. I'd never see J. J. again after this night.

We set up the tent, then Stem, J. J., and I gathered sticks and branches and built a fire while Dyer sat with his back against a log. He picked at us as he drank a beer and whittled at sticks with his big-bladed lock knife. "Why don't you get off your ass and help?" Stem said.

"'Cause I got the weed and bought the beer."

"Lazy bastard," Stem said. Dyer slung a dirt clod and hit him in the leg. "That's ass, later," Stem said.

"Fag," Dyer said, then giggled his incongruous, high-pitched, staccato hee-hee-hee.

I laughed with him, laughed too hard.

As the sun went down, I sat on the log near Dyer and took a slug of beer, my body sheened and sweating from the fire we'd built to ward off mosquitoes in the humid night. Stem paced and danced, throwing punches and pestering Dyer about when we were going to smoke. "Sit the fuck down," Dyer finally said to him, and much to my surprise, Stem did, cross-legged in the dirt, drunkenly smiling.

"How y'all know each other?" I asked Dyer and J. J.

"Grew up four houses apart," J. J. said. "I used to beat Dyer's ass."

"Beat your meat maybe," Dyer said. J. J. poked at the fire on the opposite side from us, his posture and expression more twitchy after several beers, a bad energy that reminded me of Jarreau and Lassiter humming around him. I had already decided that he was dim, a judgment I tried not to let show on my face, as my judgments often did. J. J. looked at me and grinned. "Me and Dyer and a couple other dudes used to rob houses when we were eleven or twelve. One of 'em got shot in the stomach and Dyer got all scared and was like, '*I don't wanta get shot, I don't wanta get shot,*'" J. J. said in a little girl's voice.

An amused expression spread across Dyer's face.

"Y'all really robbed houses?" I asked.

"I'd done stopped by the time that dumbshit got popped in the gut by a .22," Dyer said. "J. J.'s lucky his stupid ass wasn't there." J. J. frowned. Dyer curled a large section of bark from his stick as he looked at J. J. "How you like your new school?"

"Sucks. Dudes are dickheads and the chicks are stuck-up bitches."

"Maybe they just don't like your ugly ass."

"Then fuck them bitches."

"With somebody else's dick I suppose."

J. J. crouched and probed the fire as if he were searching for something at its core. "I told my old man I wanted to finish at Istrouma. Said he wanted to get out while he could still make his money on the house."

"Everybody's bailing," Dyer said. "My old man and old lady'll probably move out here when me and my sister finish." A smile crawled across his face. He flipped his knife, caught it by the blade, and threw it over the fire. It stuck in the dirt inches from J. J.'s foot. J. J. exploded backwards onto his butt. He popped to his feet and chucked his burning stick at Dyer, but Dyer knocked it away, laughed, and brushed the embers from his jeans.

"I hate when you do that shit," J. J. said. He turned to us. "Watch this fucker with a knife. He ain't got no sense. Stuck his own toe one time. Accidentally cut his girlfriend's hand fucking around too. Was swiping around close to her and she put her palm up."

"She shoulda trusted me." Dyer shoved himself to his feet and retrieved the knife. "It's good you left Istrouma," he said as he wiped the dirt from the blade onto his jeans. "It'd eat you up." He closed the knife and put it in his pocket.

"Fuck you, Dyer."

J. J. covered the several feet to Dyer as if he'd been launched, but Dyer grabbed him around the waist, lifted him, flattened him face first, and sat on his back. Dyer looked at Stem and me, the blaze playing in his eyes.

"Let's get high."

Stem and I laughed at almost everything for several hours, sometimes rolling on the dirt as Dyer sat back and grinned. J. J., who hadn't smoked, had devolved into a sullen drunk. Stem and Dyer mumbly-pegged, sticking the knife in the ground at each other's feet, Dyer dancing to keep from being stuck then slugging Stem in the shoulder, once so hard that he knocked him over a log. Stem had shaken with laughter until he was able to catch his breath. I didn't want to throw the knife, but I was so high I wasn't worried about being a pussy. I shoved to my feet, belly aching, and staggered away from the fire and into the trees to piss. I tried to remember if I might be heading toward the cliff that would drop me to the river, but I didn't really care. As I peed, Stem's and Dyer's laughter echoed to me. I dropped my head back and looked at the sky jammed with stars and blacker than it was in the city. The sky moved toward me, and I held my arms up to it, stumbled backward and plopped onto the dirt, slinging piss onto my leg. I sat there, laughing. I loved the sky and the dirt and my friends. A euphoria filled me unlike any since football.

Eventually, I made it to my feet again and strolled back toward the others. The fire threw bold light on J. J., sprawled against one of the logs we'd dragged up, and on Stem and Dyer throwing the knife at beer cans. I took off my glasses and wiped the sweat from my eye sockets before slipping the glasses back on. In English class, I had read *Lord of the Flies*, identifying with Ralph and Piggy and never the savage tribe. But there in the field I laughed in recognition of the scene before me. It was good to be the savages. We had power and Dyer gave us that power. I found a long stick, grinned, ran, and hurled it like a spear at them.

Dawn cooked me awake next to the smolder of the previous night's fire. I scratched at mosquito bites and squinted against the hangover that probed my forehead, but none of that diminished my residual elation. None of us had made it into the tent. J. J. and Stem dragged worse than I did, but Dyer acted the same, giving everybody shit for being wimps while he broke camp mostly by himself. We dropped J. J. at his house, stopped at Krispy Kreme for donuts and chocolate milk, then drove back to town, Dyer cheerful as Stem and I suffered. Stem fell asleep and snored in the backseat until I tossed a straw wrapper into his open mouth, and he coughed awake. At Stem's house, Dyer turned to the backseat and thumped his nose. "Hey! Go sleep in your momma's lap." Stem unfolded from the car and slinked toward his door.

"That runt cracks me up," Dyer said, and I was surprised at the jealousy that heated the back of my neck.

The mile back to our street Dyer drove slowly, hitting a last cigarette. "Thought you and Stem was gonna bust a nut laughing. I had to pull Stem out the fire once when he fell over."

"He wouldn't have felt it."

Dyer took a long drag and exhaled through his nose. "What'd you think of J. J.?"

I hesitated. "He's a weird dude."

"Whatcha mean?"

"I don't know. Just weird."

"He ain't weird. Shit just scares him. He never could hack it."

I let my arm hang out of the window. I didn't even worry that he'd see that shit scared me, too, or that I might not be able to hack it, whatever "it" turned out to beß. As we drove the streets where so much had dogged me, the old tension seemed far away. I was still the things I had been—a coward and a Christian, supposed to turn the other cheek but doing so only to run—and yet I could see Dyer giving me the protection and status to teach me to take care of myself.

I looked at him again. He flicked his smoke out the window and cruised toward the second-to-last turn toward home, a smirk on his face. Up ahead, almost directly across from the garage apartment of Robert, his wife, and their son, somebody stood on the corner. The knot in my chest recognized the shape before my sight did. Part of me couldn't believe it; another part believed it to be inevitable. Everything inside me dropped. My mouth went dry. Jarreau. I hadn't seen him in over a year, not since he yelled at me from his car as he dropped his girlfriend off at the junior high. This was a coincidence whose timing could only be created by a cruel design intent on demoralizing me, by a god who was either indifferent or punishing. I thought of slumping in my seat, but the thought of Dyer noticing that sickened me. I sat straighter and caught Jarreau's eye. He squinted, mouth open. Then he flipped me the bird.

"That Jarreau?" Dyer said.

"Yeah."

"He flip us off?"

"Me."

"He knows you?"

I hadn't said anything to Dyer about him, but I wondered if he knew something about Jarreau's stalking me, just as he'd known about my quitting basketball. "I fought somebody he knows a couple years ago and he was kind of after me for a while."

"You fought *him*?"

"No, a kid named Lassiter. He pulled a knife."

"Huh. I know Jarreau. He was one of the ones used to break in houses with us. I used to whip his ass just to keep him in line." He looked full on at me. "You wanta go back?"

The blood left my face. "Fuck him."

"You sure? Asshole shot you off."

"I gotta get home. My old man's probably gonna put me to work in the sun when he sees I ain't slept."

Dyer raised his eyebrows and nodded as he turned onto our street. I knew I may as well have said I was terrified and unworthy. I doubted Dyer would be rushing back to hang out with me again. I looked out my window and didn't say anymore as we pulled up to my house. When I stepped out, heat glared off the pavement and pierced my temples. Dyer helped me lug the big canvas square and poles into the garage. "I'll check you later," he said, walked back to his car and eased away. I peered the opposite way down the street, expecting Jarreau to appear. Donuts and chocolate milk rose in my throat, but whether it was from Jarreau, Dyer, or both, I couldn't say.

I was worried the cops would spot the silhouette of Virgil's tumbleweed 'fro and pull us over. Or worse, one of my daddy's friends would report that I had a black guy in the passenger seat. Or maybe worst of all, Dyer would see us. Far from not coming around after I'd shrunk from Jarreau three weeks earlier, Dyer had been lifting weights in my garage, awkwardly shooting hoops in my driveway, picking me up after work to cruise and get high, confiding in me about his ambivalent relationship with his girlfriend, and taking me to parties I'd have never been invited to without him. The previous weekend I'd been so intimidated by the older tough kids at the party and the beautiful girls flocking to Dyer, who was there without his girlfriend, that I'd gotten drunk and lain down in the driveway. He'd peeled me off the gravel, plopped me in the passenger seat, and driven me around until I was sober enough to bring home. I still didn't understand why he'd taken to me so quickly or that lurking inside him were probably feelings not so different from mine.

The breeze from the open windows couldn't keep the smell of Virgil's and my dried sweat from filling the car. We were on our way back from playing in an independent AAU tournament with some other tenth-grade friends and no coach. Our opponents had high school star upperclassmen, an intense coach, plays, and sponsored uniforms. We'd thought it would be loose, streetball, but they pressed us, trapped us, got our seven-man roster into foul trouble, and eventually beat us by double figures. Typically I would have been pissed at losing, but Virgil leavened it with humor, perspective, and a realistic outlook. "Man, them dudes was pros," he'd said right after the game. "They ran our asses down and kicked 'em." Even losing, it was good to have played with Virgil again and to hang with him outside of school, where his easygoing, goofy way was an antidote to nearly all seriousness.

"Where we going, man?" he asked as I drove streets that obviously weren't taking us to his neighborhood.

"I want you to do something funny."

"Funny. What you up to?"

"You'll see."

The direct route to my house would have taken us past Dyer's, so at the last second I opted to go around the block. I pushed away my nascent shame at betraying Virgil and pulled into my driveway.

"Thought I wasn't supposed to come to your house, Marc Antony," Virgil said. In English class, he'd loved the Super 8 film from which my daddy had forbidden him; his lack of resentment was astonishing to me.

"Daddy ain't home. I'm gonna play a little joke on my momma and my nephew. I want you to meet her anyway."

"Y'all don't own a gun, do you?"

We laughed and stepped out of the car. When I didn't see Momma in the living room, I led Virgil through the front door and down the hall. I stationed him in front of her closed bedroom door, where I knew she was taking refuge with the AC window unit. I knocked softly. "Momma, could you come see something?" The bed creaked and footsteps sounded. I held my hand over my mouth and knocked into Virgil with my shoulder. Momma opened the door holding a book and jolted back a step. "Oh!" She glanced at me and blushed, then broke into an embarrassed smile. "You must be Virgil."

"Yes, ma'am," Virgil said. "Tim made me do it."

"I figured that."

I bent at the waist and slapped my knee.

"How did y'all do?"

"We got creamed," Virgil said.

"Well," Momma said, "you must be thirsty."

We all sauntered to the kitchen. Momma made us sit at the table as she fetched us ice water. She tried not to act nervous as she told Virgil what a good friend I'd said he was and asked him small-talk questions. She had often provided me support in the things Daddy sometimes couldn't or didn't. She always praised me for my good grades and other accomplishments, encouraged me to be creative and silly, and, most importantly, tried to exemplify Christian love and forgiveness in the ways I wanted so hard to embrace. When Martin Luther King had died, she hadn't reveled in it. When Robert Kennedy died on my tenth birthday, she had shed a tear and said to me how she thought he was a good man. I had shared Daddy's joyous reactions to the murders, but when she felt for the dead men, I felt too. So when she sided with Daddy about keeping Virgil away, I saw how her silence and desire not to rock the boat made her complicit with him in other things. Bringing Virgil to the house *was* a joke, and I did want Momma to meet Virgil, but I was also aware of wanting to get back at her and to show I could do what I wanted. I wasn't aware that I was also using Virgil to confront the person who had the least to do with keeping him away.

"We better go," I finally said. Virgil shook my mother's hand. "Thank you, Miz Parrish," he said. I let him lead to the door. As I was walking out behind him, Momma grabbed my elbow, turned me around and waited for Virgil to move away. She whispered, "Don't let your daddy know about this."

"Why not? You think he'll wanta throw out all the glasses?" I had wondered if Momma might throw out the glass and even wondered if I'd want to drink out of it.

"Tim." I pulled my arm away and went to the car.

"That was funny," I said, back behind the wheel as we headed toward Virgil's house.

"Man, why you wanta freak your momma out like that?"

"She laughed."

"It still freaked her out and you tell how she's sick a lot. I mean, you coulda at least just yelled to her, 'Hey, I brought a large Negro in the house, so don't have a heart attack.'" Virgil liked to make fun by using that word, but I wasn't sure how much fun he was making then.

"It's bullshit they wouldn't let you come to the house."

"Dude, they just raised in another time. My parents the same way."

"I'm tired of hearing all that."

"It's true whether you tired of it or not."

"Then they shouldn't be talking about forgiving everybody and shit."

"Man, you get upset."

I twisted my hands on the wheel as my stomach roiled. Virgil chatted on about the game we'd lost until I pulled up in front of his house. His neighborhood, in which my parents had lived when it was all white, usually made me uneasy, but I was so preoccupied that I was oblivious. I stared at his neat, little house until he elbowed me. He held his hand up. "We'll get 'em next time," he said. I held my hand out and he slapped my palm.

I waited for him to enter his house before I drove again. A picture came to me of Momma shaken, physically frail, and maybe even guilty about Virgil. The image struck me like a slap, but I let myself savor my smidgen of vindictive power.

"So we get to this house on a complaint about an officer. This nigger man's got a big black eye and his wife's jetting around the room and he's just slumping there like he's pissed we came. We kinda know where this is going 'cause complaints have been coming in, off and on, for a couple of months about some crazy motherfucker on the force who's just showing up at houses, but it's our first time to go on one and I wanta see what they say. I start asking them what the complaint is and the woman's looking at the man and they don't say anything for a long time till I go, 'Look, we ain't got all night. There's citizens out there killing and maiming each other while we're standing here.'" Dyer and I laughed, and Robert took a deep drag from the smoke between his thumb and index finger, shifted in his recliner. He still had his uniform on, but without his boots or his gun belt. His wife, Deborah, leaned in the doorway to the kitchen with a smile that looked fake. She had just gotten their son, Tommy, to sleep in the other room and now it looked as if she was fighting boredom, as if often seemed she was. Robert took a sip of his beer.

"Finally the dude's wife gives him a nudge and says, 'Tell these po-licemen what happened,' and he says, 'You shouldn't of called nobody, woman. What if he come back?'" Robert laid the accent on thick. "Me and my partner look at each other and we're trying not to laugh. 'We afraid to say,' the woman says, and I go, 'Why?' and the man leans forward and goes, ''Cause Cap'n Wildfire said he'd come back and whup our ass.' Me and my partner look at each other, then my partner goes, 'Cap'n Wildfire, huh?' Man goes, 'He work on the force. Big white man with red hair and his name badge say, "Cap'n Wildfire."' 'There ain't no Captain Wildfire,' I say. 'Oh, yes, they is,' the woman says. 'He come by here last night and said he needed to talk to us. He just starts gettin' all upset and he go crazy. Cap'n Wildfire whipped his ass.' 'For nothing?' I say. 'For being. You ain't gone tell him we said nothing, are you?'"

Robert stubbed out his cigarette and lit another one. I wanted to say something about his smoking so much, but I kept my mouth shut. Our relationship had become not a roller coaster, but a Scrambler—the ride that slung you hard one way then the other. I still worshipped him and thought he was hilarious, but since he and Deborah had snuck off, gotten married, and had their son shortly thereafter, Robert had become angrier and more filled with bluster, while I had become more mercurial in my shifts between being entertained and being irritated.

"So, like I said, we been getting complaints about this Cap'n Wildfire. Tonight I get off my shift and I'm going out in the parking lot and it's kinda dark and there's this guy Davenport who's messing with his nameplate on his pocket and doesn't hear me coming. He takes it off and pulls another one out and then he sees me. I give him a big smile and say, 'Captain Wildfire, I presume.'"

"What did he do?" Dyer asked.

"He spit tobacco on the ground and then he said, 'You ain't gonna turn me in are you, Parrish?' I said, 'No, but that better be the last of Cap'n Wildfire.'"

I busted out laughing. This kind of story I liked. Even in its racism, it showed the Robert who cared about people and about being a good cop, at least in the context of the goon squad the BRPD evidently was. It was also one of his funny stories, like the one about him and his partner corralling a loose horse and Robert riding it through the station as the next shift was lined up for briefing. Or the story about the sergeant who was scolding someone about leaving a round in a shotgun and pumped it and blew a hole in the ceiling. I didn't like the more frequent stories about how he rousted people and goaded them into fights.

"Fucking Cap'n Wildfire," Dyer said. "I thought about being a cop. All that hairy shit out there."

"It ain't all hairy. A lot of it's boring."

"Tell Dyer about going in that house and having to fight off that whole family," I said.

"I don't wanta tell that one tonight."

"A whole family went after him and his black partner and Robert had to break a dude's arm with his stick and hold his pistol to the dude's head to keep the family off while he got out of the house. You even busted their TV, didn't you?"

"I even had to punch out the motherfucker's momma. Bitch kept coming after me. Shit was insane. We went to serve a warrant on this dude and the whole neighborhood started pouring in. My partner was a rookie and when shit started popping, he was aiming his gun all around like he was gonna kill everybody and I had to get him to calm his ass down while I was breaking people's bones."

"You're real fun when you come home after that stuff," Deborah said, an edge to her voice.

"You're fun, too."

She snorted and went back into the kitchen. I shifted on the couch. More and more, anger and disdain shot back and forth between Robert and Deborah, creating an uneasiness I resented.

"Tim told me you knocked out eight at once," Robert said to Dyer.

"They came in one at a time."

"You just punched 'em?"

"Right hook for everybody."

Robert nodded and smiled. "My motto is Maximum Violence Immediately. Eyes, throat, knees."

"I like that," Dyer said. "Nothing like the sound of knuckles on a head, though."

The excitement and intensity of their talk sharpened the room, but even though I loved vicariously sharing the power of what they were saying, I was shrinking. I had no story to tell. I wasn't a bad motherfucker, just a relative and friend of bad motherfuckers. Even Alan, who'd moved to Chicago to work for an oil company and work nights on his MBA, had old fight stories to tell, like the night a bunch of drunk frat boys threw a bucket of water on him as he sat on his motorcycle, and he went back, waited at the water hose behind the frat house, and knocked the kid cold. The stories cracked me up, but they also made me jealous of the fearless brotherhood.

As summer passed, Dyer and I tore up the roads, smoking weed, drinking Miller ponies, and speeding to the fast dirty boogie of early Foghat and the glam screech of Slade. My worry that he would call me out for backing down to Jarreau lessened the more we ran together. Meanwhile, Daddy fretted more and more about the country, his moods swinging, his anger growing. He saw withdrawal from Vietnam as a total defeat, resented Nixon's backing down, and said that George Wallace would have never given up to the Communists abroad and at home. He also became more allergic to TDI, the chemical he produced in his plant unit. Some nights he came home from work and sat on the floor, struggling to breathe, gripping his knees and sweating as if he'd run the thirty miles from Geismar. Momma and I sat with him and put cold cloths on his neck and arms. I hated that he suffered, but I also resented his weakness. Then blacks moved in three blocks away and his paranoia of losing our house grew exponentially.

At the same time, my resentment and skepticism at the church escalated—typical teenage rebellion—but also something more caustic. I was consciously sorting through the connection between the church's love of war and Robert's volunteering for the army, and beginning to believe that Robert had been right to reject the church. And yet simultaneously the church's lust to vanquish our enemies took deeper root in me. I wanted the clarity of the last battle in which the righteous fought against those who would try and take what was ours. I still also wanted to forgive and turn the other cheek, but even more I wanted the power to feel safe.

My desire meshed perfectly with Dyer. My urge to cleave from anybody who didn't approve of him increased every day. As summer passed I separated from other friends, like Mike Coats, and the more my circle shrank, the more influence Dyer gained. When he tossed a bottle from the car and knocked a black kid from his bike, I pushed aside my revulsion and laughed. When he talked about how much he loved his girlfriend, then talked about wanting to fuck around, I rationalized that this was the way a man ought to take advantage. I still sometimes prayed, anxiously and forcefully, but I was ready to forego the tatters of any ethics in order to get Dyer's approval. And more than all that to find a clear path that would sheer away the confusion that crackled in my head.

"Best president we ever had," Daddy said, "and them Democrats and Communists run him off." He flung old toys, tools, cans, anything within reach into a large cardboard box.

The day before, Nixon had waved and stepped on the presidential chopper for the last time, leaving Daddy in a frenzy ever since. He'd dragged me out of bed at eight and into the yard with him to mow, weed, cut limbs, annihilate ants with DDT, and then edge the sidewalk, driveway, and curb. I was actually relieved to be out of the August sun and mopping our irreparably oil-stained garage floor until Robert showed up around noon with a domestic wasp up his ass. He sat on the washing machine, working his legs as if the agitator had joined the wasp.

"Right," Robert said. "Communists."

"That Watergate's all nonsense trumped up by the Democrats. Them men was in that hotel trying to find evidence that Castro was giving money to McGovern."

"What?"

Daddy turned and pointed with a monkey wrench. "That's what was going on. The Democrats got money from Castro and the Republicans were trying to get proof." He went back to flinging objects. Robert squinched his face, shook his head, then scratched his throat. "I don't give a shit about Watergate. All I know's what Tricky Dick did in 'Nam."

"He tried to win."

"He got a bunch of my friends killed and dragged that shit out."

"He's a Christian man trying to keep Communists from taking over this country."

"Christian," Robert said. "That mean he hates everybody that doesn't agree with him?"

Daddy froze mid-fling. "What'd you say?"

"Nothing."

"If you think that, you don't know what Christians are."

"I don't? I know what Jesus said, and I don't see it in church."

"What's wrong with you? That ain't true."

"It ain't?" Robert said.

Daddy appeared profoundly pained. "You don't even go to church no more." For a second, I had a pang of guilt because Daddy didn't know how often I skipped church, then I slapped the wet mop on the floor again.

Daddy said, "It's Christian to accept Jesus as your personal savior and live the best you can. Give to Caesar what is Caesar's."

"Amen," Robert said. "Whatever that means."

"That's enough."

"Nixon got what he deserved."

1974, Summer: Seeing Black and White

Daddy shook his head. Sweat blotched his T-shirt like a Rorschach test. "You oughta be ashamed." He tossed tools from one side of his work surface to the other, as if he were looking for an answer. This irked me worse than anything.

"Why am I mopping this stupid floor?" I said. "These stains are a thousand years old."

"They's oil that'll clean up."

"Where? I've been mopping for thirty minutes and it looks just like it did when I started."

Robert hopped off the washing machine and began to rummage in the cardboard trash box. "What you doing?" Daddy asked, a rusty tin can of nails in his hand.

"Making sure you ain't throwing out our childhood like you like to do."

"I throw out junk."

"You threw out that accordion."

"We never had no accordion."

"Yeah we did," I said.

"In the attic," Robert said.

"Y'all crazy," Daddy said.

"You threw out my comic books," Robert said. "I had a *Superman 1*."

Daddy harumphed and slammed the can onto his work bench. "You a policeman and a daddy and you bothering about comic books? You better get straight what's important. Both of you." He threw open the door to the kitchen and shut it hard behind him. Robert rolled his eyes at me. He took out a cigarette, twirled it in his fingers, glanced at the gasoline can and other flammables against the wall, and put it behind his ear. "My wife's fucking crazy," he said. "Every time I go home, it's a fight."

"Hard to believe."

"Huh?"

"Nothing."

"No. Don't step in my shit then act like it ain't on your shoe."

I dunked the mop again, cheeks and ears burning, and wished I'd kept my mouth shut. "You come by here all worked up all the time. I don't always wanta hear how you pulled this guy over and that guy over and fucked with 'em or how you're pissed at some boss and telling him off. You're always showing somebody something."

"Hey, why don't you try my job and see what you can do. Besides, you ain't Mister Calm yourself. You tell Daddy you brought your black friend by?"

"That was months ago. Momma told you?"

"Yeah. And by the way, you think doing that wasn't just to fuck with her?" I didn't say anything for a minute, didn't look at him as I mopped again. He walked just outside the garage door and lit up. "I come over here and now it's you *and* Daddy giving me shit."

I stopped and looked at him, his eyes aglint with a light both menacing and sad. In my head rattled the thought that if I could tear him down it would build me up. I tugged the sweaty, dirty shirt away from my front. "You never had a *Superman 1*," I said.

Grime from the garage where his father worked stained Dyer's hands as he loosely held the wheel of his car. He still wore his dirty jeans, but his fresh T-shirt shone clean white. In the backseat, Stem wailed off-key to the James Gang. My skin was baked, my arms soggy from Daddy's all-day purge of Nixon's downfall, but beer had cushioned my head. I raised my can. "Fuck Tricky Dick."

"Who?" Stem yelled from the backseat.

We hit a patch of wet air laced with vinyl chloride and I sneezed and pinched at my burning nose. "Nixon. Fuck him."

"Fuck Nixon," Stem said. I glanced at Stem and then over at Dyer, both of them deep brown from the summer sun. "Y'all don't even know he resigned."

"Who gives a fuck," Dyer said.

"He was the goddamn president."

"So what?"

"He's a liar."

"What politician ain't?"

I dropped my arm out the car window and kept pissy time on the warm metal. "Jesus, I can't believe you dumbshits don't care the president resigned."

"You think too much, Parrish," Stem said.

"Least I *can* think."

1974, Summer: Seeing Black and White

"Think about my dick."

Dyer turned the stereo down and gave me a glare unlike any he'd given me before. "That Nixon shit ain't got nothing to do with us."

"He sent my brother to a war."

"You got a war here you best pay attention to." Dyer slipped a cigarette from the pack on the dash and lit it without taking his gaze off me.

"Where's the fucking music?" Stem said.

"Shut the fuck up," Dyer said.

"Yeah, shut the fuck up," I said.

"Shitass queers. I'm always stuck in the backseat." Dyer cranked the music again—louder than before—and Stem slugged him in the back of his shoulder. Dyer turned it down, then flicked cinders Stem's way. Stem batted at them.

"That best not burn my seat," Dyer said.

"You flicked it, dickhead," Stem said, still extinguishing sparks.

Dyer wheeled us onto Choctaw and burned a cloud of rubber. The shotgun houses on one side and the warehouses on the other clicked past. I glanced over at the speedometer climbing to sixty, seventy, eighty. The light ahead changed to red and Dyer kept speeding toward it. Stem hooted and yee-hahed. I pressed back into my seat as my balls retracted. Dyer jammed the brakes and power slid us to a stop just at the intersection. "You're out of your mind," I said.

Dyer took a long drag and blew it at the ceiling. "I'm gonna show you what matters." He pointed left. "Niggers." He pointed straight. "Niggers." He turned and drove at a crawl. A half-block away, our school appeared to the right, a whole block of beige brick. Dyer raised his chin at it. "A third niggers and going up."

The word still grated, but I was buying into the word. "They're not all bad," I said. I tried to swallow the words back in. Dyer did a slow take on me.

"I ain't said they're all bad. There's blacks and there's niggers, but they're all seeds and they're done planted. Take a good look at your school, Parrish, your brothers' school, me and Stem's school. Our old men worked their asses to keep us going here and build our houses in a good spot and look what's happening. Look what happened to you in basketball."

I did look and the lore of the place bloomed in me visceral and sentimental. All through elementary school, my classes had come to the pageant that told the history of Istrouma, which meant "red stick," "Baton Rouge," the names of the blood-stained tree marking tribal boundaries. The pageant told the story of Chief Nawaganti and his stand against the French, who came to take his land. I could make fun of it all, ignore the irony of white people taking the land from native people, but the history and messages still resonated—you stand against invaders or you lose your place and its meaning.

Dyer eased onto the gas, heading us across Winbourne and into his old block. I rubbed my palms together as we pulled onto Dyer's old street. He had driven me by here before and every time, pictures of my own street taken over came to me, my parents and neighbors packed and dispersed to who knew where.

"Give me a cigarette," Stem said.

Dyer said nothing. In front of a small brick ranch, the yard well-kept, windows yellow with light, he stopped. He sat quietly for what seemed like minutes, a thin line of smoke rising from his cigarette. "Twenty-something years and get run out," he said, his voice softer than I'd ever heard it, and yet with a razor underneath. "Now I got to watch my ass walking down the street."

Stem tossed a beer bottle into the yard. "Fucking niggers."

Dyer spat, and floored the car. I glanced at his hard-set profile, then focused straight ahead on the gray road. Ever since Dyer had arrived at my garage, I saw him as the cool badass and guide. Invulnerable. Invincible. Unshakable. In that moment, though, I saw him as someone who'd had what mattered taken. Someone like me.

Fall 1974: Skirmishes

I squinted, rum-buzzed, as we entered the stadium. The bank of lights directly across the field glared like truck headlights stacked four high. I blinked and looked lower at the several thousand fans in the stands on the other side, then lower still to the green, white-lined grass where the first two teams collided. For a minute, I missed the days when my daddy had come to watch me play in this very place, missed the Istrouma games we'd watched together, missed playing the game. Then I busily pushed all that away. It was the start of eleventh grade, and those were childish things.

Ahead of Stem and me, Dyer and Sarah turned out of the portal and headed up toward our student section. Cheers and honorary abuse greeted Dyer, a celebrity, the King of Cool. He shot them the bird with one hand while he held Sarah's with the other. We four together were a puzzle, especially Sarah, pale, redheaded, demure with an edge beneath. Cute but not fine like the girls who hit on Dyer at the parties he'd taken me to over the summer. Stem was the lowbrow, funny follower. And I was the popular, hyper, smart kid. I'd considered our peculiar grouping before, but never in the light of school and the gaze of so many of Dyer's crew and my friends. Grandiosity and displacement wheeled in me.

A bleacher cleared enough for all of us. Dyer lit a smoke. People called to him from the rowdy throng of white students. Some kids called my name, too, and I slapped hands and raised my waxy paper Coke cup to take a douse of rum from a friend. The clack of helmets and shoulder pads echoed from the field. Dyer traded insults with other badasses and took the attention of girls I wished would just look at me. All the while Sarah sat quietly, almost churchly, as Dyer's anchor, his security. I wondered if that's what I was, too, because I was a listener and a follower. I shrugged off the thought, gulped my rum and Coke, and hoped for the bliss of being high.

The football jamboree was a strange, first-week-of-school exhibition of six teams playing three twenty-minute games. This jamboree pitted some mostly white against all black schools for the first time, an unprecedented mixing of fans. A black neighborhood, where one of the schools playing was located, bordered the stadium on two sides, making us the intruders. On the other two sides sat the Governor's Mansion and an industrial section. Not far away rose the tall, gray State Capitol building, whose beacon shone a beam on Huey Long's grave.

The first game ended and our Indians charged onto the field in maroon and gray. I knew some of the seniors had been stoned since morning then hooked down speed an hour before kickoff, a combo to dull pain and bring on ferocity. I scanned for the ones I had played with—Mike Coats, my alienated friend; Jason Stanley, my old competitor for quarterback; Virgil; Dufour; Comeaux. We jumped and howled, the old wooden bleachers and cement floor shivering beneath us. I tried not to care about the outcome, only about hanging out, the prospect of getting higher, and the hope that some girl would bounce off Dyer and land with me.

For the opening kick, we all stood and swirled our hands in the air, watched the opposing team's runner get smacked by our players. Then heads turned and Stem pointed past me toward the next section, separated from ours by a chain-link fence thirty feet away. A group of black kids was coming up the steps, pointing and trading shouts with whites on our side. Dyer stepped up onto a bleacher and craned. The boys around me went stiff and quiet, as if they smelled something on the wind. A scuffle erupted, not completely visible from where we were because of people standing. Dyer hopped down from the bleacher and took a step. Several others moved with him, but Sarah grabbed his wrist. "Kurt," she said. He gave her a glare and tugged his arm away, but he didn't go. "Pieces of shit," he said. The scuffling stopped. The black kids walked back down the steps, calling over their shoulders, laughing and cursing. An uneasy energy rippled through.

"Party!" Stem said. I nodded, the tightening in my neck and shoulders squeezing away some of my buzz. I chugged off my drink and pressed my eyes shut against the brain freeze. A pop of pads and helmets sounded, then cheers, and I looked to the field where my old friend Mike jumped up after a hit on a running back. The aromas of dirt, sweat, and chinstrap plastic came to me as powerfully as if I were on the field. I blew through my nose to get rid of the smells and held my cup out for more rum. Dyer touched my arm. "Hey, Sarah's gotta pee," he said. "Y'all want another Coke?" Stem and I nodded, then I watched them disappear through the portal, boozy gauze behind my eyes. In a couple of minutes, a kid I barely knew loped up the bleachers.

"They was talking shit across the fence and some nigger threw a drink. A couple of dudes got some good licks in. Heard shit's breaking out under the stadium too."

"Motherfuckers," Stem said, and there were similar mutterings from our section.

I searched our section above and saw there were no black kids here—no surprise really. Adults from above began passing us and heading out. On the other side of the stadium, at least two-thirds of the people had cleared in the three-quarters or so of an hour we'd been there. Maybe fans of the teams who had finished, but their leaving was still a surprise in its suddenness. I sipped my drink, time passing in blurry yips as I half-watched the game. Another scrum started on the opposite side of us, close enough to hear some heavy blows and yelling, and to send some boys from our section pushing in that direction. I looked to the portal and wondered exactly how much time had passed since Dyer and Sarah had left.

I tugged Stem's short sleeve as he stared toward the latest fight. "How long they been gone?" I asked.

"Dyer?"

"Yeah, Dyer."

"A spell, I guess."

"That fucking helps."

"You don't know either."

I peered toward the portal again. "Let's go see if we can find 'em." I pointed at him. "Don't start anything." He made a scornful child face.

I was glad I said it, because the portal was a gauntlet of black teenagers who called us "honky motherfuckers" and "boy." When we reached the bottom of the cement ramp, I looked up at the underside of the stadium, high and sloping and crimped like an accordion from the bleacher rows molded into the concrete. My head spun. Dust from the dirt floor thickened the air and it entered my lungs like something malevolent. I rubbed my face hard and focused. Older fans, black and white, trooped out through the gates, which were unattended, while young blacks from the neighborhood entered in groups and hung out in clusters. Outside the tall hurricane fence, many more young blacks mingled. We went into the bathroom, wary we might get jumped, but only two slightly older white guys stood at the urinal. "We're getting the hell outta here," one said to another. "There was all kinds of fighting in our section. I hear they're jumping people in the lot." They zipped, glanced at us and strode out.

"Where you think Dyer went?" Stem asked.

"Hell if I know." I tried to pee, then zipped up without success. "We gotta get 'em and go."

Stem spat into the urinal. "What bullshit."

We exited the bathroom back into the drunken, hallucinatory dust. Feet away, barking exploded as a police dog charged a group of black kids. They scattered, a couple scaling the fence. People stumbled back, screaming, laughing, cursing, bumping into each other. My head swirled. Metal crosshatching cut into my back. I realized Stem and I had ended up against the high fence between us and the outside. In the parking lot, glass broke. I turned. Through the wire, a chubby black kid smiled at me. "Bring your honky ass out here. I got sumpin' for you."

"Fuck you," Stem yelled through the fence. The kid and his friends just laughed. I grabbed Stem's arm and tugged him back toward the portal.

"Be cool, man," I said. Stem flipped off the kids. I gripped his shoulder. "Look, dude," I said, "you go back where we were sitting. If they're there or not, just wait for me. I'm gonna look for 'em down here."

Stem's face ruddied, but he headed back inside. As soon as he disappeared, my vision and hearing kaleidoscoped. I was sure Dyer and Sarah had gone to my car for some reason, sure they were hurt, although I couldn't quite register the thought of Dyer being hurt. I waited until a group of whites hit the exit chute and followed them. The variety of the blacks' attitudes beyond the gate jangled me, some of them on a lighthearted goof or just hanging, another portion antagonizing whites with insults, spit, and thrown rocks. In the lot, busy with foot traffic and slow-moving cars, the noise rang differently, echoes gone, the shouting harsher and more distinct. Far away, a car window shattered with a watery burst. Police sirens drifted in; several car horns blew and kept on blowing. My buzz vanished. I wished Robert were there.

The hanging dust was an extension of the fog in my mind and held in it were the red of inching taillights, the glint of cars, the glare of too-white headlights, and the stink of exhaust fumes. I realized that the whites I had followed had hurried on while I stumbled distracted. The air itself bristled with a rage that I didn't yet have the context to know had festered for 400 years, been inflamed by the segregation in my lifetime, by the beatings and hosings my daddy and I had cheered, and by the humiliation my brother's police force heaped on daily. Not that having context or comprehension would have lessened my anxiety and fright in that parking lot, but it may have changed what I would soon do. Every day, the angry people around me walked a dangerous white world, and now I walked through a black one of fury and raucous freedom. And all I saw was the savagery of blacks, just as I'd been taught.

I spun and slogged back toward the stadium, remembering as I did that we had brought my car and I was the one with the keys. An older black guy wearing a do-rag busted a car window, saw me looking and pointed. When I reached the gate and re-entered against the thinning crowd, kids perched on the waist-high rails and taunted, but didn't touch. "Where your ticket?" one kid said and elbowed his friend. Inside, a single cop tapped his pistol handle and billy club. I stopped. The underneath of the stadium bustled—chaotic, a confusion of revelry and threat. I tried to remember our portal and couldn't. I chose one and headed into it. A thick, wide-shouldered white cop stood against the wall. I relaxed, but as I tried to pass him, he stepped forward and poked me in the gut with the butt of his club. I staggered back. "Can't go in here," he said.

"Why'd you hit me?"

"Can't go in here."

"My friends are in there," I said, trying to catch my breath.

"Get on."

I wondered if Robert knew this guy. "Son of a bitch," I said. When he stepped at me I ran. Ten yards away, I slowed to a quick step through the weird diffused light. I searched my mind for our portal number, but there was nothing. Sharp panic rose in me for the first time. A hand wrapped my arm. I spun, ready to swing. "Parrish," Dyer said calmly. Stem and Sarah were with him, Stem's face murderous and jumpy, Sarah's pale. I opened my fist.

"Let's get outta here," Dyer said, still nearly monotone.

"Where the hell were y'all?" I asked, but I thought, How the hell did you know where *I* was?

"Sarah thought she left something in the car she didn't want stole. We remembered halfway there we were in yours."

"I went out there looking for y'all."

"No shit?" The corner of his mouth perked up. He draped his arm over Sarah's shoulders and led us through the gate, the mouthing off coming this time only after Dyer had passed. We strode toward the car, the sensations from before more intense. Traffic stood still as black teens strolled among the cars, some cursing at the whites inside. Before us stretched acres of dark parking lot, criss-crossed by car paths to the main road leading out. We passed several parked cars with shattered windows, heard several more shatter, saw slashed tires and kids running with items they'd snatched. A fire smoldered in my head. I wondered what I would do if Dyer wasn't there. "I see it," he said. I scanned, but the cars were indistinguishable glints to me. We passed some with glass cubes spread on their seats. I envisioned my 8-track gone and Daddy's new Dodge Dart on its rims. Then we were next to it and it was fine.

"Where are the fucking cops?" I yelled.

"The cops are useless," Dyer said.

I almost defended Robert, then I nodded. We piled into the car and I cranked it, jerked at the shriek of music, and punched eject on the tape player. "You want me to drive?" Dyer said from the backseat with Sarah. "No." I breathed deeply and eased into the slow line of traffic that was trying to merge with the long single lane to Plank Road. Taillights pulsed in the exhaust before us. "Maybe we can get out the back way," Sarah said.

"Yeah, cut back around by the stadium," Dyer said. I hadn't thought about the route through the warehouses and had a momentary hope we'd escape quickly. I weaved through spaces cars had vacated and made good time against the flow.

"I never seen so many crazy coons," Stem said.

"Acting like fucking animals," Dyer said.

I turned parallel to the stadium, the crowd thick and raucous around us as we slowed in traffic again. The line moved. "Stop!" Dyer said. Next to a jacked-up car with a flat stood a white kid with a raised tire iron. Around him a loose circle had formed, some just watching while others threw rocks and taunted. A streetlight beamed straight down on him, lit the faces around like firelight. He was as scared as anyone I'd ever seen. My own fear went off like a sunspot of memory.

Dyer, Stem and I threw our doors open, but Dyer told me to stay behind the wheel and Stem to stay put. He pushed aside a couple of people at the edge of the circle. They said something but didn't move at him. "Come on!" he yelled to the kid. Several people closed toward the kid, but he swung the tire iron. The kid broke past Dyer and nearly dove into the backseat. Stem hopped back into the passenger seat, but Dyer hesitated a few seconds. "You want something?" he said to the man nearest him.

"Get in the car, Kurt!" Sarah yelled. He casually slid into the seat behind me, accompanied by jeers. Small rocks flew at us and dinged off the car and windows. A bit of space opened ahead and I punched the gas, scattering part of the crowd. "We're not getting out that way," Sarah said, and she was right; the route we had wanted blocked by police barricades. I turned the car hard and took a spot in line for faraway Plank Road.

"Thanks," the kid in the backseat said, his voice shaky. "My friends hitched a ride when they saw my flat. Some cops pulled up and they took off too."

"Sorry-ass bastards," I said.

The line was herky-jerky, my foot heavy on the brake and gas. As the stadium receded, slow car-length by car-length, so did most of the chaos, but my brain had ignited. We rolled our windows down. I touched my solar plexus where the billy club had poked me. Up ahead, several cops joked and smiled as they halfheartedly directed traffic. Robert's tough-guy stories came to mind, his rousting people on a whim. Why wasn't he here helping me now? Why hadn't he ever been able to help me?

The car ahead of us moved, and I floored it. Yells. I slammed the brakes. We whiplash stopped. I banged the steering wheel and screamed. "Goddamn fucking cops, why don't you fucking do something!" Tears burned onto my cheeks.

"It's cool," Dyer said, and patted my shoulders as Sarah rubbed my bicep. "Just stay with the road." Everyone went quiet as we inched ahead, the air poisoned with fumes and dust. When we neared the intersection with Plank Road, we passed a group of milling police. "Fuck you, you motherfuckers, do you know what the fuck is going on back there!" I yelled. They looked at me. "Go!" Dyer said, and I peeled out onto Plank Road. I weaved through traffic until Dyer said, "Slow down," and I did, still cursing. Everybody but me started laughing, from relief I was sure, but I also thought at me and my silly reaction. I wanted to shove them out of the car to the road.

"Just keep it together," Dyer said. "Hey, man, where you need to go?" he asked the kid.

"I live in Tara," he said, one of the upper middle-class neighborhoods we hated. "You can drop me off anywhere though. Y'all saved my ass."

"What about your car?" Stem asked.

"The hell with my car." They all laughed again. "Y'all smoke?" the kid asked

"No thanks," Dyer said, letting it go because Sarah didn't like him to get stoned around her.

"Fire it up," Stem said. The kid lit a joint and passed it to Stem. My eyes were blurry wet, seething, and I warded off the joint with my hand when Stem tried to pass it. "Looks like me and you," Stem said to the kid.

"You hanging in?" Dyer asked me. I was still hot at all of them, but more so with myself for not being able to laugh it off like everyone else.

"I don't fucking get it," I said.

"You will," Dyer said.

"You know a Berry Marchand?" Robert asked me several days after the jamboree. He and I stood in the middle of our bright kitchen, while Momma and Robert's wife sat at the table with Tommy, who was playing with blocks. Robert had been talking loudly and gleefully about how he'd been in an armada of twelve cop cars that screamed toward the jamboree but stopped on Plank Road to beat the shit out of people breaking store windows and looting. Every word and gesture had been a coiling of the spring inside me. I didn't care that he'd had a job to do; I only cared that he hadn't been there to help me. He'd become the convenient representative for both the loss of order and bullies. I wasn't sure why he'd asked about March-and except that he'd noticed me glowering.

"I know him," I said. "He's a dick."

"Tim," Momma said.

"He said he's a friend of yours," Robert said. "I let him off for speeding."

"He's not a friend. He's one you shoulda hassled and smart-assed."

"What?"

"You heard what I said, officer." The smell of smoke and his cocky bearing repulsed me. He breathed heavily through his nose.

"You better watch your mouth," he said.

"Why? 'Cause you'll do nothing like you and your partners did at the stadium?"

He lolled his head and exhaled. "Y'all so bad, why didn't y'all do something?"

"We saved a kid who was surrounded."

"Then you didn't need me. We were busy corralling people for stealing shit." He grinned. "And from walking on the street." He pulled his cigarettes from his shirt pocket. I snatched them away from him. I'd been riding him to quit smoking, but this had nothing to do with that. He grabbed at them. I jerked them away and twisted the whole soft pack. "You lost your mind?" he said. "You know how much them cost?" He grabbed again, and I swung at him. His hand wrapped my wrist and spun my arm behind me. He took me to the floor and pressed his knee into my back so quickly that I could barely process it. Momma and Deborah bolted from their chairs toward us. "Try that again," he said.

"Robert," Momma said, "let him up."

"Promise you won't try that again."

"Eat shit," I said.

"Tim," Momma said, "what is wrong with you?" I squirmed to get out, but he pressed his knee harder into my spine, my cheek flat to the linoleum.

"Promise," Robert said and let more weight down onto me. I grunted and gritted my teeth.

"Robert," Momma and Deborah said at once. He let go, and I scrambled to my feet and threw the cigarettes on the floor. I clenched my fists, but I could see in Robert's eyes that he would easily take me down again without even having to hit me.

"You're so tough," I said, and stormed out. I walked at almost a jog, humiliated not only by him but by acting like an asshole. My path took me to their car and I paused, opened the door and jerked it outward against the hinges again and again. When I slammed it, it stuck but didn't really close. I stared at it, then I covered my face and wondered where I could go. I thought of Dyer's, but I knew he would just think it was funny, and I didn't want any more laughter; it would only confirm how powerless I was. Then I thought of the pine tree in the backyard that I hadn't climbed in years. I hoisted myself on the lowest limb and clambered twenty-five feet up. The refinery flares in the distance broke away and curled skyward. They made me think of Daddy and that thought made me even madder. He and Robert seemed more desperate and enraged by the day. Fearful men with no clear course of action, just like me, and that was intolerable. I examined the distance between the ground and me, imagined jumping and falling. I heard all of them come out, surprisingly unexcited.

The car door squealed when Deborah opened it, then it still wouldn't shut completely. Robert kneeled and examined it as Momma held Tommy's hand and Deborah stood to the side. I held my breath. "I guess it slipped off its hinge or something," Robert said. He slammed the door and tugged against it. "It'll stay closed to get us home." He kissed Momma, and they buckled Tommy into his child's seat. I watched the taillights until they turned the corner.

Momma stayed in the yard by the road. She stared one way and then the other, her hands clasped in front of her. She seemed lost and frail, but I swatted away the sadness and sympathy for the comfort of anger.

A not-quite-definable bruteness existed in Dyer's house. While I waited for him on their worn Naugahyde couch, I surreptitiously scanned the bare walls and the complete lack of culture in their living room. I'd noticed before that there were no books, newspapers, or magazines. Not that my family was literary, but Momma read romance and *Reader's Digest* condensed novels, and she and Daddy both read the newspaper and the Bible almost every day. Mr. Dyer sat in his easy chair nearby. He was quiet, tall, and broad-shouldered with a potential for violence, which Dyer confirmed when he once told me how his old man "knocked him down" for mouthing off. Mr. Dyer was usually pleasant enough when he spoke, but every time I was there he managed to bring "niggers" into his comments, as if they were a fallback for not knowing about anything besides cars and home repairs. Every time he and I were left in a room together, we quickly fell into silence, something that didn't seem to faze him, but left me antsy that I was lacking in any manly skills or knowledge.

Mrs. Dyer made me feel even stranger and more alien. She was a wiry, pale, talkative woman with jet-black hair and a knack for observing everything negatively. Even though she punctuated her talk with laughter and smiles, her brown eyes held a threat. She always had a cutting remark to make about Dyer and his younger sister, although she mostly left out her husband, maybe because she was wary. Like a lot of people I knew, she liked to lob racist remarks my way and study me to see if my reaction would show agreement or discomfort, even if my words didn't, most likely because I didn't say "nigger" much. The statement was often something that demanded recognition ("How you stand to go to the same bathroom as them at school?") or a joke that demanded a laugh ("I saw one that barely had his tail cut off"). I knew I was easy to read, my uneasiness broadcast by my eyes, even though I myself was a racist and was striving to be more of one.

Dyer entered the living room looking both hangdog and irritated. He slapped my shoulder and told his mother he was going. When she said to be back early, he said he'd be back when he was back. His father called out something about not giving lip, but we were out the door before he was finished. "Fucking bullshit," Dyer said, heading to his car. "Sarah and them all on my ass." He slid behind the wheel and slammed the door, but didn't crank the car immediately. "She wants to dump me, dude," he said. "She found out I fucked Ann Daltry."

"You fucked Ann Daltry?"

"After a party. Some bitch told Sarah."

All I could think of was Ann Daltry naked and my own virginity. I glanced at Dyer again. "Man, she's fine as shit."

Dyer cranked the engine and accelerated fast. "That ain't the fucking point. I can't lose Sarah, man." He went quiet and for a moment I thought he might cry. My legs tensed. If he cried, how could I help him? And if I had to help him, how could either of us survive?

"Look," I said, "I'll tell her you were with me. She'll believe me."

"She ain't never been this pissed."

"She won't dump you, dude."

"How the fuck do you know?" The sadness in his expression mutated into hardness. His eyebrows angled in before he looked forward again. I breathed in and fidgeted. His silence punished me with disapproval, but I also wanted his vulnerability to go away.

"I don't know anything," I said. "I'm just saying stick to your story and it'll work out."

He plucked a cigarette from his pack, lit it, and took a deep drag. "Maybe," he said. "I'm supposed to pick her up before school tomorrow and kind of iron it out."

"That'll be good. She won't let you go."

We sat quietly as he drove too fast down Eaton Street, my mind already racing over the lie I'd agree to tell. It seemed different from the lies to my parents. This lie seemed intimate and consequential beyond me.

"Where we going?" I asked.

"Nowhere." He let that sit, the same discomfort I felt with his old man creeping into the car. Then he looked at me again, his expression—defiant and assured—as different as if a switch had flicked. It jarred me, but I was glad he'd moved from that other place. "There's gonna be shit with L. B. and them tomorrow night at the JV game. We're gonna kick some ass for them dudes getting jumped in the bathroom."

"Who got jumped?"

"Davis and Hall."

"I didn't hear that."

"You're hearing it now. You and Stem pick me up about six."

I forced a smile, even though my guts were knotting. "Better bring a lid if Stem's coming."

Dyer snorted a laugh. "Little Jellyhead." He dropped his cigarette butt out the window and lit another one. He offered me one, but I shook my head, basketball tryouts not far away. He met my eyes again. "You got a roll of coins? Pennies or something?"

"With me?"

"At home, Brain. Bring 'em to use as a slug." He demonstrated by slowly closing his fist around his thumb. "Gives you more of a punch." I nodded. He nudged my arm. "Thanks, man."

"Yeah," I said. It took a second to figure out that he was thanking me for having listened since all I could think about was the next night.

All night and the next day at school, I tried to work myself up. Since the jamboree, I had been trying to use the lens of stereotype to support the idea that blacks were uncivilized. I used as confirmation loud, boisterous black kids, kids with intimidating expressions, dumb kids, kids who talked street. Even Jason Stanley, stalwart student and school citizen, I tried to see as becoming radically black because of his growing Afro, his mirrored sunglasses, his ultra-cool demeanor, and his army jacket. I worked to ignore the majority of their behavior, which was as various as the white kids', ignore the good black teachers like my geometry teacher, ignore the girl in my math class—the prim, quiet Christian girl on whom I had a crush— ignore the kids in the clubs I was in, ignore Virgil. In part, I was able to ignore the positive and simplify, but two new white teachers, Kate Arnault and Fred Shirley, weren't helping. Context and complication were my enemies, and Arnault and Shirley were delivering both.

Arnault taught American History, but I had her every morning in homeroom. She'd started the year before, at twenty-one, and had said in class, "Fuck Nixon." Nobody ratted her out. She had a tall, olive-shaped face, wiry body, big smile, slightly tobacco-stained teeth, and almost no governor or boundaries. She wore tight body shirts, sometimes low-cut, and swooshed around in prairie skirts and dangling earrings. She'd been raised fundamentalist Catholic in rural Louisiana but had managed to get her mother to take her to a Beatles concert in New Orleans, which I considered cool even though I thought the Beatles were wimps. At LSU, she'd dived into antiwar and civil rights politics. She railed against status quo politicians for betraying the nation and harkened back to the crafters of the Constitution and the Declaration of Independence as fodder to support her argument for another revolution in political thinking. She cheered Nixon's resignation, and she talked about the upcoming bicentennial as a year when America might start anew, with respect for justice and equality. She was like an alien who'd landed in our midst.

In English, Fred Shirley insisted we examine both supporting and contrary evidence in making arguments, and that we make sure to see it outside the *coloration* of opinion. He demanded a kind of critical thinking, awareness of style, and rigor of argumentation that I didn't even know existed. He was intimidating, though not physically intimidating—tall, about six-two, with a bushy mustache, and a little of the cologned dandy about him, his movements gangly and languid at once, which made him slightly effeminate to us. Some people called him queer behind his back, but no one challenged him in his class. His mind was incisive, his wit so dry and cutting that for a while I didn't understand how witty he was. He appeared as straight-laced as a teacher could in his tie, black slacks, and black shoes, yet there was an undercurrent of anti-authoritarianism in his reaction to the administration, conservatism, and jock culture, even though he'd played college basketball and even coached in Mississippi. He challenged smart-asses and slackers about why they had taken his class, sometimes put them down without their even knowing it. Yet he met any student who was willing to work right where they were.

In their classes that day, my chest and mind twisted with my secret attempt to hate the black invaders, especially people like L. B., a guy who'd briefly been on the JV team and whom I despised. His behavior fit my definition of *nigger*—crude, belligerent, criminal, and intimidating. It didn't matter that I could be all that too, except maybe the latter; it only mattered that L. B.'s style was different and his skin was black. I stayed quiet in Arnault's and Shirley's classes, afraid that any word or expression might give away my mission and out me as a racist they wouldn't understand and would certainly criticize.

Fall 1974: Skirmishes

• • •

Gnats of white light played at the corners of my vision as we perched on the wooden bleachers of our small school stadium and watched Sarah's brother, Skeeter, root away at left tackle. Not that I paid much attention to the game. Dyer had called me out. He had seen me avoid Jarreau the day after the camp-out, and another failure to act would certainly confirm me as a coward. As the fourth quarter wound down, I squeezed the paper cylinder of pennies in my pocket until my sweat dampened the wrapper.

Down a ways, L. B. and some other black guys had been yelling and pointing at some of Dyer's friends, and they had been yelling and pointing back. L. B. stood about Dyer's height, a rangy, sinewy guy with a lean, very dark face, close-cut hair, and an explosive temper. Robert had told me he came from a notorious family with at least one member in prison for murder.

When the gun sounded to end the game, L. B. pointed at Dyer from a distance across the crowd, surprising me that he knew where Dyer was. L. B. nodded and smiled, then joined the flow of spectators in the small exit space between the lowest bleacher row and the fence surrounding the field. He and his crew headed toward the spot below and in front of us. Next to us, over a thin, metal rail, the bleachers dropped off to the ground by the cinder block concession stand. Riche, a tough, transplanted country kid in my grade, and some other white guys moved lower. Stem took a step down with the crowd bunching below us. "Wait," Dyer said.

L. B. strutted with his posse and called out Dyer, Riche, and the others, but my anger still wasn't coming. Part of my hesitation was fear of a gang fight and part of it was that none of this seemed personal. The abstraction of losing our neighborhood and culture was not yet urging me to jump into a thrashing crowd where people would be getting smashed or maybe even stabbed. No matter my doubt, the moment of decision was cockily walking toward where Riche and his group of whites had gathered below us. All around L. B. and between us and the bottom of the bleachers, lots of fans were simply trying to leave, unaware of what was brewing. L. B. had his signature red bandanna wrapped around his fist and he held his arm high as he shoved white fans out of the way. "Cocksucker," Dyer said. "Give me that slug." I handed him the coins, a small relief, and he moved to the edge of the bleachers and the eight-foot drop. Stem started again to try and move down through the crowd, but people were noticing the commotion and pushing back up toward us.

L. B.'s group rushed forward and met Riche and the other whites in the four-foot space between the bleachers and the fence. Sounds like medicine balls being dropped on concrete reached me. Shrieks cut the air. People surged upward, bringing Stem with them. Dyer stood still as if he knew exactly what would happen. The fight swirled around the end of the bleachers into the space between the bleachers' edge and the concession stand. Dyer swung over the bleachers' side rail and dropped into the crowd, miraculously landing on his feet between people in the middle of the confusion. His arms pistoned into motion, his powerhouse punches clearing black kids in front of him, his hair and height and the space he was creating keeping him visible as if there were a force field around him. People pressed me into the rail to see. I gripped the metal to keep from being knocked over, mesmerized by Dyer as my guts writhed over whether to dive in and join him. Then cop hats were moving in and the fight was scattering. Stem appeared beside me, cursing he couldn't get down.

When I looked back to the ground, I'd lost Dyer. I panicked for a second at the thought he'd gone down, then he appeared next to me, having somehow climbed the bleachers. He grinned, grasped my wrist, turned my palm upward and poured loose pennies into it. The wrapper was blasted open like a firecracker. "I nailed L. B.," he said and laughed. "Come on." He turned and shoved his way through the people still clumped on the bleachers. Stem and I followed, but when we reached the bottom, Dyer pushed past the cops and the several fighters they had separated, then sprinted toward the parking lot, moving through the crowd as if it were drapes. Yelling came from up ahead, signaling where the fights had gone. Stem and I pushed after, but we lost him. "That fucker's like Tarzan," I said.

"Like a fucking wild ape," Stem said. When we cleared the crowd and reached the dimly lit parking lot, we found running fights, random people throwing punches and taking off, people jogging or hauling ass past us, dervishes of activity. Stem seemed as confused as I was and not so eager now to brawl, so we kept walking between the two angled lanes of cars toward Daddy's Dart. From behind a car leaped a tall, thin black woman, L. B.'s mother, whom I recognized from basketball. Her expression addled, she drew a pistol from her purse and pointed it at us. "I'll shoot you honky motherfuckers," she screamed. We dove to the concrete and quick crawled under a car as if we'd choreographed the move. Feet scuffled around L. B.'s mother's feet, then two feet came up behind her. We heard a thwack, and down she came to our level, flat on the concrete. Jimmy Gonzales knelt and looked under at us, a sign stake in his hand. "Knocked her ass out," he said, grabbed the pistol and ran.

Stem and I looked at each other, chuckled and shook our heads. L. B.'s mother struggled to her feet and staggered off. We crawled out and jogged toward my car. The fighting seemed to have mostly gone around the main building and people were hustling to their cars and pulling out as fast as they could. Stem and I plopped into the Dart and stared ahead. "Crazy bitch was gonna shoot us," Stem said.

"That was L. B.'s momma," I said. "We almost got shot by somebody's momma." I opened my fist to the pile of pennies, astonished they were still there.

"Guess that's L. B.'s change," Stem said. I slung the pennies across the parking lot. "You think we oughta round up Dyer?" he asked.

"How? That bastard's probably chasing people across Choctaw."

We waited, everything around us normalizing as the remaining crowd cleared out. In a few minutes, Stem and I were alone with a few empty cars in the lot. Sirens howled in the distance. I turned on the 8-track and we got out, left the doors open, and sat on the trunk. I was glad chaos had partly conspired to keep me out of the fray, but anxious sweat broke out on me nonetheless.

Soon, some of the white fighters came strolling back to their rides, woofing how they'd chased the blacks back to their neighborhood. Dyer sauntered in alone. "Y'all get in it?" he asked, and motioned for Stem to give him a smoke.

"We almost got shot," I said.

"Shot?"

"L. B.'s old lady pulled a gun on us and Gonzales knocked her out,"

Stem said. Dyer gave his high-pitched hee-hee-hee. Stem handed him a cigarette and Dyer held it in his mouth as he examined his knuckles.

"I chased some sonsabitches clear down past the gym. I almost punched your pal Virgil." He flexed the hand that had used the penny slug earlier. "I let him go 'cause you know him." Both his arms shot out and punched us in the chests. "Pussies."

"Hey, *Tim*," Virgil said to me the next morning as I walked toward homeroom. I'd tried to act like I hadn't seen him and Jason Stanley. I stopped and stepped to the side of the hall as the crowd brushed past. "Your damn friend wanted to kill me last night," Virgil said. I glanced at Jason, who stood watching through his sunglasses in the dim hall.

"Kill you?"

"Dyer. I was walking home from the game when all these fools come tearing ass around the building and I just kept on walking slow to let 'em know I didn't want to fight. I knew most of 'em anyway. Your buddy runs up and cocks back like he's gonna hit me and I just stood there. He took a minute and grinned and said, 'You know Parrish,' and laughed and ran off, but he still gave me a look like he wanted to bury my black ass."

I didn't say anything. I wondered what Virgil and Jason would say if they knew I wished I had fought. The clang of slamming lockers sounded like junkyard chimes.

"He told me," I said.

"Why you run with him?"

"He lives on my street. He's just gets crazy sometimes."

"That's true. White people get crazy. Most niggahs get in fights, they just fights, but when these white dudes get started around here, they wanta kill everybody." He glanced at Jason, who remained unreadable. His stare through his impenetrable glasses and his unbuttoned army jacket with his last name on it needled me. I didn't know his daddy was in the army.

"Yeah," I said, "no black dudes wanta kill anybody. Like L. B."

"L. B. does, yeah. But Dyer, shit, he digs hurting black people."

"You don't have friends dig hurting white people?"

"Not that I run with." Virgil stroked his chin. "Why you think it is white cats get so insane when a fight starts?"

I knew Virgil was trying to bring things back to a place that wasn't so heavy, but I was churning. "I don't know, man. Why you think L. B. and some of them are such assholes?"

Virgil raised his eyebrows at me, but he didn't ask why I was being an asshole too. I looked at Jason, still my competition for quarterback, even though we hadn't competed since eighth grade. "You been playing good this season," I said. He nodded without speaking, an unusual gesture that struck me like a finger poke in the chest. I pointed at the sunglasses. "Is it bright in here?"

He raised them to the top of his head. "No, Tim." I waited for more. We stared at each other, my muscles twitching. Then Virgil tapped me and said we needed to get to class. I told Jason I'd see him later, and Virgil and I headed off.

"I'm serious, man," Virgil said, "you oughta watch it with Dyer."

"I heard you." I tried to work some moisture back into my mouth. "What'd you get on Shirley's paper?"

"C-plus and I was glad to get it. He said it lacked coherence, a clear thesis, and enough examples. Besides that, it was fine." Normally, I would've laughed, but the image of Jason judging me, and the thought of Dyer threatening Virgil and using my name, pressed me hard. "What'd you get?" Virgil asked.

"Goddamn B-plus."

"Shit! B-plus. I'd give a nut for a B-plus."

I inhaled. Talking about school seemed ludicrous.

It struck me as almost scandalous and at least startling when talk of the fight entered discussion in Arnault's homeroom and Shirley's English class. Arnault directly asked if anybody had been there. By strange odds, Stem was in homeroom with me, but no black kids were, and he said, "Me and Parrish was there. It was cool. We almost got shot." I wanted to slap Stem in the mouth to keep him from rolling quickly into how we were there with Dyer, but another classmate saved me when he jumped in and told how Dyer and others had run the blacks off campus. "How'd the fight start?" Arnault asked.

"L. B. and them went after Riche and his posse," Stem said.

"So it's completely racial?"

"They're jumping people in the bathroom," a girl said. "It's not safe."

Ms. Arnault's fingers moved her brown hair behind her ear. I loved that kids trusted her enough to be so honest, loved that she had the courage to take on something that was dangerous for a teacher to discuss. But I hated that if she found out that I wanted to fight, believed I needed to fight, her judgment of me might be worse than Jason's and Virgil's. Then I was disgusted at caring what she thought. "There is a bigger context," she said, and the sound of minds snapping shut around me was almost audible. She quickly summarized slavery's legacy of Jim Crow and the murders of Martin Luther King, Medgar Evers, and Emmett Till. I'd never heard these things from a sympathetic perspective (had never heard of Emmett Till or Medgar Evers at all), and I didn't want to hear it right then.

"I never had a slave," Stem said, and the class cracked up. She glanced over at me, I'm sure looking for a sympathetic connection as she often did when she brought up something topical or I made a crack about something. When she looked away, I didn't know what expression I'd had.

In Mr. Shirley's class, there wasn't an actual discussion. Someone asked if Shirley had heard about the fight, and he said, "Yes. You weren't dumb enough to be in it, were you?" He gave the guy the look that challenged him to try and present an argument for the indefensible, but the guy said nothing until after class in the hall when he said, "Nigger-loving fag." I said nothing back.

Tryouts

I looked forward to varsity basketball as a place I could at least prove myself still an athlete, if not a man. But two weeks into practice, the new coach was cursing in my face, poking me in the chest, grabbing my shirt to sling me into place whenever I made a mistake and finally making me run laps when I told him not to call me a son of a bitch. Redick stood to the side and smiled. I believed he had turned the new coach against me as a quitter before tryouts even started. There wasn't a second of fun or satisfaction. I doubted I was learning anything. After the practice where I'd run laps, I dropped my gear with the manager, an encore of the previous year's proof that I couldn't take it. At least I wasn't going to be pushed around anymore.

The following day, I told Virgil I'd quit. "What?" he said.

"I just wanta play ball, not listen to a bunch of shit."

Virgil nodded, shocked I think. I didn't tell the coach. Why bother? I was a quitter, and I wasn't going to give him the opportunity to rub in what I already knew. I wasn't interested in riding the bench either. Two days later, I stopped in to talk to the defensive line coach, who had grown up in my neighborhood and who still called me Timmy. I was filling him in on my brothers when the basketball coach came to the office door.

"You quit my team?" he said. He was squat, dark-skinned, and hairy-armed. "You fucking quit my team and Birch has to tell me? I heard about you, you little son of a bitch."

"Don't call me anymore names."

"I'll call you whatever the fuck I want," he said, and started toward me. I held my ground, tensing my skinny right arm to catch him before he got inside on me, even though I knew that he would hurt me and yet I would be expelled. The other coach swept his arm around me and stepped between us.

"Move," the basketball coach said to him. "I'm gonna teach him a lesson about mouthing off."

"That's enough," the other coach said. "Timmy, get outta here." I didn't move. "Go!" he said. I stayed locked with the coach's eyes.

"You *better* fucking go," the basketball coach said. I was scared, but I didn't care if he beat my ass. That would be better than more bullying. I kept my mouth shut as I slowly walked past him. "Little sissy," he said.

The next day, the principal called me into his office and told me that the coach was willing to forgive my trying to start trouble and quitting if I went back and took my punishment. I hadn't even known Tank knew who I was, wondered later if he wanted to keep me on the team only because I was white since fewer and fewer whites were going out for basketball and the attendance at games was dropping. At that moment, I wanted the motherfucker to die.

I didn't go back to the team. I also didn't tell my parents about the confrontations with the coach or the principal, but they evidently sensed something was wrong and kept asking me how practice was going. I said fine. For the next two weeks, I wandered the neighborhood until the time practice would let out. When I finally told Momma and Daddy that I'd quit because I was tired of being yelled at, they glanced at each other. Then Daddy looked at me. "Screw that little dago," he said, and went back to eating. Again, I loved him for being on my side, but I wasn't quite sure why he was okay that I'd quit. Not that it mattered. Nothing he said or did could have lessened my feeling that I was less than a man.

I drove while Dyer toked the last of a joint in the passenger seat. He'd called me on a school night to fetch him from Sarah's because his car had broken down, and he'd told me to bring some weed. Rain reflected my headlights and blurred the road except for when lightning slashed and strobed. Thunder rocked the car. The air stank with chemicals burning off at one of the plants, their odor overpowering even the pot. "Pick it up, Granny," Dyer said.

"Why don't you kiss my granny ass?"

"Fucking kick your granny ass."

My blood was amped, the visuals cool, but Dyer was right that I was driving stoner-slow. I pressed the gas and cut around a corner, the tires squealing. He turned the music above the hiss of the water from my tires. I floored it toward a red light, mimicking Dyer's stunt, slammed the brakes and slid. The rear end of the car fishtailed right, hydroplaned, jerked straight, went left, and slid to a stop at a 45-degree angle in the deserted intersection. I slapped my palm on the wheel and hooted.

"Jesus, bitch," Dyer said, blowing a last toke.

"Can't take your own shit?"

"My shit don't slide under a red light. Man, when you gonna get off the rag over this basketball bull?"

"When I'm fucking ready." I peeled out, running the red light I'd already half-run.

He laughed. "Go to Pak-A-Sak," he said. "I wanta get a Coke and some smokes."

"Yes, sir." His bossiness rankled me even more. I thought of Daddy and Robert the Cop—not Robert the Good Guy who'd agreed to be our nominal coach in the recreational basketball league where my cousins played. Only a minute ago I'd had a good buzz. Now it was just paranoia with an oncoming headache, the pot roulette landing on a bad number. "Parrish," he said. I glanced at him. He popped the burning roach in his mouth, swallowed it and grinned. *Fucker.* Lately all his stunts clawed my nerves, stunts like flicking bottle caps at bullet speed toward Stem's and my eyes, or bringing his new nunchuks around and spinning them close to us. One time he told me to run, slung them into my ankles at fifteen feet, and dropped me to the ground. It was okay for him to act crazy, but then he'd suddenly act like he was my old man.

I pulled up in front of the Pak-A-Sak fast and braked hard. The rain drenched us on our short sprint from the car, and I followed Dyer into the cold, bright store. The shift in light and air was almost trippy. Dyer turned toward the drink cooler in back, but I wiped the rain from my glasses and lingered at the front to scan munchies. When the bell on the door jingled, I lifted my head. Jarreau. He saw me, too. I went numb, just as I used to, maybe more intensely because Dyer was there. Jarreau squinted at me, paused, then came around the corner of the aisle—up closer than he'd ever been. His features were screwed in, his eyes deep blue, the whites bloodshot. I towered over him now, but his body was hard and adult inside his tight white T-shirt. He cocked his head. "I know you?" he asked.

"I'm Parrish. I got in a fight with Lassiter."

The wheels of his thinking were almost audible. He turned his head slightly to the side, sneered and nodded. "Your brother's the cop came to my house."

"Yeah. When you sent Chandler after me." I didn't move. The fluorescent light sharpened him and erased everything behind. A frown crept across his face, and I readied for a swing, wondered if I should kick him in the nuts or uppercut his chin before he struck, just to get a lick in. I heard the cooler door close and felt Dyer's eyes on me. I wondered if he was expecting Jarreau to punch me, wondered how long he would take to step in if Jarreau was beating me down, wondered if he would step in at all, and how it would somehow be worse if he did.

"I remember," Jarreau said. He licked his lips and blinked. He rubbed his elbow on his side and studied me with slow eyes that seemed more stoned than my own. Maybe he was trying to retrace what all had happened and why. Maybe he just didn't care about me anymore. Maybe he was calculating what he was going to do to me in the parking lot. Or maybe he simply knew that to still do nothing was somehow worse than hitting me. Then he glanced past me and his eyebrows perked up. Dyer nudged me. "You get my smokes?"

I narrowed my eyes at him. "Uh-uh." I couldn't tell if my voice was shaky or not.

"Dyer," Jarreau said, and smiled like a snarl. "Ain't seen you in a while."

"Ain't seen you either, you sorry motherfucker."

"What you been up to?"

"Same old shit," Dyer said. "You still robbing houses and chasing skanks?"

"When I fucking feel like it." His expression snapped in as if some of the THC had been shoved aside. He leveled on me, then looked at Dyer again. "You running with him?"

"We live on the same street."

"No shit?"

"No shit." Dyer tapped me and nodded toward the counter. "Kools. Here," he said, handing me the Coke he was getting. I wanted to tell him to fuck off and get them himself, but I didn't. "See you around, Jarreau," Dyer said.

"Yeah," he said, and gave me one more look.

I went to the counter and paid as Dyer left the store. I walked toward the exit, Jarreau and I staring at each other as he watched me from the cooler in the rear. Outside, I didn't duck or rush through the rain. In the car, I handed Dyer his smokes and drink. I cranked the engine and pulled fast out of the lot, my glasses blurry with water.

"I hate that bastard," I said.

"What's the deal between y'all again?"

"I fought one of his buddies and he started messing with me."

"Messing with you?"

My whole body heated. "He sent this older kid to my house to get after me and a few days after that he followed me home and cussed me. Robert went to his house and put his boot on his throat and then Jarreau said some more shit to me."

"He never punched you?"

"No."

"Huh. And you ain't never fought him?"

"No I never fought him. This some kind of goddamn test?"

"Not for me, dude."

I worked my hands on the wheel and slowed. Dyer's power play was filtering in, how he'd waited not just long enough to see what I'd do but long enough to make it clear that he was king when he stepped in. "You were checking to see what I'd do back there, weren't you?"

"I let y'all do what you were gonna do."

"So you remembered there was shit between us?"

"I remembered something. I reckoned if y'all were gonna go after it I wasn't gonna get in the way."

I almost said that he *had* gotten in the way, but it was still in me that one day I might want him to get in the way. "Would you have jumped in if he was beating my ass?"

"If he was killing you or had a blade or something."

"You think he would've beat my ass?"

"Jarreau's been in a lot of shit."

"So you think he'd beat my ass?"

"Hey, man, if you need to find out about Jarreau, let's go. Take a stick to him or something if you got to."

My stomach was green and rolling. Why had I even asked Dyer? I knew what he believed, and I knew what I believed. When Jarreau had looked at me, I was thirteen again and might be forever.

"Look," Dyer said, "Jarreau ain't shit. You gonna have plenty of chances to show your stuff when it counts." He chuckled. "Your brother put his foot on his neck. I bet Jarreau almost peed his pants." He swept his hand across his hair and wiped the water on his jeans. "Jarreau. What a cum wad." Dyer rolled down the window and lit a cigarette. He pulled hard, the cinder traveling up the cylinder, and I rolled my window down, too. Our routine was to air the car out so Daddy wouldn't complain, even though it never worked and the rain was coming in.

"It's going down at the end of the pep rally tomorrow," Dyer said as he plopped down at our cafeteria table the following Friday. Stem and I guarded our sloppy joes from Dyer's usual grab and bite. His eyes went past us to the section of the cafeteria where some black kids were loudly cutting up. "Smith and Melancon got in it with 'em in the bathroom, so that's it."

"What's *it*?" said Stem. Dyer focused on me.

"I'm gonna kick L. B.'s sorry ass for good," he said. "Right after the Indian sticks the hay. It's gonna make them Yankee riots in South Boston look like nothing." His look pierced me.

"Where's Sarah?" I asked, because she usually joined us at lunch.

Dyer frowned. "She's pissed 'cause she knows I'm gonna fight."

"You won't be getting any," Stem said.

"At least I still get some."

"Stem gets some," I said, and moved my fist up and down at the waist.

Dyer glared at the black kids as his plate sat untouched. "I got some picked out," he said. He locked on me again. "You best pick, too." My hands tingled. I knew I should nod or say something, but I wasn't even clear enough to tell myself all the reasons I was frozen. Dyer smirked. He grabbed Stem's and my sloppy joes, one with each hand, and took huge bites. He chewed several times, opened his mouth to show us and swallowed.

"Dick," Stem said.

Dyer went serious again. "This is for real tomorrow. Shit will get settled." He stood and walked off, passed close to the black kids' tables, nodding and smiling.

I was shooting turnaround jumpers in the driveway that afternoon when Momma's coworker dropped her off and waved at me. Momma strolled over and gave me a kiss. We both stood there a second, not saying anything until I asked her how work was and she told me it was fine. She linked her fingers in front of her. "The doctor wants me to go spend the night at Ochsner's in New Orleans to figure out exactly what's going on. Don't worry, it's nothing new."

"Maybe they'll find the right medicine."

"Maybe." She glanced away. "I'm give out with all this. I know your daddy is too."

She breathed deeply. "You excited to play with your new team?"

"Ain't much of a team with Dyer and Stem and them. Really only one other real player. I guess it'll be all right."

"Robert's coaching y'all?"

"Robert's acting like the coach."

My desire to tell her about the upcoming fight pressed outward inside me. I started dribbling again. Momma gnawed on the tip of one of her long fingernails. "I don't understand why those coaches at school have to be so aggravating."

"'Cause they're assholes." She made a face, then laughed with me.

"How's the rest of school?" she asked.

"Fine," I said.

She looked hard at me, sensing, I'm sure, that there was more. For whatever reason—her own fatigue over illness or the strain of taking care of us—she didn't ask. She raised her face to the sky and shut her eyes. "It's a pretty day," she said, and it was, the sky light blue and a breeze blowing late fall. But her tone, almost elegiac, stiffened me. She looked at me again. "It's supposed to rain tonight. Maybe it'll clear up before the football game."

"Maybe so."

"I miss us going out to get malts."

"Me, too. Maybe we can go sometime."

She made a sound in her throat. "When would that be?" She waited a minute, then turned to go inside, paused at the front door. "It's every man for himself for supper." The door closed behind her.

I didn't know it to say, but I believed she had betrayed me with her illness. Every night I slept lightly, waiting for the brass bell she kept by her bed to launch me from sleep and to her bedside. Already I had helped her to the car, sped her to the hospital and stayed by her, terrified I would lose her and angry she might leave me.

Blood in the Halls

As players and coaches gave speeches, cheerleaders did their stunts and majorettes danced, C and D batteries sailed back and forth across the voluntarily segregated gym. I had never been aware of such a stark battle line. In bleachers on our side of the gym sat the whites and a few blacks, divided into senior, junior, and sophomore sections, while on the other side sat only blacks. Teachers, coaches, the principal and the single cop craned to see who the snipers were, but it was impossible to police 1,200 people.

Across the floor, L. B. and several members of his posse had stayed on their feet the entire pep rally, cutting up, laughing and nodding across at Dyer and some of the other whites who would lead the charge. Dyer stood one section of bleachers over from me, hands in pockets, his profile as menacing as an assassin's. The plan was for Dyer and L. B. to lead the combatants to center court at the end of the pep rally. Stem and I waited on a low bleacher, Stem antsy to fight, me caught in my Hamlet-like ambivalence. The band clustered onstage and on the floor in front of them sat the football team with Virgil, Jason, and Mike. I almost laughed that they were focused on the game while dozens of boys geared up to spill blood right there. Strangely, I was aware of how a fight here would violate the gym that I still thought of as hallowed ground from my days watching Alan's basketball team, the floor polished to a high gloss, the photos of Heisman Trophy-winning alum Billy Cannon hanging in the foyer. I'd banished myself from the court, but I hadn't banished my sentimental attachment to the place's symbolism, representing our white neighborhood and my parents' values of hard work and working-class identity.

The previous night and all morning, I had remembered the JV fight and imagined this fight as twenty times worse. A tangle. A stampede. I imagined a blade between my ribs, and feet trampling me. But worst of all, I imagined myself motionless once again. I'd tried the old exercise of churning up anger with the call to defend what was ours, and again no heat came. That was one of Dyer's gifts, to always be ready for battle. It was one of Robert's gifts, too, although he seemed to have anger so close to the surface that he could dip into it any time. Daddy as well. I also knew that they'd fight without anger if they had to. And I was aware that this wasn't Nagasaki or Vietnam or a house full of people who wanted to kill me, aware of how my trepidation over the comparatively low-intensity violence about to happen here further reinforced my timidity. In minutes, though, I'd have another chance to follow Dyer down the path toward being a man.

The war drums started again as two students dragged to center court a hay bale adorned with a fake panther's head and pelt. The Imalakala war chief, a white kid in brown body paint, came to the front of the stage dressed in a long headdress and loin cloth. He raised his spear parallel to the floor, as the band blared the Hollywood Indian song. I usually smiled at the ridiculousness and thrill of the pageant, but now I pictured someone grabbing the spear and plunging it into someone else. A stiff chill raced down my spine and through my legs. The Imalakala dropped from the stage and weaved toward the bale. Hundreds of people sang with the band, and I wondered how many knew what was coming, wondered how many were eager for it, wondered who didn't care. The Imalakala circled the hay more and more tightly. At last he stopped and raised his spear. The gym went silent. The Imalakala shrieked and plunged the point into the hay. The band erupted into our fight song. The air was charged like the second before a lightning strike.

L. B. and his group of thirty or so shoved through the crowd on the bleachers toward the floor. On our side, Dyer, Stem and others did the same. The principal, the cop, and the coaches strung out the length of the court. The band ended its song, and the crowd poured onto the floor and toward the exits. The men at center court shoved back against Dyer and L. B. I didn't move. L. B.'s red-bandannaed fist rose above the crowd and pointed outside. Dyer pointed, too, then started pushing through the crowd toward the white exit on the opposite side of the stage. I followed into the flow, glad to be slowed and given time to work up resolve.

The damp, unusually chilly air surprised me when I stepped outside. The courtyard spread huge and soggy. Hundreds of black kids moved along the sidewalk, hemmed in against beige buildings by the whites parallel to them, some of whom were taunting and throwing bleached seashells put down to keep the ground from muddying. I hurried to reach Dyer and his following, but stayed behind them farther out in the courtyard. Principal Tank, the cop and the coaches had come outside and were in the DMZ between the sides, pushing back boys who took a step forward, but the people yelling and taunting on both sides were stringing out way beyond what a few men could stop.

Dyer halted. He slipped off his blue jean jacket and tossed it onto a low tree branch as if he'd choreographed it. He strode forward and swung. Dozens of people charged. Shrieks shattered the air. Body blows thudded like hung meat slapped with paddles. I lost sight of Dyer no more than ten yards in front of me. White kids scattered around me, while many of the black kids stampeded toward the cafeteria doors, a crush, people leaping the long red metal railing that was supposed to form the lunch line outside. People fell and were snatched back up. Bodies swirled everywhere. I didn't move, even though movement either toward or away from the riot had become a physical law. People fought just feet in front and to the side, but I seemed invisible, cloaked in hyper-consciousness of my passivity and of so much violent noise—screams, scuffling feet, cracking face punches. Then the fighting opened so that my sightline went straight to Dyer.

He was a nightmare wonder, attacking with every part: arms, feet, elbows, hands. He knocked two kids down, then he stood still a moment as skirmishers wheeled near and others fled. His expression was angry, and yet the anger was masked in calm and near ecstasy. He loped forward, cut off a kid headed to the cafeteria, dodged a swing and struck him with a right that lifted the kid into the air and dropped him unconscious on his back. Black girls screamed, cursed and pounded the glass of the cafeteria windows. He laughed, flipped them off, spat on the flattened kid and gave a feint to the windows that actually made the girls recoil.

Dyer acted with all the qualities of the movie heroes he loved: the force of Bruce Lee; the steeliness of Clint Eastwood; the coolness of Billy Jack. But it wasn't a movie. His strength, his brutality, his indomitability were all real. The people he'd hurt were bleeding, crawling, staggering, groaning, crying, or knocked out as he stood not twenty feet from me, daring anyone to come at him. Olympian, almost mythical. I was awed, repulsed, intimidated, and enthralled. I looked away, disgusted at him and even more at myself.

The crowd had mostly dispersed, but little scenes still played out around me—individual fights, white people standing in shock or strolling, tourist-like. Our beautiful, racist, green-eyed student-body president wept as she ushered a white kid whose nose gushed blood. A wiry black kid named Nate, who was prone to mouth off, came strutting toward the cafeteria from the courtyard—amazing, since the courtyard had been white from the start. He had both arms held high, his middle fingers displayed, evidently victorious and showing off for the faces in the window of the cafeteria. They were yelling and pointing at Dyer, ten yards away, but Nate didn't notice. Dyer sprinted, leaped with both feet out and caught Nate mid-back. Nate flew, sailed parallel to the sidewalk until his shoulder caught a vertical bar of the red railing. His legs twisted into the wall, his body torqued at an impossible angle. "Motherfucker," Dyer said, and stomped Nate's stomach once before moving off. Several kids rushed out of the cafeteria and dragged Nate inside.

I thought then that Dyer might see me, see I had done nothing, but he kept going toward the main building. The black kid I had seen humiliated in my Louisiana history class so many years before ran past me, pursued by ten or so whites. I watched them run twenty yards until the kid went for a door, bounced off it locked, and the pack set on him, punching him and each other in their frenzy. I shivered, cold setting deeper in me like sudden crystals. I strode toward the main building, but just as I reached the edge of the cafeteria, a tall heavyset black guy trotted around the corner and bumped into me. He still had on his band uniform. We both stepped back and squared off. I knew him and didn't like him, a cocky smart-ass, but we shared friends who played in the band. I thought of swinging before he did. He scowled, dropped his fists, and jogged on by.

Ahead was the covered patio where people gathered before school. The cloudy day had darkened it like twilight. The concrete shone with wetness that glittered. Closer, I saw the glitter was the glass of large Coke bottles smashed and strewn, evidently pillaged from the concession stand and used as weapons. A white kid I knew lay on his back, his girlfriend kneeling next to him, his face impossibly pale, a pile of jackets tossed over his torso. Dead, I thought. Another kid tossed his jacket onto him as he sprinted past. Then Virgil jogged up to me, his football jersey giving him some immunity from the riot. "You all right?" he said.

"Yeah," I said. "You?"

"I'm going home till the game. You oughta go too." He slapped me on the shoulder and jogged through the gate to the parking lot.

People were wide flung about the courtyard. From all I could see, the rioting was finished. Then, as sirens swirled in, two large black men in civilian clothes, one with "Black Power" and a fist on his jacket, came through the gate and went after several white guys who were talking. They all threw punches, and I took a couple of steps toward them before the white kids took off, and the black men chased them. I made to go after them, my legs sludgy, but police cars screeched up outside the gate and white, uniformed cops jumped out and stormed in. Several of them went after two white kids who were looking out for the kid under the jackets. Others began roughing up and cuffing anybody they could get their hands on. One helmeted cop marched onto the courtyard and took up a sentry stance with a shotgun held across his chest. Craziness. I turned and walked fast away.

Here and there single shoes lay, as if people had run or been knocked out of them. Blood speckled a white sneaker. I kicked it, then stood beneath the canopy of a small tree. A frizzy-haired friend with teardrop glasses walked up and stood next to me, his eyes glistening with shock. We watched the cops pour in thirty yards away. "They're beating people for no reason," he said.

"I saw that."

"Did you see those big black dudes that looked older? I heard they're undercover sheriffs' deputies."

"No way."

The principal's halting voice came over the loudspeaker. "Everyone is to report to their homeroom. I repeat again, all students report to their homeroom. This is the principal."

"Dumb fuck," I said.

Blood in the Halls

My friend pointed. Dyer was sprinting toward us from the far end of the courtyard. He pulled up, a big smile on his flushed face. "I think I knocked out a nigger deputy."

"See?" my friend said.

"You knocked him out?" I said.

"He swung a blackjack at me and I clocked his ass. He was on the ground and he pulled out a badge and said I was under arrest, so I kicked the motherfucker in the chest and booked. The pigs are going nuts. I got poked by a rake too." He tugged his shirt away from his shoulder to show a row of puncture wounds from somebody's pick comb. "I'm outta here before that deputy gets some help." He slapped my shoulder and ran between buildings toward the other parking lot like a kid fleeing adults. The principal blew into the loudspeaker, then spoke again. "No one is to enter the buildings. No one is to enter the buildings. I repeat again no one is to enter the buildings. Plan One is in effect."

My friend and I looked at each other and shook our heads. *Enter and don't enter.*

"What the fuck is Plan One?" I asked.

"Hell if I know. I'm going too." He went the way Dyer had.

I scanned the courtyard, a battlefield only—what?—ten, fifteen, thirty minutes before, and now nearly deserted except for cops, and students tending to injured friends, students strolling as if going to class, or wandering as if bomb-dazed. The grass was chewed to mud, the sky lower than it had been earlier. My head throbbed, my bearings disoriented as if I were at a place that only resembled a place I knew. Then—I don't know why—I walked back toward the patio where the police had taken up positions. Ambulance men were rolling away a gurney with the kid from beneath the jackets. The police smoked and chatted as if the fighting and arrests had been hours ago, as if some of them hadn't made it worse. I crunched over broken glass through the cops, felt them watching me, maybe a couple trying to figure out if they knew me. None of them said anything.

I shoved through the heavy door into the unlighted hallway, the floor dark as old oil and sheened with thin window light from the far end. I pulled up to let my vision adjust. The hall stretched long and empty. The brown lockers dully glinted. Emotions spun upward in me, surely colored by teenage melodrama, but real nonetheless. My feet moved. On the floor, spots and smears gave a meager reflection. I had already stepped in them—a smattering here, a tiny pool there—and I moved to the side. What machine could have dripped this fluid? My mind cleared. Blood. A trail of blood. I smelled it, coppery and rich above the rank odor of school. The school where my brothers had gone and where I had always dreamed of going. My school. In a way, my church of nostalgia.

My rage found me—too late—not directed at anyone in particular but everywhere at once. I shuffled along the bloody tiles, pressure pushing outward against my temples and forehead. Foot heavy, I climbed the stairs, better lit but also bloody. On the second floor, some white kids laughed giddily in the hall. I glared and they went quiet. Then I was yelling: didn't they know what the fuck was going on, that people were hurt, that our school was destroyed? They backed up, then turned and paced away with me still raving. Someone grasped my arm, and I spun. Ms. Arnault. She tugged me into her classroom and shut the door behind me. The small group of students studied me. I wanted to hurt them, then I spotted Stem smiling, his pant leg rolled up.

"Were you in it?" Ms. Arnault asked, her complexion pink.

I stared at her. "What?"

"Were you in the fight?"

"No," I said.

"Oh," she said, and leaned back, her voice seemingly disappointed, a high school girl's voice. I stared at her a moment before walking toward Stem.

"Some dude hit me with a chunk of cement," he said, pointing to a large bruise on his shin.

"You think it's broken?"

"Nah. Did you get any?"

I shook my head and went to the window. For as far as I could see, city police and sheriff's cars lined the street. Stem limped up beside me. "We counted thirty-eight on this side. Every cop in the parish must be here. I bet Robert is here."

"Maybe so. The fucking cops just came in and started the shit up again."

"You see Dyer kick ass?"

"I saw. He said he clocked a black deputy." I plopped into a desk, exhausted. I held my hands up, examined my knuckles, unbruised, and covered my face. What right did I have to be so mad? I hadn't done shit.

Nobody spoke to me again until Robert knocked, grinning through the door's window. Ms. Arnault unlocked and opened it. "I'm here to arrest those two," he said and pointed. Stem laughed and so did Robert. "That tall one's my brother." He introduced himself.

"I've heard about you," Ms. Arnault said, smiling.

"Then you know why I gotta grab 'em out to jail." Ms. Arnault patted my shoulder as we left. I lagged behind Robert and Stem as we walked the long hall and exited into the parking lot. "Y'all get in it?" Robert asked.

"Nigger hit me with a chunk of concrete," Stem said.

"You?" I shook my head. He nodded. "Dyer break some heads?"

"He punched some nigger deputy Tim said."

Robert chuckled. "I heard some nigger plain clothes sheriffs came in. Some of my buddies had it out with a couple of 'em. I got called at home, but when I got here all the fun was over."

"Your buddies came in and whipped people's ass for no reason," I said.

Robert poked his tongue against his cheek. I dropped onto the passenger seat and stayed quiet. Stem kept telling about what he'd done and seen Dyer do until Robert dropped him at his house. When we pulled away, Robert asked, "So you sulking about some people getting rousted in a riot?"

"I'm not sulking."

"You doing a good job of faking then."

"I don't feel like talking."

"You felt like mouthing off. I'm just asking what's bothering you."

"They fucked up our school and all you fuckers are laughing about it."

"It's just a fight. Ain't the first and won't be the last."

"Fine," I said. "Why'd you ask? Go fucking ask Dyer."

"What?"

"Nothing." I didn't say anything as we pulled up to the house and I stepped out.

"You gonna be all right?" he asked. It irked me and touched me at the same time.

"Just fucking great."

"Hey, don't be mad at me." I walked toward the house until he called my name. "Tell Dyer I'm ratting him out to the Sheriff."

My impressions were fractured and impossible to categorize. A heaviness that wasn't exactly physical inhabited my body, but I still thrummed with adrenalin. My head raced with the images of the day, and yet what I'd seen had scoured my earlier emotions. I didn't understand that my cells were archiving a small nightmare.

Daddy made an indecipherable noise deep in his throat, got up from the table and turned on the portable radio. I had listened to the news earlier, heard that six classmates had been taken to the hospital and that the one rumored to be dead was okay. I could barely stand to listen anymore. "It's a wonder nobody got shot or stabbed," Daddy said as he paced back and forth across the kitchen, shaking his head. "They oughta just send the police up in them neighborhoods and take care of that business." He ran his fingers through his thinning black hair and stared at me with a look that seemed more worried than angry. Then his eyes flared. "They tearing up everything. Two blocks over. They'll be on this street in a year." He swept an arm as Momma and I watched from the kitchen table.

"Hollis," Momma said, "sit down."

He poured himself and Momma more coffee and sat with us. He and Momma hadn't heard about the riot before they arrived home from work, and I'd just given them a summary of how it started in the courtyard, turned into a rout, and the police came. I hadn't given any names, especially not Dyer's.

"What got all this started?" Momma asked.

"I said they've been jumping people in bathrooms."

"You think this'll stop all that?"

"You know it won't, Rachel," Daddy said.

We all went quiet. Momma kept her eyes on me, while Daddy stared into his coffee and shook his head. Their drama repulsed me, although I wished I could partake more in it by telling them I'd done something to protect our neighborhood. I imagined how Daddy would be proud. I couldn't fathom that he wouldn't have wanted me to fight and couldn't have accepted that he'd have been right to want that.

"You ain't going to that ball game tonight," Daddy said, glancing up at me.

"They cancelled the game."

"That's good," he said.

Momma reached across and touched my forearm. "You all right?" For some reason, the memory of the detectives in our living room came back to me as hot as a brand. I wanted to jerk my arm away.

"I'm going outside to shoot ball."

"You not going *anywhere* tonight," Daddy said.

"You told me."

Battle dreams jolted me awake all night, images from the riot blending with images of actual shooting war, dreams probably as close to Robert's as I would ever get. The dreams left me with a hangover I couldn't shake, so I lifted weights and shot basketball, hoping to tire myself out. My head stayed electric. I roiled through the next two nights and went back to school raw and foggy. On Monday, as I stepped from my car, I spotted David Duke prowling the easement between the school ground and the street. A crowd of white boys took his KKK flyers and nodded as he preached. Spit filled my mouth. A fucking Nazi interloper. Then I wondered what right I had to feel disgust at him. I walked on.

Near the gates sat police cars. Cops patrolled the school ground on foot. Before class, people told stories of what they'd seen and what they'd done. I told a little of what I'd seen, but because I'd *only* seen things, I mostly kept quiet. During homeroom, I looked differently at Ms. Arnault. Her reaction of disappointment had changed my image of her, at least temporarily, from revolutionary to just another high school girl who might see me as weak. My resentment seethed until I left her class. In Mr. Shirley's class, I still simply feared he'd find out who I really was and point the same disdain at me that he'd pointed at other fighters.

Late in the day, Mike Coats checked to see if I had fought. "No, did you?" I asked, knowing full well he hadn't. He had been disappointed that I was involved with Dyer and that I was smoking so much pot, so I had written him off as a square. I knew he was trying to make sure I was all right and somehow that was unbearable. His face fell. "See you later, man," he said. I wanted to apologize, but I just stood there.

Back at home, my parents were preoccupied with planning their trip to Ochsner's in two days. Momma hadn't been officially diagnosed, and this trip was designed for the doctors to pin down her illness so they could better treat it. Daddy was terse and crotchety about what to bring and when to leave, and Momma was fed up and sharp. Their nerves reached into me and twisted like barbed wire. I listened to their instructions of what not to do and how long they'd be gone and when they'd be back, then I went to my room and put my headphones on. I detached myself from the seriousness of their trip and their emotions. Compassion felt like an enemy that would leave me more defenseless. I was wiped out, body and mind, but I couldn't stop my thoughts from rushing. Every time I dozed, some image bolted me alert. Finally, I swung out of bed, enraged and ragged, my overhead light like a laser. I wanted to smash something, hurt somebody, or at least claw my way out of my head. Instead, I went to the dark living room. I had no idea what time it was. I assumed Momma had poked her head into my room, seen me asleep and left me alone, although I also thought she may have been so tired and anxious she forgot.

I collapsed on the couch and stared out the picture window. I believed I was weak, cowardly, confused. I was terrified that I would be destroyed from without or within, while I imagined Dyer in his bed asleep. At peace. Dreaming of crushing his enemies. Invincible. I both loathed and idolized him. I lusted after his certainty and his astonishing ability to do damage. If I had those things, my adversaries would be crippled, my confusion erased, my self made unshakeable with conviction. I'd be safe and able to sleep. I knew I'd never

Blood in the Halls

have the physical power he had, but maybe I could find the will that led to clarity and conviction. That will had to be available. Dyer had tried again and again to lead me to it, lead me to meaning that was uncluttered and unambiguous. All I had to do was act.

Losing It

"What the fuck?" Dyer said. I'd just thrown a cup of ice cubes into the windshield of an oncoming car, and the car had screeched to a stop and was U-turning. "Gun it!" he said.

"You don't wanta fight 'em?" I said.

"Just go, motherfucker."

I floored my parents' Galaxie 500, the engine kicking in with a sound like a big propeller under water.

"They're catching us," Stem said from the backseat.

"Hit that right up there," Dyer said.

"I can't believe you wanta run," I said.

"We don't even know those bastards. They might be packing."

I cut us hard, fishtailing at the next road, floored it again, hit the next left, then turned once more, the headlights of the other car long gone. Stem slapped the seat between Dyer and me and doubled over, while Dyer gawked. I banged on the steering wheel and let go with laughter until my eyes watered. My parents had taken the Dodge Dart to New Orleans, leaving me with the family car and with strict instructions not to go driving with my friends. I had called Dyer and Stem as soon as my parents had turned the corner.

"That was fucking wild," Stem said.

"Fucking nuts," Dyer said.

"I thought you and Stem wanted to fight everybody."

"Niggers maybe," Stem said.

Stem and Dyer both lit cigarettes. "You bitches don't burn the goddamn seats," I said. "My old man's been climbing all over my ass about the burn holes and he'll kill me if we burn this car." Stem feinted his cigarette at the side of my eye.

"Wouldn't be no burn holes if you pricks cleaned your weed," Dyer said.

"Clean weed is for ladies," Stem said. He and Dyer hung their arms out the window as I sped closer to my house, my adrenalin still ahead of me.

"Stop this big mother and let's see what kind of r.p.m.s it'll get," Dyer said, as we neared our street. The crazy energy had continued to intensify in my head, and tonight it was spinning me wild and directionless. I rocked the wheel back and forth, and they gave a fake yell as the car swayed on its loose suspension. I slammed on the brakes in the middle of the road and shifted the automatic transmission into neutral. "Galaxie 500," I yelled, and pressed my foot all the way down, the engine roaring and vibrating, a smoke cloud billowing behind us. Laughter took me so hard that my belly hurt. I dropped the shift into drive, thinking the car would peel out like a standard. It lurched twice, threw us all forward and jerked to a stop. The dashboard lights flickered, went dim and bled away. The engine hummed all the way down.

"Why the hell you'd do that?" Dyer said.

"I was popping it like a clutch."

"In a automatic?" Stem said. Dyer laughed and covered his face. He caught himself enough to recreate the sound of the engine groaning into oblivion and Stem joined him.

"Shut up, dick," I yelled. I turned the key. Nothing. Turned it again. And again. "Goddamnit." I banged my hands on the steering wheel. "Shit, motherfucking shit."

"Everybody out," Dyer said. "Let's push this bigass mother home."

It seemed like twenty miles instead of two long blocks, not only the weight of the car resisting me, but also the wheel I was one-handing without power steering. We grunted as we made the last push up the short incline of the driveway, then I jammed the shift into park. Dyer and Stem leaned against the car, laughing. I slammed the door, gritted my teeth, went in and called Robert. Back outside, I propped against the ironwork as Stem and Dyer rode me until I told them to go to hell and they backed off.

"You did what?" Robert asked after he sauntered up in shorts and a ragged T-shirt and heard my story.

"He murdered it," Stem said.

"Motor spun down and all the lights dimmed out," Dyer said and giggled. Robert shook his head and laughed, too, while I scowled, sick to my stomach.

"It ain't funny," I said.

"It's funny," Dyer said.

"Fuck you, asshole."

Robert tapped his chin. "You outta your mind?" I didn't speak. "I got no idea what you did to it, but it's bad."

"Thanks for clearing that up."

"Hey, I came over here on my night off. Don't act like my wife."

I ran my hands down my face. "Shit."

"Well, you can't tell Daddy what you did, so you got to make up a story."

Stem said, "How 'bout somebody snuck up in here and floored it and threw it in gear."

Robert came over and sat on the ironwork next to me. "What were you thinking?" he asked. "Momma's in the hospital and you go and do this."

"I don't need you on my ass." I walked over, slid behind the wheel and gave it one last try. The car was dead metal. When I got back out, Dyer was telling Robert about punching the deputy at the riot and Robert was slapping the side of his leg. "I'm going in," I said. I sat down on the kitchen floor, my back against the pine cabinets, and stared into the fluorescent light. Robert came in and ran himself a glass of water. "They took off," he said. He drained the water, wiped at the corners of his mouth with his thumb and index finger. "Look, you messed up. It ain't the worst thing in the world."

"Bullshit."

"All right, it is bad." He rubbed his hand back and forth on the counter as if polishing it. "How 'bout this? You were just backing out the driveway and it bucked and went dead."

"Maybe. It seemed like it was just electrical the way the power died."

"Why not? You got no chance to get out of this when he takes it to the shop, so you might as well save yourself until he does."

"I'm fucked."

"Pretty much. At least he can't kill you."

"That's what you say."

Robert put his hands in his pockets and smirked at me.

"What?" I said.

He scowled. "Jesus, why you always on the rag?"

"Just fuck it."

He loudly exhaled. "You wanta come over and drink a beer?"

"No."

"I don't blame you. Nothing but arguing over there. Bitch complains about being home by herself with the kid and complains about being home with me."

"*She* complains?" I said.

"All right." He held up his palms. "I'll check in tomorrow night on what they told Momma. You can thank me then for coming over."

I listened to his car drive away, then stayed there a long time, imagining Daddy's expression and finally wondering if Momma was going to die.

"Man says they's a fist-sized hole in one of the cylinder walls and you still gone say it happened backing out the drive?" Daddy gripped his hips, his stance wide as he stood there in his work khakis. It was three days since I'd blown up the car.

"That's what happened."

He adjusted his black-framed glasses. "I told you not to go running the road while we were gone."

"I didn't."

He sighed. "Son, I'd be ashamed if I did that to the car while my momma was in the hospital."

Guilt washed over me caustic and unacceptable. When they'd told me about the diagnosis of systemic and epidermal lupus, diabetes, and a list of other things, it sounded like an evil incantation. I'd wanted to bash the walls, bash myself. Instead, I pushed the emotion down like a land mine and held it, not considering what would happen when I released. I did the same here again with Daddy. "I didn't do shit," I said.

"You don't talk to me like that." He put a finger close to my face.

I didn't flinch. I'd already justified denying the truth. After all, didn't Daddy and his church do the same with their denial of everything inconvenient—science; any part of the Bible that didn't suit their immediate goal; and worst, Christ's words when bigotry and ignorance compelled them? I knew I was no better, an asshole and a hypocrite, but the spit of defiance was my available weapon.

"You gone help pay for this repair." We stared at each other, neither of us backing down. "I don't know what's wrong with you," he said. His brown eyes glinted then saddened, yet so subtly that no one except our family would have noticed, and we wouldn't have spoken about it.

"Think you got enough chain there, Parrish?" Stem asked.

"Got enough to knock your cocksucking head off." Stem oohed and slapped the back of my head from the backseat. In my peripheral vision, I saw Dyer smile. Before he picked me up, I had searched through our garage and found a ludicrous chain sturdy enough to tow a car. It was an unwieldy and ridiculous weapon, but wrapped around my hand, several links loose for swinging, it kept me focused as a means to bolster myself.

Behind me sat Sarah's big, kid-like brother, Skeeter. I was glad he was there. He had told how blacks harassed his family on their street across Plank Road, how his mother had no money to move them, and how they were unlikely to get enough to move if they sold their house. Knowing this motivated me. Every day since the riot, I had smelled blood in the hall and seen the courtyard as tainted, unsteady ground. I said nothing while desperation and rage built in me. Despite what I felt toward Virgil, Jason, and other black friends and teachers, I had tried to build a cold hatred based on the simple math of race. This *was* a war, I told myself over and over. *Niggers* were coming to take what was ours; *niggers* were the catalyst for destroying the idealized school in my head; *niggers* would take my parents' neighborhood just as they'd taken Dyer's. L. B. and his ilk would rule.

"There's those assholes," Dyer said. The parking lot of a building on Winbourne was filled with cars for the David Duke meeting, the reason Dyer had chosen this night to "do something and not just talk shit."

"I thought you'd be for him," I said.

"I don't care about his KKK bullshit. He don't even live in our neighborhood, and he comes around wearing a suit and handing out flyers. Piece of shit's just a politician, and the idiots who're eating it up are just as full of shit as he is."

"Them idiots are just about everybody we know," Stem said.

"Yeah, well all they gonna do with Duke is talk and pay dues." Dyer blew smoke from his nose as I glared at him. Dyer's position made no sense. Didn't Duke believe in the war Dyer had pushed me to join? "He just wants to get on TV," Dyer said. "Shit, *we* should be on TV and not that South Boston crap. Them dickhead Yankees ain't doing nothing but throwing rocks at buses, those pussies." Dyer, Stem and Skeeter busted out laughing. I pressed my index and forefinger into my eye sockets and gripped the chain more tightly.

"Here we go," Dyer said, his voice low. Up ahead on the sidewalk, five black kids ambled toward Skeeter's neighborhood. "Let's kick 'em back across Plank," Dyer said, and bumped his car up onto the curb. We piled out. A couple of the kids ran, but the others turned to fight. Dyer knocked one down with two punches. I chased one of the runners, screaming I was going to kill him. He stumbled and went down on the sidewalk. I drew back with the chain and he turned to face me. He was younger than I was, twelve or so, although big for his age. "Nigger!" I screamed, and grabbed his collar, my hand still raised. He covered his face with his arms, his eyes peering through the gap. Around me, I heard curses and punches. I shook him, notching myself up. He was a kid, but a kid who would grow up to come take what was ours. I jerked his collar and tried to bring my arm down. He turned his head. A hand grabbed my wrist and lifted me off. "Git!" Dyer yelled. The kid scrambled away. Relief momentarily lifted me. Dyer looked at me with disdain. "He's just a kid," he said. I almost swung at him. I remembered Dyer taking out kids seventy pounds lighter than he was, knocking a kid off a bike with a beer bottle for a goof. "Fuck it," I said. I trudged back to the car, threw the chain on the floor and plopped in. The kid's frightened face floated in front of me. He and his pals had just been walking along when we set upon them. I knew all about that.

Stem and Skeeter jumped in laughing. Dyer steered us off the curb as Stem and Skeeter woofed about the licks they'd gotten in. Stem laid his hand on my shoulder. "Parrish was gonna whip that boy," he said.

"Fuck all y'all," I yelled. "Let me out."

Dyer looked at me in amazement. No one was supposed to show this kind of emotion unless they were about to fight, and again I hadn't even been in the fight. I opened the door with the car still moving and swung my leg out, going. They grabbed me as Dyer braked.

"We're shitting you, dude," Stem said.

"Yeah, cool out," Dyer said.

"Assholes!" I pulled my legs in, slammed the door and told Dyer to take me to the house. My drama had made me seem even more ridiculous than the chain had. They tried to talk to me again, but I told them to shut up. When they pulled away from my house, I slung the chain into the corner of the garage and went to the refuge of my backyard. The terrified kid came to me again, as if carved onto my eyeballs. I imagined the sound of flesh giving, the dullness of bone cracking. I covered my face. What I'd done was despicable. Who was I? What was I? I rubbed my face harder and harder until I felt it chafing. Then I cried, heaving, until I wondered if I'd ever be able to pull my mind back in.

An hour and a half later, Dyer cruised in and parked on the street. I had been playing ball hard in the driveway, trying to blunt the edge in my head. I was exhausted but still going. He leaned against his car and lit a cigarette. I faked left, spun right and banked in a fall-away jumper, the shot I practiced over and over. "Nice shot," he said. I dunked the ball, then stopped, soaked in sweat, my heart hammering, and dribbled hard as I looked at him. He pushed off the car and motioned for the ball. I tossed it to him and he let go a shot that banged off the board. "Nice touch," I said. I retrieved the ball and came back over.

"So your panties still in a wad?" he asked. I didn't speak. He ground his cigarette on the driveway then put the butt in his pocket. "You oughta point being mad in the right direction."

"Like you did that night you hit that kid with that bottle."

"That was a little plunk on the head, not a bigass chain."

"You like to shift it your way." He gave me a warning look that he'd never given me before. I tensed. He tossed his hair back and tugged at his ear lobe, his eyes level.

"You didn't wanta hit that kid. You think hitting that little nigger would've made you feel better?"

"Why don't you get it straight? Sometimes it's everybody black and sometimes it ain't."

"Hey, if you want to get it on, get it on when there's something like at school or the JV game. If you don't, don't be a baby about it." He shook his head. "You think too goddamn much, Parrish."

"Okay, I won't think next time I'm checking to make sure somebody's old enough to get hit."

"Right." He smirked. "Stay mad. Maybe it'll help." He walked around to the driver's side of his car. "I ain't told you. I'm getting a Dirty Harry pistol Friday."

"Say what?"

"The old man and old lady been telling me no, but now they say it's cool to have some protection with all the shit going on at school. Maybe we'll take it out and pop some rounds this weekend." He pointed his finger at me and dropped his thumb like a hammer. He ducked into his car and cruised off. My stomach soured. I truly didn't know if he meant shoot at bottles and cans or at people.

I tossed the basketball into the garage and went inside the house, my body plastered with sweat. I intended to go past Momma, who was reading in the living room, but she asked me if I was okay.

"Yeah," I said and kept walking, but she told me to come back. "What?"

"I don't like that tone, young man. Sit down for a minute and talk to me."

I sat on the vinyl-covered ottoman. There, in front of her, the whirl inside my head increased. I knew I couldn't stop it, but I'd been hoping that a hot bath might slow it down. An interrogation would only spin me harder.

"What's going on with you, Tim? You're either mad as a hornet or you're not saying anything."

What could I tell her? That two hours before I'd almost caved a kid's skull? An hour ago I was sure I'd gone insane? That I worried every time I looked at her and Daddy; that Jarreau was still out there; that I felt split in two between the kid at school and the kid who ran with Dyer? Getting purchase on a thought, much less thinking through the consequences of what I said or choosing the right lie, was like catching grains of sand thrown by a centrifuge.

"Nothing's going on."

"Something's going on."

I fixed my eyes on the floor. The embarrassment of having already cried burned in me, and I worried she could see my swollen eyes. Her hand touched my cheek, and I recoiled as if snakebit. Her mouth dropped open.

"Why's everybody on me?" I said.

"I'm not on you." Momma's eyes had gone worried. I wondered if I looked crazy. I tried to steady myself.

"I don't mean you."

"Where are your old friends? You never bring Mike or your old friends around. Why isn't Mike on your basketball team?"

"He plays football and runs track at school."

I thought of my recreation league basketball team, one other true basketball player and me along with thuggish Dyer, Stem, and a group of fill-ins. I laughed and shook my head. "We got enough." I wiped the sweat away from my brow.

"Why don't you go get cleaned up and maybe we can watch a little TV or something."

She moved her overbite across her lower lip. I realized that for a few seconds my thoughts had slowed down, but the realization was a string pull on a spinning top. I popped up and headed down the short hall. For a second, I considered turning on the attic fan and having it suck upward above me, as if that might pull away the dread and self-loathing.

Spring 1975: Battle Lines

I was settled into Daddy's easy chair, reading *The Grapes of Wrath* for Mr. Shirley's research paper, when the phone rang. I started, thinking for a moment that someone was calling to tell me Momma was sick again, even though that made no sense since she was in her bedroom, having had a bout of fever the night before. I hopped up and went to the phone, expecting the call to be from Robert in his new bachelor's apartment. Instead, Dyer spoke.

"Skeeter got stabbed." It didn't sound like him, his voice absent of bravado and confidence.

"That's not funny." We hadn't hung out in weeks, had barely talked since basketball season had ended.

"Some nigger stabbed him a coupla hours ago. It's bad. We're at the emergency room at the Lake." He hung up.

I lowered the phone as if it were made of crystal. I heard Skeeter's laugh, then pictured a black man jumping from behind a bush and stabbing him in the back, pictured Skeeter arching and crumpling in pain. Then, weirdly, I saw Dyer's face as unsure as his voice had been on the phone, a vulnerability I'd only glimpsed in his troubles with Sarah.

"Who was it?" Momma called from the back of the house. I walked down the hall, my brain already fabricating a lie that would keep questions away from what I might do. She sat propped against pillows, her expression tired in the way it always was the day after a fever.

"Dyer. His girlfriend's brother got in a bad wreck. I need to go to the hospital."

"Oh, God." She took off her reading glasses and sat straighter. "Did he say how he was?"

"Not really. He's at Our Lady of the Lake. You all right here by yourself?"

"I told you I'm fine. Do you really need to go this late?"

"I want to." Daddy was on the way to the dog shift, so I didn't have to worry about him.

"Well, you be careful. Call me and let me know."

In the car, my head ached as if a trap had closed on it. Since I'd raised the chain the previous fall, my life had normalized some. I had coached a kids' basketball team at the request of parents on my street. Robert and I were talking more since he and his wife had split, and I was also talking on the phone more with Alan, who was urging me to figure out my college major, even though I had begun to crazily wonder, often and secretly, if college would somehow be a betrayal of my working-class roots. I'd also reconnected some with Mike Coats and was gearing up at Ms. Arnault's urging to be Scholars' Club president my senior year. I slept better at night. I still ran with Dyer, but his bullying irked me more and more. I twisted my hands on the wheel. This drive to the hospital seemed a drive back into his heavy gravitational pull.

I parked and trudged through the yellow-beamed lot. The buildings before me made my frantic trips here with Momma rattle through my memory. The red EMERGENCY sign floated above an ambulance. This was the unreal part, the part before I knew the facts and saw the faces that would make them real. The electronic doors whooshed open, and I passed beneath the sign and into the antiseptic smell I'd come to hate. Across the room, in molded plastic chairs, sat Dyer, Sarah, and her mother, all quiet, nobody touching the other. Dyer was hunched over, elbows on knees, fingers linked. They stood to greet me, and I hugged Sarah and told her mother, a short, rotund redhead, how sorry I was. They thanked me for coming, then I looked at Dyer. His color was drained a shade from normal. He wore a too-small, hospital T-shirt that somebody must've given him. From his lap to his knees, his jeans were splotched dark. It took a second for me to register that it was blood.

"He's been in surgery for a couple of hours," Sarah said.

"You know how he is?" I said. She shook her head. Nobody said anything else.

"I need a smoke," Dyer said. "Y'all need anything?" They shook their heads. Sarah's mother's eyes looked as furious as they did worried. I followed Dyer out into the warm night, and we stepped around the corner from the U-driveway where another ambulance had just arrived, throwing its red light over us. Dyer lit up and leaned against the side of the building. "Thanks for coming, man. It sucks just sitting with them."

"What the hell happened?"

"Nigger fucked him up good."

"Where?"

"In his back and side. They were wrapped up, sounded like slapping. Him and me didn't even know he was hurt till he went down."

"Jesus Christ." Dyer looked off into the lot. I studied his profile. "I meant, *where* did it happen?"

"Right in front of their fucking house."

"Goddamn."

"Look at this shit." He motioned to his legs. "It's still damp. He musta lost a gallon." He pushed in hard against his eyes with his palms, the cigarette dangling from his mouth, raked his fingers front to back through his hair several times. The manic energy kicked up a notch in my veins.

"Can I get a smoke?" He gave me one and lit it without looking.

"I thought we lost him on the way here." He blew smoke and flicked hard several times. "Sarah's old lady keeps throwing shit at me. Like I need that. I can't do nothing for Sarah."

"You hurt?"

"Huh?"

"Did you get hurt?"

"Fuck no. Those bastards are gonna get hurt."

"You know 'em?"

"I'll find 'em." He looked at me with an expression I couldn't read. Skepticism? Trust? Doubt that I would help him?

"I can go get you some clean clothes."

"I ain't changing tonight. Sarah and her old lady was on me to change into some hospital pants, but I ain't doing it." He dropped his cigarette on the sidewalk and headed back inside. I noticed I hadn't even taken a drag from mine.

We waited on the hard seats, my thoughts beginning their old sprint. Irony hovered over my being here. I had begun to separate from Dyer, and now my irritation struggled with my sympathy for him. There had been no more fights, but his aggressiveness toward Stem and me had amped up. He had taken to pulling his .44 from beneath his seat and pointing it at us, sometimes challenging us to play Russian roulette. Some nights I believed he would do it if we agreed.

But his thuggishness on our basketball team had alienated me the most. Rebounding was his only ability because he could clear space with strength and intimidation, so he played enforcer in a league where nobody needed an enforcer. His dirty play bothered me, but one night he took it way beyond bother. Another team's best player was dribbling the ball up the sideline, and Dyer forearmed him so hard that the kid flew into the lowest bleacher with a boom. Dyer stood over the kid, smiling, and daring him to get up. The referees called a technical foul, but they didn't take a step toward Dyer. The other team's coach ran at him, but when Dyer turned, the man pulled up like a reined-in horse. Robert said nothing. Worse, I not only said nothing, I smirked when Dyer walked past me and said, "Showed that cocky prick." The league commissioner called and told Robert and me that if anything like that happened again, we would be kicked out of the league. When we told Dyer, he said he'd only take shots at people under the basket, then he laughed and said, "That's the far-est that dude ever flew." I laughed again, but after that night I looked at myself differently. I was sick of going along with him.

After two hours, a doctor entered the waiting room and took Sarah and her mother to the side. Still, I overheard him say that one of Skeeter's lungs had been punctured and he was stable but still critical. It seemed wrong to hear it at the same time they did. Sarah had remained something of a stranger to me, an ancillary feature of Dyer, and I had talked to her mother only a few times. Even Skeeter and I weren't really close, yet here I was in their inner circle. I didn't know what to say to them.

When the doctor left, I told them I needed to go see about Momma and remembered I hadn't called her. Dyer walked me outside. "I appreciate you coming," he said, the vulnerability I'd heard on the phone still there, but already partly hidden by a hardening mask. "I'll call you tomorrow." Then he shook my hand, a strange gesture for him, for us. "Don't tell nobody at school, you got me?"

"Sure."

On the way home, everything rose up under my ribs and into my temples. As big as he was, Skeeter came to my mind as a boy, and I pushed against the picture of him bloody and falling. I wished I could see the ones who stabbed him now when I was angry. Back at the house, I eased down the hall to Momma's room. She snored on her side and didn't stir. I went over and stood by her bed, lightly touched her hair, then went to my room and lay on top of the covers with my clothes on. Through my blinds the streetlight filtered in as slats. I wondered if I should call Robert tomorrow to see if had heard about it or if he could help, but I knew I wouldn't call. The impending fall of Vietnam had been pulling him down. This was my business to deal with.

The next morning, I called Dyer's house and woke him. He said he didn't have an update, but he would pick me up that night around seven. The hospital told me Skeeter was still in ICU. At school, I didn't tell anyone what had actually happened, not even Stem, and I was glad he was going away to Mississippi that night to visit relatives over the weekend. The rest of the day at school, my sense of detachment intensified. Class and books and teachers seemed insignificant, nearly unreal, compared to what waited outside. I staggered through in a sludgy haze. By late in the day, fatigue weighted my head and body.

Back home I skipped supper and listened to the clink of plates and silverware being cleared, then to my parents' voices as they drank coffee in the living room. When Dyer's horn beeped outside, I swung my legs off my bed, trudged into the living room and toward the front door. "I'm going to the hospital," I said.

"Don't stay out too late and leave your momma here," Daddy said.

"Yes, sir."

"I mean it."

"I hear you."

I dropped into the passenger seat. Dyer eased away from my house then pushed it around the corner at the end of the street. "How's he doing?" I asked.

"Still in ICU."

"Sarah and them all right?"

"What you think?"

I breathed in and looked out my window. "We going to see him?"

"Nobody but family and me. Besides, I ain't planning on going there right now."

I already knew where we were going. There was no music in the car and not another word for a while. We turned onto Winbourne Avenure, went past Istrouma, and on toward Dixie. We passed near the Dalton Theatre, where only a few years earlier my friends and I had felt safe strolling or riding bikes to see science-fiction triple features, a place on the same road where Robert had been robbed as he worked at the convenience store. We passed the spot where I'd raised the chain, the image of the kid coming back, as it often did, with almost unbearable shame. We crossed Plank Road and passed the tiny, whitewashed library my mother used to take me to. Several short blocks later, we turned onto Sarah and Skeeter's narrow street and parked in front of their darkened house. All the houses nearly touched one another. Gravel driveways cut the small lawns. The nearest streetlight shone nearly a block away, deepening the darkness that was straining my vision. I stretched my neck against the tension and wondered if any other white people still lived on this side of Plank Road.

Dyer shut off the engine. "I caught him right here," he said, his deep voice quiet and shaky. "We was both laughing 'cause we'd kicked their asses and run 'em off, and all of a sudden he took a kinda jerky breath and started going down. I grabbed him before he hit and his shirt was all wet in back, and when I seen it was blood, I tore it open and seen the stab holes. One of 'em was pumping, and I stuck my finger in it." His silhouette stood out against the darkness behind him. He sat still, looking straight ahead. "We was both on our knees on the ground and I was holding him and I started yelling at Sarah in the house till she finally heard me and came outside. She helped me sorta get him up and we both lugged the big bastard to the backseat 'cause I couldn't move my hand. He was just white as shit. I kept telling him to hang on with Sarah driving like crazy. I kept my finger in there the whole time till we got to the hospital. It was weird. I could feel him inside."

He didn't move, and somehow his held emotion passed into me like rushing water. I wanted to say something, but I touched his shoulder instead. He gave me a look that backed me off, then he swiped at his eyes and pulled out a cigarette. He stepped out and I followed him to the rear of the car, the night damp and overcast. I pictured Dyer holding Skeeter after he fell. My right hand clenched against the sympathetic throb in my own finger.

"What started it?" I asked.

"We was on the porch having a smoke and they came by here talking shit," he said, motioning to the street, his voice an edge now. "Three of 'em, saying honky fucking this and honky fucking that and giving us these grins like they was gonna kick our shit, so we went after 'em. One of 'em had a sawed-off broom handle he swung at me, and I just knocked it down and punched him out. Chickenshit took off and I went after another one. I was punching the fuck out of him and I could hear Skeeter and the other one sound like they were slapping. I punched mine a couple more times and he took off and I looked over where Skeeter and his was tied up. Nigger was slapping Skeeter's back it looked like, till he ran and we started laughing and walking back in the yard. Fucker had been stabbing Skeeter while they was clinched."

I scanned the cars parked on the sides of the road and the bushes and trees in the little yards, as if somebody might be waiting. When I looked at Dyer, he seemed to be studying me. "They booked down that way," he said.

"You seen 'em before?"

"They gotta live around here." He peered down the street. "They mighta gone in one of them houses." I blinked in the dim light, wondering if they were seeing us right now. "Let's go."

Back in the car we inched along, Dyer ogling the houses we passed. I thought of the .44 under his seat. He liked to pull it out and quote Dirty Harry: "You feeling lucky, punk?" I squirmed inside, at first from what Dyer had described, but then for another reason. It came to me that I had to take care of him emotionally, had in a way already taken care of him, just as I believed he'd taken care of me physically.

After I cut the grass on Saturday morning, I tried to focus on the novel for Shirley's class. Finally, I sank for a while into the world of the Joads, who'd been pushed out and away from their farm, reminiscent of the Mississippi farms where my parents had grown up. Outrage crept into me until my hands ached from gripping the book. I set it down, my anger at the banks' stealing from the Joads combining with my anger at the abstracted blacks coming to steal from us. I understood how the haves took from the have-nots, but I didn't yet understand the complicated forces at play in my own scapegoating.

Shortly after noon, Dyer picked me up and we tore out, the sky scrimmed with towering cumulus clouds. "How's he doing?" I asked.

"Better," he answered, but his voice didn't carry the tone of the news. "Sarah and her old lady are all but saying it's my fault. Can't take anymore of that shit right now."

"So we're not going to the hospital now?"

"No, we not going to the hospital now. Can't see him yet anyway." His expression was intense in a way I'd never seen and couldn't quite read. He hot-rodded down busy Florida Boulevard and out of town, jutting between traffic, blasting through lights just turned red, fishtailing around curves once we hit the small town of Denham Springs. I tensed in the seat, gripping my thigh and the door handle. Hendrix blasted so loud it made it impossible to talk. Dyer's love for Hendrix and Tower of Power was another irony I'd brought up to him, but he laughed it off with, "All black people ain't niggers," a statement I heard a lot but never saw play out as an actual distinction by the people who said it.

He rocketed onto a back road that took us into the country, where the road was still as winding as the original cow paths that had been paved over. The speedometer read around eighty-five. I was white-knuckling, yet part of me was also giving in, letting myself be taken by the speed and music and danger—both because it was time to stop being scared and because I couldn't do anything else. "Look!" he said, and motioned ahead with his chin. Across a pasture on my side, a freight train sped toward the intersection where we were headed. Dyer pressed the gas to the floor, shoving me back into the seat. There was no gate in front of the track and there was no way we could make it. I locked onto the train's engine barreling at us. I was certain Dyer meant for us to die, but an unexpected calm set in, as if my life had been spiraling inexorably toward this moment.

"Hundred ten!" Dyer screamed. The train's horn blasted above the demented licks from the 8-track. The engine's face loomed impossibly close. We dipped before the hump of the tracks, scraped and lifted, sailed. The crash back onto the road threw me forward into the dash. We swerved. Then Dyer braked and straightened us. He flicked the music down and slowed to the first reasonable speed all day.

"Goddamnit, Dyer."

"Balls, motherfucker." He grabbed his and laughed his high-pitched hee-hee.

My insides churned hot awake, obliterating the placid feeling I'd had moments before. Dyer banged his palm on the steering wheel, his expression now serious. I turned my head and watched the calm green of pine trees and swampy vines as we passed. Somehow, he had willed the train to appear and willed it to miss us. Somehow, he was scripting the world. I believed this. How else could he brutalize so many people and barely get a scratch? Cheat on his woman, get caught, and get by? Then I thought of Skeeter. Dyer hadn't scripted that. I glanced at him again. He was watching me. "You can't live scared, man," he said. "You live scared and you die scared." He stared at me, the road going where he wanted it to. I knew he could see through my thin chest to my yellow heart, bullied time and again, even by him, without my standing up. I almost told him to fuck off, then what I saw made me go cold. Part of him had gone insane and that made him even more powerful in a world that had gone insane. I thought how I would be insane, too, if my brothers or my parents or Dyer himself had been stabbed and might die. If I'd lost my house and my neighborhood.

Dyer reached under the seat and brought out the holstered .44. He tossed it onto my lap. As a kid I had shot our .22 rifle out by the river and in the gullies and dump near our relatives' farms in Mississippi, but the weight of this pistol always implied a different purpose. I froze for a second. He pointed close to my face. "If we find those cocksuckers, are you in?"

My skin heated as if a sheet of flame passed over it. I tossed the pistol into the space between us. "I'm in."

He braked hard, veered us over a shallow ditch and onto the side of the road among short palmettos. He picked up the pistol, unholstered it, popped the cylinder and dropped the bullets into his lap.

He pinched up one bullet, slipped it into a chamber, spun the cylinder and slapped it shut, his hand covering the gun so I couldn't see where the bullet had landed. He cocked the pistol and left it pointed at the roof. "What about it?" he asked.

"I told you that's not funny."

"I ain't being funny. I'll go first."

"Quit fucking around and let's go see Skeeter." His sideways punch to my shoulder knocked me against the door and smacked my head against the window. My left arm went dead. "You fucking asshole!" I said. "Don't ever hit me again."

He uncocked the hammer, picked up the bullets, put them back in their chambers, then holstered the pistol.

"I'm serious, Kurt," I said. "Don't ever fucking hit me again."

He looked at me. "Hey, when you get hit, you do something about it." He slid the pistol under the seat.

That night, Robert stuck his head in my door as I reclined on the bed. The novel lay open on my chest. "You can't come out and say hey?" he said, dressed in jeans, T-shirt, and cop boots. I had heard him come in and talk to Momma ten minutes before.

"I got a lot on my mind," I said.

"Uh-huh. Join the club." He came in and sat at my desk. "How's your friend?" I thought about telling him the lie I'd told my parents, then I got up, shut the door and sat on the edge of my bed. "It wasn't a car wreck. Some black guy stuck him with a knife outside his house."

"No shit?"

"No shit. Dyer was there. Stuck his finger in the wound to get him to the hospital."

"Pretty smart." He stared at me. I looked down, realizing I'd been scowling at the thought that what Dyer had done as a medic had again made him more like Robert than I was. "Why didn't you call me?" he asked.

"What for?"

"To let me know."

"It just happened."

"Two nights ago. You can't use the phone?"

"I figured you'd heard."

"I heard some white kid got stabbed, but I didn't know it was Dyer's buddy." He breathed more heavily through his nose, a sour expression on his face. "So what's Dyer gonna do?"

"Get back at 'em if we can find 'em."

"We?"

"Skeeter's my friend, too."

"That don't mean you got to do something stupid."

"Why's it stupid? You wouldn't do anything? Every time somebody looks at one of y'all wrong, the whole force jumps on 'em."

He wiped at the corners of his mouth. "This ain't like that. We're cops. Just 'cause Dyer's doing something don't mean you got to do it."

"I know that."

"You're not acting like it."

"You don't even know what we're gonna do."

"If it's Dyer, I know somebody's getting hurt."

"I'm doing what I think, not just what Dyer thinks."

We sat quietly for a while, each of us tapping a foot madly until we noticed it. We both chuckled. "This kid gonna come out of it?" he asked.

I shrugged. "He's still in ICU."

"You ain't telling the old man 'cause you afraid he won't let you go out?" I nodded. "Huh. Maybe I oughta tell him and Momma what really happened."

"Bullshit."

"I'm serious. I don't want you fucking up."

"Like you don't fuck up."

He looked around the room and stroked his jaws. He exhaled hard through his nose. "Shit, you and Alan got this room all to yourselves. I got fucked out of it except for about ten minutes. Fight a war and you don't even get your own room."

"You got your own room now," I said.

"That's for sure. Been fucking like a rabbit."

"Y'all only been split a little while."

"Hey, what you gonna do? Goddamn uniform's a pussy magnet."

I'd been relieved when he and Deborah split, but he and I had never really talked about it, except for him to say how rough it had been before she left and for me to say it was best they were apart. He always asked how I was. I inhaled. "What's it like at your new place?"

He scratched his head. "It's a lot less crazy. I miss my kid. Ain't the same not seeing him every day." Robert stared at the wall. I had seen the gloom thickening over him more every day as the North Vietnamese moved south. He'd mentioned the advance when DaNang and Chu Lai fell, his voice tinged with sadness and not as much anger as I expected, but we hadn't spoken about it otherwise.

"How you doing with this 'Nam shit?"

He bit at his fingernail without looking at me and shook his head.

"You know, I never got to go to Saigon. This dude in our outfit evidently did something bad down there, maybe even with a general's wife, and they wouldn't let anybody else in our unit go. Wouldn't even tell us what he did." He chewed the inside of his cheek for a second. "He was a fucked-up dude. Drove an ambulance that carried nothing but bodies and amputated limbs over to Graves Registration and he had to bag all of them. He smoked so much dope it just came out his driver's window like a train and nobody messed with him about it. Me and Larry tried to take care of him when we could. We'd go take over from him and send him to his hooch 'cause he was so wasted. One New Year's, we sent him off and we took these two bodies he'd already bagged, and an arm, and when we got to Graves they opened up the bags to get the rings and stuff off 'em, and one of the guys had Uncle Sam eyes."

"Had what?'"

"You know, like on the poster how his eyes follow you everywhere you go? He'd got shot in the forehead and his eyes followed you all over the room. The bag was filled with blood and I told those guys to hurry it the fuck up and sign the transfer papers. Larry asked me if I was all right, and I just said I wanted to get the hell out of there. They handed us the transfer papers and they had blood all over them too." He rapped his knuckles on his chin and kept rapping. "All that fucking blood."

We sat quietly again until Robert picked up an 8-track from my desk, glanced at it and tossed it back onto a pile of papers and books. He pointed at me. "You call me before you do anything, all right?"

"I'll try."

"You call. I mean it, asshole."

I slouched alone on the back pew the next morning, the first time I hadn't skipped church in months. I didn't hear a word the preacher said, because I was trying to work up a prayer both for Skeeter and guidance for myself. I hoped that Jesus would touch me and give me the solace I'd had so many years ago. But then I wondered when? When I was eight and thought I'd saved myself from hell by joining the church? Before the first vote to keep blacks out? Before Jesus's message of tolerance and peace slammed head on into the war of Revelation? Bile saturated me. Why was I here? I didn't believe Christ would touch me. What I still wanted was the church's conviction for a territorial war, wanted to embrace the simplicity of a clear enemy and the justification and finality of a last battle, but without the church. If I took revenge, I was determined not to do it wearing the cloak of Christianity. I stood and walked out in the middle of the service.

At home, I almost called Dyer, but instead called the hospital and asked for Skeeter. Amazingly, I reached him in a regular room and he told me to come see him. For a minute, I hesitated, wondering how bad he would be, then I grabbed the car keys. I started off going straight there, but at the turn I kept going. I took a circuitous route through an upscale neighborhood where live oaks reached across the road and bent their limbs to the yards. I drove on, reached LSU and winded slowly through campus, its Spanish architecture and exotic Indian mounds a peaceful world far away from mine. I had always assumed that I would go here, but I still only knew it through sports, Alan, and Arnault, and that was hardly at all. I pulled over next to the parade ground and left the engine running. The bark of the crape myrtles that circled the field looked like the hide of skinned animals. Here and there students strolled. I thought how they were older than I was but probably still far from making the kind of decision I was speeding toward. Thought how they would probably never have to make such a decision at all. For a minute, I hated them. Then I put them out of my mind, and dread took their place. What would I say to Skeeter? A knife had entered him, made him breathe his own blood, forced Dyer to plunge his finger inside him. I knew that seeing him would force me to decide. I backed up and headed the way I had come.

He was alone, hooked up to an IV, drainage tubes and machines, his face pale and tired. He grinned nonetheless. "How you doing?" I asked.

"I been better. Worse, too, I heard."

"I thought you were faking it just to get the good food."

"You got it right."

"They give you the liver and onions and tell you it was steak?"

"Ain't even gave me liver." His breath was labored. I sat on the edge of the plastic chair.

"Where's everybody?" I asked.

"Home. I'm glad. They was in here cooing and bugging me till a coupla hours ago."

"You're looking pretty good."

"You think? I ain't even looked in the mirror."

I asked how his mother and sister were holding up and he asked me how Dyer was doing. "He's all right," I said, although I couldn't quite describe how he was. "Acting like Dyer."

"He looked like he was fixing to shrivel when I seen him yesterday."

"You saw him yesterday?"

"Last night. Never seen him like that. Guess he's guilty 'cause he thinks he got me into it. Sarah said he saved my life. Said he plugged me up and started yelling to get me back when he thought my heart quit."

"You remember that?"

"Nah. All I remember's walking back to the house and all of a sudden I couldn't breathe. Woke up in here the next day and everybody's looking like I come out of the dead."

"Guess you kinda did. Maybe they didn't want you over there."

He laughed and started coughing hard. Finally, he caught his breath, his face whiter, and wheezed with his eyes closed. My whole body braced, wanting to help him like I did Momma when she was here, feeling the same helplessness. Finally, he pulled himself up in the bed with a grimace. Adrenalin filtered through me like sewage. I sat back.

"It don't even seem real," he said. "One minute me and Dyer are hanging out on the porch, the next minute I'm falling down and waking up in the hospital."

"You remember if it hurt?"

He shrugged. "Hurts now and they got me drugged up. I didn't feel nothing that night except like getting slapped. I couldn't figure out why he kept coming in to grab me when I was punching him." He breathed deeply and adjusted the IV tape on his forearm. "He'd get up close and I was slugging the shit out of his ribs and all he'd do was slap me in the back."

"Piece of shit."

Skeeter snorted. "Yeah. I guess if two big bastards jumped on me and I was one of them little niggers, I might've stabbed somebody too." He laid his head back on the pillow. "I could hear Dyer beating the fuck out of the other two and I was a lot bigger than the one I was fighting."

"They came by saying shit, they deserved it."

"They didn't say nothing. They was walking by and gave us that fuck-you look gives Dyer the reds. You know how he is. Nigger looks at him wrong, that's it. Dyer said something like, 'What you looking at, nigger,' and they said something and we went after 'em."

"They were still in your neighborhood. You ever seen 'em before?" I asked.

"I don't think so. They's so many of 'em in there now, and they go back and forth to where they stay." Something caught in his throat and he worked hard to clear it. He held his side and blew out. "Now *that* hurt." He took a cup from the bed stand and sucked water through a straw.

It was strange to be here with this kid I barely knew but to whom I now felt connected. I had come to see him because we'd hung out through Dyer, gone after those kids on the street, and because I was sorry for what had happened. But I was looking for something, too. Most likely for the decision to be made, but something else I couldn't pin down.

"What's it like," I asked, "having 'em all up in your neighbor-hood?"

"Niggers? It sucks." He stared at the ceiling. "I don't know what Momma's gonna do. Sarah'll probably marry Kurt and I finish school next year. We ain't gonna get shit for that house."

We just sat there. I knew that soon houses would be for sale up and down our street. None of our neighbors said they were leading the way, but everybody was gearing up to go. If I'd known more, I suppose I could have heard inevitability, recognized the economic fallout of centuries of racism and white fear, seen the poverty of ex-clusion and rage. Instead, I felt disgust at the surrender around me. Skeeter and his family were casualties because whites hadn't stood together. Illogical, of course, but what logic was left? I had been im-mersed in irrationality and hatred for so long that reason had been shattered.

Skeeter gave a long exhale and looked at me. "You know, you the first I told about it all."

Between classes on Monday morning, Stem strode up to my locker. "Why the hell ain't nobody told me about Skeeter? I had to hear it from Landry when I was walking by."

"I thought it was up to Dyer to tell you."

"I saw Dyer this morning and he didn't say shit. What's wrong with all y'all?"

"There's a lot going on. I'll let you know when I find stuff out."

"Dyer gonna do anything?"

"I don't know." Stem shook his head and cursed under his breath as he paced away.

At lunch, Dyer said he'd call me later, but didn't sit at my table. From a distance I saw a few of the other badasses talking to him, but Dyer didn't seem to be saying anything, none of his usual pre-fight excitement. I knew none of the badasses would come to me to find out more, and I was glad for that, even though it made me think how few people actually knew that Dyer and I ran with each other, made me resent the dual life that made me one person with Dyer and another person without him, the dual life I'd tried to escape and had fallen back into. I dropped the silverware onto my plate, strode to the clean-up station and tossed my lunch in the trash.

Darkness had just set in when Dyer knocked on the door, came into the living room, told my parents about Skeeter's recovery after the car wreck (I'd told him my lie), and convinced them to let me go to the hospital. His bullshit and charm rubbed me wrong, even though I used the same things myself to get what I wanted. What irked me most was Daddy laughing, smiling, and nodding at Dyer, whereas with me it seemed he searched for the negative. "Hold on," he said after Dyer had passed through the door ahead of me. "I ought not let you go the way you been acting. Don't you be late." I thought of mouthing off, then simply nodded and went to Dyer's car. Neither of us spoke. I hadn't been in his car since he slugged me, and I was certain if he hit me again I would try to fight him, no matter how useless that would be. I had never known before that I would fight him, and yet it didn't seem to even matter now.

"You didn't say you went to see Skeeter," he said after we'd gone a block.

"I've hardly talked to you."

"You couldn't call me before you went?"

"I just wanted to see him, man. He said you saw him after that stunt with the train. Why didn't you take me up there then?"

"'Cause your little feelings were all hurt."

"Right."

We didn't say anything again until we neared Skeeter's street, our inevitable destination.

The night hung pre-summer thick as we eased past his house. Dyer cut his lights. We crawled three houses down and stopped next to a plain white house raised off the ground with brick supports.

"I been thinking," Dyer said. "I think I saw 'em run in there."

"The dudes you fought?"

"Yeah, the dudes I fought. They went in there."

The house was nondescript, small and seemingly freshly painted, its windows curtained and backlit. "You just remembered that?"

"I've had some shit on my mind, Parrish."

We glared at each other until I turned my head and looked at the house again. "We gonna wait for 'em?"

"We're gonna burn 'em. It's easy. You fill a milk jug with gasoline, cut a little hole in top, and put a cigarette fuse in it. I did it for kicks in a field a couple times when I was a kid. You just shove it under the house, get the hell away, and up it goes." His voice was as casual as if we were discussing whether to order pizza with pepperoni or Canadian bacon. I had no doubt that he was serious, and yet I was in so deep that I didn't question the insanity of it.

"You don't wanta make sure it's them?"

"Hey, go knock on the door if you wanta check. They went in there and I'm paying 'em back. Even if they didn't, you think the ones in there don't know who did it? You decide if you're in." He pressed the accelerator, taking us farther into the black neighborhood.

"I guess we're not going to see Skeeter."

"Reach in the glove box." I thought maybe he'd put a bag of weed in there, but inside lay a six-pointed metal star, six inches in diameter, its slender spires like shark's teeth. "Grab that out." I picked it up. "Finished it in shop today. Ninja star. The points are like fucking razors. You wanta take a shot at somebody?"

"You see the dudes who stabbed Skeeter and I will."

"I'll bet. Give it to me."

I handed it over. We cruised slowly along. On my side was a small school, its playground dark, the whole street too dark. Ahead on the sidewalk, a black man strolled. Dyer stopped the car a few feet behind him and gave me a look like the star might be for me. The man glanced back. Then Dyer swung open his door and stepped out. "Run, nigger!" he said. The man sprinted, ten yards, fifteen yards, me not saying anything, not calling out to Dyer to stop. Dyer stepped forward like a javelin thrower and hurled the star. It zipped through the air, glinting in the dim streetlight as it spun. My body nearly imploded. The star sailed close past the base of the man's skull. He cut around a corner and disappeared. Dyer got back into the car and shut the door. "I almost nailed that bastard."

My eyes stayed straight ahead as we moved. I barely felt anything. What did it matter who was in that house? Wasn't Dyer right that somebody in there was the enemy? This was the battle line. Someday the line would be my street and I might be there without Dyer.

I lay in bed flattened by something heavier than exhaustion. The image of Dyer's star whizzing past the man's head sickened me, and yet my brain rested with something like resolve. I was letting myself settle into a motive that seemed less self-involved, that seemed not so much about proving I was strong and unafraid as to protect my parents and the slippery idea of what my neighborhood and school represented. I was cleaving from Dyer, but my direction was no less base, no less controlled by lack of reason and by the terror and shame bled into me by the racist bravado around me and the humiliation inside me. Not that I saw these things. All I saw was that if I went along with Dyer, it would be with a determined, idealistic courage he'd never had. I no longer believed Dyer had a larger cause. He didn't even want revenge on the ones who stabbed Skeeter, didn't want to send a message. He just couldn't stand the guilt. Lying there, I harkened back fully to the justifications provided by the book of Revelation and the votes in church in order to dull any ethical pangs. There *were* invaders. There *was* a war. Skeeter was proof. I closed my eyes. I was tired. I didn't consider, and wouldn't have yet understood, that the path I was choosing was emotionally and intellectually easy, even lazy. When I awoke the next morning, my certainty had vanished like a dream.

At school, everything happened behind a screen, voices muted, people blurry. Mike tried to talk to me about Skeeter and what had happened, fishing, I suppose, to see if I was going to do something with Dyer. He may as well have been talking from a hundred yards away. Virgil asked me how Skeeter was, and I said fine, then told him I had a virus and had to get to the bathroom. During lunch, I went to the library to avoid Stem and Dyer. In class, I acted like my head was killing me so I wouldn't have to participate, although I didn't really have to act.

After the final bell, I drove to Skeeter's street and slowed in front of the house Dyer wanted to burn. I imagined what we would do: park a block away; skulk over with the bomb; slide it under the raised floor; light the fuse and scurry off. We wouldn't be there to see it, but

I imagined a ball of fiery gas blasting through the house's floor, fire curling from the underside of the house, flames scrambling up the walls, smoke becoming a living thing. Whoever was inside scorched and incinerated. I pressed my palms against my forehead. I wished someone would come out so I could see them and know who was there, maybe even fight them, whoever they were. Then I drove to Scenic Highway, past the fires of the plants and refineries, as if they might speak to me.

Dyer wasn't at school the next day, but he called me at home in the afternoon. "I'll get you about eight," he said.

"Let's take my car," I said. "Nobody'll recognize it."

He paused. "Whatever."

"You doing it tonight?"

"Just come pick me up."

After supper, Robert called and I told him that Dyer had cooled out because Skeeter had gone home, the second part true. "That's real good," he said. "Let's get together this weekend."

For a while, I tried to write Shirley's paper, laughed when the co-incidence of the title *The Grapes of Wrath* finally hit me, then gave up on concentrating. I studied the things in my room, normal things, my records and tapes, my LSU pennant, the old plastic tiger head on the wall, my trophies and books. I replayed the kisses and gropes I'd had with a neighborhood girl just a few weeks ago, replayed football with Robert and the pee-wee teams I'd been on, almost tasted the cream puffs and eclairs Momma used to leave for my elementary school friends and me when she knew she'd be at work. I was a person who coached basketball for little kids, who was clownish and smart-ass, who made good grades, who insecurely talked too much, whose parents loved him through their pain and flaws. The realization that all that could be obliterated landed solidly, and yet I still wondered who would defend my parents if not me.

Not long before eight, I went into Momma's room. She was lying down reading. Daddy had started the 3–11 shift and wouldn't be home until midnight.

"I need to go get a book from Mary Bickell's house," I said. She took off the pink-framed reading glasses she'd recently bought.

"Why so late?"

"I forgot mine at school and I got a test."

She watched me carefully as though my thoughts were visible through my skull. She slipped her glasses back on. "Don't be long."

"Yes, ma'am." I wanted to go over and kiss her, but I pushed the impulse away. Kissing her might soften the hardness I'd worked so hard to achieve.

I headed away from Dyer's out of the driveway and went around the block before I pulled up to his house. I remembered the time not long after I met him when I'd done the opposite to avoid his seeing Virgil in my car. I knew Dyer wouldn't cow me like that again, but I didn't know if I would let Virgil in my car. The lines I had to draw weren't yet clear.

Before I could honk the horn, Dyer came out empty-handed, no bag or jug, and I breathed out as he lowered into the passenger's seat.

"You decided not to burn it?" I asked.

"I ain't burning it tonight. You think I'd carry something out the house anyway?" He shook his head. "We got to let some time pass and plan it right. You ain't slipped to Stem or nobody, have you?"

"What the hell you think?" I touched a sudden sharpness in my forehead. "So what're we doing?"

"Going back over there and see if we see them fuckers."

"We're not gonna see 'em."

"Just go. I wanta check out the house." I drove down Winbourne toward Skeeter's neighborhood. I glanced at Dyer and tightened my hands on the wheel. Resentment rose in me like a heated cloud.

"Why didn't you say you started the fight?" I asked.

"What?"

"Skeeter told me you started it."

"You bringing that up now? So what?" Kurt said.

"You lied, that's what."

"Jesus Christ. What are you, my fucking girlfriend? They're walking all through there like it's theirs."

"So why didn't you just say that? I'm supposed to be trusting you."

"Look, pussy, you wanta turn around, then turn around."

We crossed Plank Road and turned onto Skeeter's street, the

lights in their house finally on. I thought of Skeeter laid up in there, thought of him, Sarah, and their mother never being able to step outside again without the thought of a waiting knife. I clenched my teeth and kept the car slow as Dyer gazed ahead at the white house. Parallel to it, I stopped and shut off the lights. The house was simple and smaller than my house. The shifting light of a television played through a curtain. I imagined a family inside, a black mother and father watching with a little boy and little girl, their living room walls bare, their only furniture a worn couch and an easy chair, and then I squeezed my eyes shut. What did I know who was in there? It could be criminals, a bunch of L. B.'s people ready to kill us in the right situation, or a black woman like people around me bitched about, a welfare woman without a husband, having baby after baby with different men, slapping and yelling at her kids in public. I stopped. Opened my eyes. I stared at the back of Dyer's head as he watched the house. He knew just as I did that the ones who stabbed Skeeter hadn't run into that house. Or did he? Maybe he'd convinced himself they had, just as I'd tried to convince myself it didn't matter who had gone in. And in spite of all my knotted thoughts and rationalization, I let myself know the obvious: this was not a war and I was not a soldier. Killing these people would be murder.

He turned and met my gaze. Snorted. "I shoulda figured," he said. "What?"

"You'd find some reason to back out."

"You know you didn't see anybody go in that house."

"Yep, backing out."

"It doesn't matter if they know who did it, *they* didn't do it."

He held up the index finger on his right hand. "I had this *inside* him. I felt his heart stop." He looked away. "How many times is it you pussied out? You gonna pussy out when those fuckers come down our street with a knife?"

"No."

"Uh-huh. Just cruise."

I smoldered as I pressed the accelerator. We went past the place where Dyer had leaped out and thrown the star at the man. I again imagined the points burying themselves in the base of his skull, him crumpling forward, all as I silently watched. Dyer was right about my being a coward, but not for the reasons he'd said.

"I'm not doing it," I said.

"Thanks for clearing that up." I looked at him, expecting a look that said he might slap me, not even dignify me with a punch, but that wasn't what he gave me. I couldn't be sure, but he looked relieved. Disgust coursed through me. He lit a cigarette and blew smoke out his window. "Drop me at the house."

I drove without saying anything more. I felt rejected, but not as much as I would have only a few months before: before I lifted the chain to hit the boy; before Dyer had sent a kid sailing into a bleacher; before I saw that he simply wanted me to help him commit murder. And yet I also felt loss. Yes, he had almost led a friend to his death, had led me to the brink of the unforgivable, had bullied me, but he had also roused me to challenge him and his power, to challenge at least a portion of my fear. In a way, I loved him like a brother, a love with the tug of unreasoned loyalty. I understood his pain. I gained confidence from his needing me. But I was done with him. He had no conviction or code.

At his house, he stepped out, slammed the door and leaned in the window again. "Maybe you'll grow some balls by next time." He slapped the roof of the car, turned and went inside.

I pushed the clutch, shifted, let my foot up, and slowly accelerated down our short road. I drove past the small houses yellowed by streetlight—the Salarios', the Ramirezes', the Simms', the Lawsons', the Slatons', the Goudeaus', and our own. I turned onto Mission Drive, and for some reason, the kind of clarity I craved came to me, although only about Dyer. It wasn't the fuller clarity I would later have, that violence was his way to keep from feeling anything beyond anger, just as it was becoming my way. Not the clarity that there was a growing element of the sociopath in him. The clarity was that Dyer was just as scared as I was of being seen as weak, of being alone, of being unmoored in a world of ambiguity and change. And the fact that he was scared of the same things I was made him unbearable.

I kept driving and a sense of purpose rose in me. It was up to me to protect my parents and preserve the values of my neighborhood. Those values were abstract—community, hard work, justice, fairness, tradition, standing up for what you had earned—and yet they carried a profound feeling. I didn't yet realize how shot through with irony my own behavior had made them; all I knew was I had to fight for this place, even if everyone else surrendered, even if it was a lost cause, even if it meant giving up college and dreams beyond where I was. Who would I be without this place and its meaning? Who would I be if I gave in? It was here I had worked so hard to redeem myself from cowardice and unmanliness, to break free from the sway of Jarreau and Dyer, to forge a self and a mission. I'd formed an unsure identity around the idea, no matter how damaged and warped and absurd, that I needed to "keep" our home, and I was going to act according to that concept.

I had no idea that I was still just scared. Of losing what little self I'd gained. Of the unknown of leaving what was familiar. Of new variables perhaps more dangerous and challenging than anything on those streets.

Book Three: Into the Breach

Fall 1975: Flailing

I had dressed for school with a dramatic sense of purpose, going for practicality but also for a sort of uniform—blue jeans, blue-jean shirt, and blue Bob Wolf sneakers for traction on the concrete. That week, some black guys had put two bullets in the quarter panel of Dan Riche's car and forced him to swerve down a side street to escape. Worse, the next night several guys broke into his house, supposedly thinking he was home, and beat his grandmother so badly she'd been taken to the hospital. A group of us had decided we were going to do something about it. Dyer had graduated. It was up to me to help hold the line against uncivilized attackers.

Now, those of us planning to fight stood beneath the porte cochere on the vague border between blacks and whites. Students were packed into the area created by the main building on one side, the cafeteria on the second, and the tall chain-link fence that opened to the parking lot on the third. On the fourth side, the courtyard spread wide. Black kids congregated near the main door, many of them talking and laughing loudly above the crowd's murmur. At the fringe of them, closer to us, stood the black guys we suspected of having gone to Riche's house, along with their posse, probably twenty or so young men. A couple of the black guys had their rake combs ready, and I had seen what those could do when sharpened. Some people had picked up on the tension and moved away, but most of the students appeared oblivious that a fight was looming.

Stem was my only close friend in the group, but I was puffed up to be in the company of everybody planning to fight. I didn't delude myself anymore that I was a type of soldier but that didn't mean there weren't still battles to fight. During the summer, a black family had moved in next door to the Dyers. When I ran into Dyer, he acted nonchalant, said he and his family would be out of there soon and that the kid who'd moved in wasn't so bad. I agreed with that. I knew the kid, also named Tim. He was a promising running back a year behind me at school and the only black kid I knew who liked heavy metal. I didn't believe anything should be done to him or his family. I'd welcomed him to the neighborhood, even brought him into my house to get stoned and listen to Led Zeppelin while my parents were at work (surely, at least partly to make myself feel superior and defiant to Daddy and Dyer in a token way). But, of course, in my ambiguous world, the fact that Tim and his family appeared to be good people wasn't the point. When Dyer acted like blacks moving onto our street was nothing, I despised him. Worse still, all Daddy did was grouse. The fire had finally reached us, and he gave none of the anticipated rants, no call to arms, no summoning of the apocalypse. I knew that any of those things would have pissed me off as well, would have fueled my ongoing disdain of Christians' hypocrisy, but they would have also confirmed a clear means to gain his approval by joining him in resisting the blacks' encroachment. Disappointingly, on the day Daddy met Tim's father on the street, he came home and said, "I met the man and he's all right. Held his hat in his hands and said, 'Yes, sir,' like they used to." I was disgusted both at his racist condescension and at his acceptance, but more so by the latter. Where was the indignation that had fueled him and Dyer and had warped me? My parents had begun looking at property outside town for when I graduated, and Dyer was working offshore and getting ready to move before his parents sold. Everyone was running. At least I had some conviction, I told myself.

The rancid odor of sugar from spilled Coke slushies sickened the humid air. I scanned the black guys, trying to decide if there was someone in particular I should go after, wondered if I should take off my glasses, as I had with Lassiter, then left them on. "There he is," Stem said, and I turned toward Riche, who strode across the courtyard, his wide belt wrapped around his fist, buckle dangling, several guys keeping pace with him. Riche pointed toward the blacks and started shouting. I turned toward the covered area again. I remembered the kid who had lain right here the day of the big riot, remembered the broken glass glittering on this concrete, remembered the police pouring in and whipping kids with sticks. My body remembered my hesitation.

Book Three: Into the Breach

Riche waded in, and punches, scuffling, and screaming erupted. I charged. For a moment, there seemed to be a skirmish line in my peripheral vision. Then I was throwing punches at three guys at once, none of us landing anything of much consequence. I was distantly aware of the stampede toward the main entrance and out the fence gate as my body moved full throttle and my mind remained calm. The black guys weren't coming at me full-on, and I danced, feinted and punched, still squared off against all three. We shuffled to the side of the main fight, and I glanced and realized there were only black kids around me. My calmness evaporated. The only one of the three I knew, C. J., a wide-shouldered, large-headed kid with a criminal reputation, fell away. I swung and jabbed at the other two, one a rangy kid at least a year behind me, the other a chubby guy, neither of whom seemed interested in fighting. The rest of the fighters swirled further away from us.

Lightning. I staggered backward, my mind threatening to go out, and bumped off the brick refreshment stand. I stiffened my knees, put my hands up, expecting a rush of punches, but C. J. stood several yards away, smiling, the other two gone. Static cluttered my brain, though I could still hear the fighting. I tasted blood, shook my head, and went toward C. J. A hand gripped the back of my collar and lifted me off the ground. I slammed against the brick of the Coke stand. "Get back!" Principal Tank screamed in my face, then went toward the other fighters, scattering all but a few of them. A ringing sounded and it took me a second to sort it from the ringing in my head. People streamed into the building, some of them staring in my direction. An ice pick pain traveled between my temples. I cupped my nose and came back with a handful of blood. I set out through the fence gate.

My consciousness sizzled on the edge of going out as I moved through the bright sunlight and squinted to see my car. I pinched my nostrils against the blood and spotted the Fairlane Robert had sold me for fifty dollars. When I reached it, I fumbled to get my keys, managed to find the hole, opened the door, and dropped behind the steering wheel. I found a dirty towel in the backseat, wiped the blood away, then leaned my head back and pressed the towel to my nose, little hammers banging behind my forehead and eyes.

I almost went out and sat up again. Would there be someone coming in a minute to tell me what to do? I realized how ridiculous that thought was from the aftermath of my fight with Lassiter. I sat there, the morning quiet except for the oceany sound of traffic. I blinked again and again against the glaring sun.

When I thought the bleeding might have stopped, I looked in my rearview mirror. My nose angled sharply to the side and my eyes were already blackening. Inexplicably, my glasses hadn't been touched. I lowered my head to examine my blood-spattered shirt then threw my head back again when the pressure fired pain through my sinuses and cheekbones. I toweled off the best I could and stepped out of the car. I leaned against the door until the whiteness cleared and my legs steadied. Then I moved across the parking lot.

The halls were empty, so I trudged toward class. My watery vision distorted everything. I entered class and Mrs. Jackson—my skinny, homely math teacher—gave me a horrified look, but said nothing. My balance wavered a second, then I aimed down the aisle and found my seat in the last row. Cherie and Lindsay, two girls on whom I had crushes, stared at me. Cherie asked if I was all right, her voice coming through cotton. "I'm okay," I said. I laid my head on my desk and fought the nausea.

By second period, the pain had steadied to an insistent beat. No one talked about the fight. I had expected there to be some immediate difference, some recognition of my noble cause, some change inside me, but all I sensed was revulsion and puzzlement from the kids in the advanced classes and shock from my teachers. Between second and third periods, somebody told me that Ms. Arnault heard I was hurt and wanted me to come by and see her. I hoped she would show some admiration after she'd seemed to show disappointment that I hadn't been in the riot the previous spring, but I doubted she would. I'd been elected president of the Scholars' Club, of which she was advisor, and I had been spending more time hearing about her politics and impromptu history lessons/rants on Manifest Destiny, the corruption of the Constitution, false patriotism, and the principal's anti-intellectualism. I agreed with nearly everything she said, but I kept my thoughts about race and protecting the neighborhood hidden. Now one punch had erased the illusion of public separation between my two minds.

When I walked up between classes, she covered her mouth, took my elbow, and led me away from her door to a slightly more private spot at the end of the hall. "Are you all right?" she asked. I laughed. "I've been better." She lightly touched my nose, furrowed her brow, and exhaled, then examined the spots of dried blood on my shirt. "You need to go home."

"I'm staying," I said. She gave me a pained expression that seemed lost. She hugged me. The first inkling of shame hovered near, but I brushed it away.

As I walked to my next class, I spotted Virgil coming toward me. I wished I could avoid him, but he waved and stopped me. "Damn, son, that's broke," he said.

"No shit."

"I heard you got slugged."

"Got fucking cheap-shotted."

"C. J. did it?"

"How'd you hear?"

"He bragging and laughing all over. What you doing up in there anyway?"

"You heard what they did to Riche's grandmother."

"I heard."

"Then why you asking?"

"That was Riche's grandmother, not yours. You know they were after Riche 'cause he's always starting shit."

The pain intensified between my eyes, and I shut them and pressed there. "Man." When I looked at him again, he was frowning and shaking his head. "I gotta get to class," I said.

"I'll catch up with you," he said.

Shirley's class was late in the day, and I was wearing thin as my dread of seeing him grew. In the month of school we'd had, he'd already turned me on to literature outside of class—to Robert Penn Warren's *All the King's Men*, which I saw was a story about a man coming under the sway of a more powerful, corrupt man, and to *Slaughterhouse-Five*, which was banned by our school board. He suggested them without pointed comment or leading commentary, but I could see in Warren he probably knew something about my relationship to Dyer, see in Vonnegut that he supposed I needed a dose of subversiveness toward machismo and violence. Nonetheless, as I approached him in his doorway, resentment welled in me. I remembered him calling last year's fighters ignorant thugs. What did he know? These weren't his fights. This wasn't his neighborhood. How could he know me? And yet I knew that he did.

"You going to make it?" he asked as I came up. I slowed and nodded. I supposed he knew that I had chosen to be in the fight, and I was grateful he didn't say anything more. I was also grateful that Mike Coats was absent. Sherry, my brilliant next-door neighbor, asked if I was all right. I simply nodded. During class, I forced myself to concentrate, even though all I wanted was to fall into foggy sleep. When the bell rang, I rushed out before anyone could say anything more.

My spirits lifted as I drove home, relief that I'd finally acted, and maybe some late endorphins kicking in. I put on a tough face and imagined how Daddy would at last admire that I'd fought the fight I believed he wanted me to fight. At home in the mirror I saw my black eyes, crooked nose, and blood-splashed shirt full-on and smiled, even though I better understood some of the disturbed looks I'd gotten. I took three aspirin, lay on the couch, and iced the bridge until Momma arrived from work. When I sat up, her mouth fell open. "You should see the other guy," I said. "Not a scratch on him." She dropped her purse in a chair, came close and touched my face with both hands.

"What did you do?"

"I turned the other cheek when I shouldn't have."

She pressed her lips tightly together and dropped her hands. Her expression settled somewhere between concern and irritation. "We're going to the doctor. I hope we can get in." For once I didn't argue.

As she drove, I told her about the attack on Riche's grandmother and the fight, her arms straight out as she held the wheel. "You shouldn't be fighting," she said. "Especially in something like this where you can't tell what might happen."

"They beat up his grandma."

"That's terrible, but this is dangerous, Tim. You need to let the police take care of things like this."

"Like they did with Jarreau? Daddy'll know why I did it."

"I wouldn't bet on that."

"You wait and see."

We waited for two hours, sleep threatening to drag me down. The doctor was a man I didn't know, younger and with a black pencil mustache. His expression was serious, business-like, and maybe impatient with my late emergency as he pulled the stool up in front of me. "What happened here?" he asked.

"I zigged when I should've zagged."

He sat back. "What?"

"I was in a fight."

"A fight?" he said, his voice disgusted, whether for my barbaric behavior or my lack of care for the organ he had devoted his life to, I didn't know.

"I got punched from the side."

He touched my nose, jolting me in the chair. "Hold still," he said. He braced the bridge with his thumbs and jerked my nose back into place. Fire shot through my forehead and tears flooded my eyes. When I cleared enough to see him again, I could see that his disgust was for my whole person. "Ice it and take aspirin. You're done," he said, and walked out. I lowered my head and tried not to vomit.

Daddy worked three till eleven, didn't get home until I was asleep, and wasn't awake when I left for school. "I didn't tell him yet," Momma said at breakfast. "He was tired and I didn't want to start the day with all this. You're going to tell him when you get home."

"Fine."

"I want you to know I'm really unhappy." A thick fog slowly whirled in my brain. My head ached and the purple crescents had deepened beneath my eyes, but still I was eager to go to school and hear what the other fighters had to say. I was proud I'd stood up for a principle, even though I hadn't stood up very well, and worried about seeing C. J. in case he wanted to continue the fight. When I arrived in the courtyard, Stem and some of the others were already gathered. "There's Parrish," one of them said with a grin. "Way to lead with your face."

"Yeah," Stem said, "I heard you hurt his fist real bad. Said he tried to miss your nose and couldn't."

"Fuck y'all," I said, acting like I wasn't humiliated and embarrassed at having my nose flattened without landing one good punch. Under different circumstances, I would have laughed with them, but I wanted to spit. They turned to one another again and talked about who they'd cocked or what kid they wished they had gotten, their words focused only on the excitement of the fight. Foolishly and naively, I had expected talk about how we'd defended Riche's grandmother so that such an attack would never happen again. I wished Riche would show up and say something, even though I'd heard him woof about fighting more than most. When the bell rang, I split from them and headed toward math, my entire face pulsing.

Cherie and Lindsay watched as I went to my chair. "You look terrible," Lindsay said. "Is it broken?" Cherie asked.

"Knocked out of place. It hurt worse when it got knocked back in."

They exchanged a glance that seemed both worried and judgmental. "Why did you do that?" Cherie asked, her green eyes narrowing. The summer before I'd held her on my shoulders at an Aerosmith concert in New Orleans' City Park, her thighs squeezing my neck. I didn't want her or the brown-eyed, soft-featured Lindsay looking at me the way they were.

"They shot at Riche and went to his house and beat up his grandmaw."

"Riche is always starting trouble," Cherie said. "Everybody in that group likes to start trouble."

I started to defend myself, then pulled back, thinking how they were unable to see the big picture, how they didn't understand they would want me to stand up for them in a similar situation. "I did what I had to," I said, and rummaged through my book sack.

In the hall between classes, Mike matched my step. "Man, you look like shit. It hurt bad?"

"Only when I breathe."

"It looks rough around the eyes."

"The doctor made it fucking worse. I think he liked popping it back in."

"What'd your daddy and momma say?

"Momma didn't like it. Haven't seen Daddy yet, but I think he'll get it."

Mike didn't say anything. As we parted toward different classes, he said, "Later," and patted my back like a sad parent. I chose to be pissed off instead of embarrassed.

The crowd in the hall squeezed in at me, and I scanned ahead, not only for C. J. and the others we'd fought, but for some threat less tangible expanding in my chest. The school had changed again, but not in any way I predicted. The pride I had the day before hadn't been reinforced by anyone. The people I'd fought side by side with had no vision of protecting anything. I'd known this before, but I'd managed to deny it, just as I had with Dyer. It didn't matter though. Hadn't I fought for justice and a larger ideal? Still, by the time I reached my second period class, I was burning, as much from an inkling of my own willful ignorance as from the reactions to me. No sooner had I sat down than my teacher handed me a slip to report to the principal's office.

My shoulders and back stiffened as I made my way toward Tank's. Even though he had possibly saved me from worse injury, I had no respect for him. I assumed he was calling me to use my fighting as an excuse to take revenge for my having quit basketball the year before. I passed the glass case that held the department store mannequin in Indian garb and entered the outer office. The secretary told me to go straight in, and when I entered the office, there sat Daddy in front of Tank's desk, his hair still wet from a shower, his eyes tired but fiery. "Take a seat," Tank said.

I sat next to Daddy without looking at him. Tank leaned back majestically with his hands crossed in front of his chest. His head was a huge, gray-haired rectangle, his jaw transplanted from a T-rex. I'd been so self-absorbed, I never considered repercussions at school. Dyer had never been called to the office, so why should I suspect that I would (since I was the one whose nose was broken).

More than that, I assumed Tank would like that I had fought hooligan blacks.

"Mr. Parrish," Tank said, "I called your father in to tell him what went on yesterday, and I wanted you to be here when I did." He looked at Daddy. "Your son helped instigate a large fight yesterday morning. I saw him fighting with several other young men and I removed him and told him to stay. He went right back in and started to fight again." *Removed*? Even his diction infuriated me.

But his lie was the worst, no matter how meaningless to the main issue. Tank was lying about my going back in, and I wanted to jump across the desk. He leaned forward and focused on me. "This is a very serious offense, Tim," he said, and his using my first name sickened me. "You are an honor student and you are supposed to set an example of behavior, not attack other students. It's very disappointing." He leaned back. "In the light of all of this, I am suspending you for one week beginning immediately." He slid some paperwork across his nearly barren desk. *Honor student*? I'd always assumed being smart was a mark against me. My mind could only process how I had been wronged, how the truth had been altered to show that *I* was in the wrong. Why didn't Daddy stand up for me? Maybe he didn't know who and why I'd fought.

Daddy signed the form, still having never looked at me, then stood and shook hands with Tank. Daddy thanked him and assured him that I wouldn't be involved in anything like this again. Tank looked at me, maybe expecting an apology, but I wheeled and left the room. Daddy caught up in the hall. "What the hell were you thinking," he said, and strode toward his car.

"Daddy—"

"I don't wanta hear a word outta you, embarrassing me and your momma like that, acting like a fool." I followed him into the parking lot where the air pressed warm and wet. "Don't think this is gone be a week off. You're gone get that hair cut too."

I strained not to curse him or plead with him to listen as I fell behind. He was supposed to be proud. Hadn't I finally done what he wanted, what men of honor were supposed to do? Fight for what was ours. Tears pushed against the back of my eyes, but I wouldn't let them out. "I thought you'd be happy I fought niggers." He turned and faced me, his eyes ablaze.

"Where'd you get such an idea?"

"I fought *niggers*." I had mostly stopped using the word, but I used it then as a pointed thing.

"You don't need to be saying that word."

"You say it every day."

"That don't mean you say it. I don't want you fighting nobody unless you have to."

"How you know I didn't have to? They bea—"

"I said that was enough. I won't have this out of you."

My fist ached to fly at him. He slid into his car and cranked the engine. I'd understood the message behind his stories of men standing up and fighting. I understood his message of the righteousness of cops who clubbed and set dogs on black rioters, of voting to keep blacks out of church, of reveling in the deaths of King and the Kennedys. I understood it even when it troubled me. So why was he treating me as if I had acted incorrectly? Where was his pride? All I saw was more hypocrisy, and it would be many years before I could recognize that he had done the good and right thing, could see that he had risen above his own shortcomings in order to guide me.

My rage curdled at almost everyone I knew, but especially at Daddy. He gave me the usual chores and added scrubbing the house for mildew, priming and painting ironwork, and cleaning out the broiling attic. He sent me to the barber to get my "frizzy nigger hair" shorn. I said nothing to him. When I heard that my suspension matched the longest and that none of the black guys had been suspended, I nursed my outrage even more. I had big plans as a club president, some to show Tank and the rest of the jock principality I wasn't a quitter, others because I wanted to do something good for the school. Now I stewed over whether I'd be allowed to simply stay in the club. As the week passed, though, the work isolated me with my thoughts and left me to sort through my actions in the unforgiving Louisiana sun. I struggled to hold onto my outrage as my self-delusion began to slip.

On the last day of my suspension, I was squatting on the edge of the hot roof, dipping slimy leaves and mud from the gutter, when Robert's police unit pulled up. "Trash!" he said as he walked up alone. He adjusted his gun belt, which never seemed comfortable on his slim hips.

"Officer dickhead."

"You having fun?"

"Shitloads. Come over here and I'll show you." I lifted a handful of muck.

"You want that nose broke again?" He came over and grinned up at me. "Digging in the crud where you belong." I sprang like a frog over his head, hollering as I dropped the eight feet to the grassy yard. I hit and rolled, knees and ankles jarring. He reached out, took my wrist and hoisted me. My thighs burned from squatting and I rubbed them and sucked in air.

"Fuck-up," he said. "You shoulda just gone ahead and snapped your neck."

"I'm baking to death on that roof. Never thought I'd get worked so hard for getting my ass whipped."

"He here?"

"You see his car?"

"Smart-ass."

"He's at the plant. Momma's at work too."

Robert scanned the yard and house. "You sure are putting a shine on the place. Maybe you oughta get in trouble more often."

"He's made me do everything twice and just nods if it passes the test."

"Whiner. That's why you got suspended. Tank hates whiners." He lit a smoke. "When you going back?"

"Tomorrow." I stretched my arms and back. "Why you by your-self? Nobody want to ride with you?"

"Being punished again. Chief says me and Gary have been bad riding together so he's putting us in separate corners."

"And you're calling me a fuck-up?"

"Hey, I'm fucking up *defending* the law."

I knelt and wiped my hands on the ground, then sat there in the warm soft grass. "What bullshit this is. Everybody's always talking about fighting blacks, so I go and do it and now I'm a piece of shit."

"I hate to stick up for the old man, but he's just trying to keep you from getting poked by a knife or a cap popped on you." He blew smoke. "You oughta cool it and keep with basketball."

"What? You're the one always thought Dyer was so fucking cool."

"Dyer again? Christ. He's bad, but he's crazy. Plus, he ain't my brother."

I snorted. "Right." I stood and walked past him into the house. In the kitchen, I poured myself some sweet tea and leaned against the counter. Robert came in and ran a glass of water. I shook my head.

"Why you and Daddy always talking out both sides of your mouth?"

"Watch it." His blue eyes took on that dangerous glint. He drained back half his glass then exhaled an "aaaaah" of refreshment. He smirked. "You're a moody prick, you know that?"

"Wonder where I got it." I crossed my arms and tapped my foot. He kept looking at me with his smirk. "Eat shit," I said.

"Uh-huh. You gonna have any trouble at school with the one who put the lick on you?"

"I can handle it."

"Oh, I can see that."

I feinted like I was swinging a punch, and he grabbed the butt of his pistol. "Don't make Momma clean you up off the kitchen." He killed the glass of water and set it on the counter. "All right. Gotta go arrest some citizens. Let me know what happens. I like a good horror movie."

That night Momma, Daddy and I sat eating barbecue sandwiches from Gibson's Drive-In. Momma kept trying to strike up small talk, but it died against the walls. As the week had worn on, she softened, but Daddy and I had barely spoken except for me to say I'd finished a job and for him to give his critique and tell me to do it over or give me another task. He cleared his throat. "You got yourself straight for going back tomorrow?"

"No, I'm gonna go back and attack the principal."

"I ain't in the mood for a smart mouth."

"Or anything I say. You still don't even know what happened."

"I know all I need to know."

"Some black dudes shot at a white dude and jumped his grand-maw and we went after 'em."

"That don't make it right."

"You saying you wouldn't have fought?"

"It doesn't matter what I'd do. I growed up in different times from you."

"That's it. I'm finished." I shoved the chair away from the table and shot up.

"What's wrong with you?" Daddy said. "You sit back down."

"You make me."

"Tim," Momma said.

"You, too, Momma. *Nigger* this and *nigger* that and then *we love Jesus* and *we grew up in different times*. I'm sick of y'all."

Daddy came up out of his chair. "That's enough right now."

"It's enough with you. At least I *did* something. What have you done?" I spun and went to my room. Daddy's footsteps followed and Momma's behind his.

"Boy, you better calm down!" Daddy yelled from my open door.

"Make me, goddamnit." I swept everything from my desk with a single swipe, then slung a chair against my chest of drawers.

"Tim, stop it!" Momma said.

Daddy took a step toward me, and I adjusted my stance. Momma moved past him to get between us. I'd never experienced my brain blazing like this, a blast furnace blowing in every direction, had never dared face-off with my father. I was wild with grief. How long had it been since I understood what he, or any man, wanted from me? I pressed my hands to the sides of my head. "Get out!" Their eyes went wide, their expressions frighteningly helpless. "I said get out!"

Momma squeezed past Daddy. He waited a second longer, then turned and followed her. I backed into the corner of the room, my thoughts and feelings sprinting further out ahead of me than it seemed I could reel back in. I pushed my fists against my mouth and screamed so that the sound grinded inside my throat.

Two hours later, I was sitting in my desk chair when Momma came through the door. I figured Daddy hadn't joined her in order to avoid another confrontation. She eyed the things still strewn on the floor and slowly flapped her arms against her hips. "You still mad at the world?" she asked.

"I'm still here."

"Well, you better be over throwing a fit. I won't have you acting that way. You owe your daddy an apology and I expect this room to get picked up tonight."

"Yes, *ma'am*," I said. She came closer to me.

"I'm sick of your attitude."

"Aren't you always sick?"

She slapped me hard across the cheek. She had only spanked me with switches and flyswatters a few times in my life, once with a flyswatter so old that it fell apart, reducing Robert and me to aching laughter, but she had never slapped my face. Pink bloomed on her cheeks. Her hands shook. Her eyes filled with tears. I stood, my cheek burning. I wanted to die.

"Momma—"

"Why do you have to test us so much?" She spun and I gently took her arm. She straightened it and shook me off, but she didn't step out.

"Please, Momma."

She kept her back to me. I expected Daddy to come down the hall, but evidently he was outside. When she turned again, her expression held emotions so jagged and complex that I couldn't even read them all. "You can be so mean," she said. My throat nearly clogged.

"Please sit down," I said.

She touched her flushed cheeks, then went to my bed and sat on the edge. She wiped the tears from the corner of her eyes and studied me. I sat in my desk chair.

"Your daddy's right," she said. "Me and him did grow up in different times."

"That's—" She pointed her finger to stop me.

"That doesn't excuse everything," she said, "but it doesn't mean that you can't know better." She leaned forward. "I came in here to tell you I remember that time you brought your friend Virgil by. I could see he was your friend."

"He didn't beat up somebody's grandmaw or shoot at their car."

"I'm not talking about that. I'm talking about what it said about how you are."

"And Daddy would've gone through the roof if he knew."

"All your daddy and me want is for you to be all right."

"He won't even hear my side of the story."

"He knows what he needs to know. We both want you to be a good Christian."

I bit the inside of my cheek. The word "Christian" was a tin edge raked along my spine, but that morphed into shame at knowing I'd used Virgil to put Momma in a bind. No matter what else, I was sure I was an asshole and possibly a crazy person too. I nodded. "I know you do."

She stood, came over to me, and touched my head. I kept my eyes down until she patted my cheek and closed the door behind her. It would be years before I considered how difficult it must have been for her to navigate such angry damaged men, how difficult and unhealthy for her own anger to have so little space. Right then, it still boiled in me that she was complicit in Daddy's hypocrisy, no matter how good her intentions, and yet I also saw, if only in brief, that blaming them did me no good. I pushed myself to my feet and knelt to pile things back on my desk. When I finished, exhaustion slammed me. I sat on the floor. I had tried to please so many people, had hoped somebody could protect me, then chosen the worst person to do so. I believed I could hate and fight my way through everyone and everything. Foolish. Racist. Disloyal. I had been enraged at just about everyone, but most of my contempt I turned on myself.

"Love Casteth Out Fear"

The next morning I walked, my driving privileges suspended except to go to my weekend yard job and twice-a-week janitorial night job. As I passed my old elementary playground, kids shouted and ran wild. When I was a kid, Daddy had come to my football practices;

Momma had been there for every event she could—in-class skits, parties, awards ceremonies—even when I gave her grief because the other kids might think it was babified and queer to have her there. I passed the Pak-A-Sak where I had last seen Jarreau, passed Mc-Clure's drug store, where at my first official job in the snowball stand I ate so many free ones the starting day that I nearly hallucinated from the sugar.

I both did and did not want to go back to school. The fantasy I'd had of showing courage in defense of our territory pained my gut. I was also wary that the kid who had punched me might drive by with some of his buddies and jump me or confront me at school.

Just as I'd planned, I arrived as the bell rang. I entered the main office, my expression as hard as I could make it. The assistant principal had to speak to me before I was readmitted, and I wasn't looking forward to that since he'd once been my Sunday school teacher and was likely to give me a sermon. I was determined not to show remorse or gloat. I did not want to play the penitent good boy nor show any pride in what I'd done. From behind the counter, a red-headed girl I didn't know said she would tell him I was there.

Jason Stanley poked his head out of the back office where he worked first period. He'd evidently heard my voice, and his expression was sour beneath his large 'fro as he came straight up on the other side of the counter. "How's it going?" I said. We stared at each other.

"You ain't supposed to be fighting niggahs," he said. His words penetrated my chest.

"I guess that's why they suspended me." He stayed there until the girl called my name to come inside. "Gotta go see the man," I said to Jason. I went around the counter and past him, his eyes x-raying me.

The assistant principal gave his smiley we're-ashamed-of-your-behavior-but-we-know-you'll-do-better speech, and I listened without a word, thinking how spineless a toady he was, while Jason's words and gaze continued to unsettle me. When the assistant principal dismissed me, Jason was waiting with my hall pass. "I'm serious," he said, as if we hadn't been interrupted before. "That's not you." He put the pass in my hand.

◆ ◆ ◆

"Love Casteth Out Fear"

No one made a big deal out of my being back. At lunch, there was a replay of the ribbing Stem and the others had given me the day after the fight, but my college prep pals in class asked me what it had been like to be suspended. I showed them my blistered, calloused palms. "Big vacation," I said. Mr. Shirley acted as though I hadn't missed a class, and I went up afterward to thank him for sending my work home with my neighbor Sherry.

"You're welcome. Good to have you back."

"Good to be back."

"If you have any problems, I'm here."

"Thanks."

"Just to let you know, the principal's out to get you."

"Figured that. He knows I did it all to piss him off."

He nodded and chuckled.

I avoided Ms. Arnault all day, but she sent word for me to come see her. After my last class, I lingered at my locker to let the halls clear before I walked to her room. She stood from her desk, dressed in gauchos and a tight shirt, her long hippie hair narrowing her face. She came around and gave me a big hug.

"How's it look?" I asked and pointed at the bridge of my nose. She touched the bump.

"Next time I'd get a plastic surgeon who didn't go to Istrouma." She breathed heavily through her nose, shut the door behind me, and went to the sill of the large windows that were slanted outward. She pulled out her cigarettes. "I'm sorry, but I need one."

"Don't have a joint, do you?"

Her eyes shot wide, then she laughed. She lit her smoke and blew hard. "I wish." I joined her on the sill.

"Am I out?"

"Tank asked me to drop you as president."

"He *asked*?"

"I don't think he can make me, but he's pressuring. I'm not tenured, so he can hold that over me and give me all kinds of shit work. More hall and lunch duty and committees and wearing sack cloth."

"I'm sorry." She blew a long drag out the window, flicked some ash, then looked at me. Her face fell.

"I'm mostly worried about you. Are you going to fight anymore?"

"I didn't do much fighting this time. They did the fighting on me." She waited. "If somebody comes after me I'll have to fight, or if they go after my friends."

"I'd feel better if you'd promise you wouldn't fight at all."

"I can't promise that. I can't just let people run over us."

"You think that's what's happening now?"

"Riche's car has bullet holes in it. My neighborhood's got 'For Sale' signs everywhere." I glanced around her room at the U.S. map's brightly colored states, at the wooden ceiling fans, at the board. "Maybe I should just quit."

"I don't care about the club. I mean I care, but that's not what I'm talking about here. I'm talking about you and all this other stuff." She touched my arm. "I know it's not really my business, but I don't think this fighting's doing you any good, or anybody else." I looked out the second-floor window, directly out across where Dyer's old house sat two blocks away. When I looked at Ms. Arnault again, her face crimped and she bit her bottom lip. "I just want you to enjoy your senior year and be okay." Tears swelled in her eyes. She patted my hand and lifted her cigarette to take another puff. She had always seemed brittle beneath her outspokenness, but I'd never seen it so clearly. I leaned over and gave her a hug, then I pointed at her cigarette.

"That's bad for you," I said.

The fumes of toxins and petroleum products in the garage had set my nose running, but I still perched on the edge of a lawn chair reading "The Lottery" for the third time. It was my second week back at school, and Mr. Shirley had moved the assignment up, a move I later believed was for my benefit. As I read how the town gathered, drew lots and stoned to death one of their neighbors, my body tightened with horror, my visceral reaction so intense that I couldn't process any literary or intellectual meaning except to ask why these down-to-earth, small-town people—people like my parents and relatives—would murder one of their own because of a drawn lot. I didn't even hear Daddy open the door from the kitchen. "Your brother's on the phone," he said, startling me.

"Tell him I'll call him back."

"He's on the phone now and wants to talk to you."

"I said I'd call him back."

"Get in here and talk to him." I was still grounded and knew better than to argue. Daddy went back to the living room where he and Momma were watching TV. I picked up the heavy, black receiver.

"Yeah."

"Hey, stud, heard you got in some trouble." It wasn't Robert, it was Alan, or Al, as he'd started calling himself. His voice carried his perpetually chipper tone. I hadn't talked to him since the fight and suspension.

"Daddy told you."

"Yep. Said your nose didn't come out so well."

"Somebody said it'll give me character."

"You're all right now?"

"My nose is. I'm going crazy only being able to go to school and work. They're finally letting me out this weekend to go to a state Scholars' Club meeting at LSU."

"Uh-huh." He paused and I knew the conversation was about to shift. "You know, it looks bad for college, pal, getting suspended. I'm going out on a limb to get you this scholarship." He'd been working his old petroleum engineering professors to give me one of the full-ride, oil-company scholarships, even though I had doubts that my math skills could carry me.

"I appreciate it."

"You should. You think you can stay out of trouble?"

"If they don't come roughing up anybody's grandma or taking shots at anybody's car."

"Well, if they're not taking them at you, you oughta keep your ass out of it."

I thought of bringing up his own youthful past, but he had always guided me toward the larger world of college and a wider-ranging life, had always been loyal to my parents and me. Nonetheless, I resented that he didn't seem to want to take on the same questions as me—religion, neighborhood, morality.

"How's Chicago?" I asked.

"Great! Job's great, and I'm getting close to finishing night school and getting my MBA."

"That's cool."

"Yeah, I'm aiming to move out of engineering and into management. You'll have to get up here and see us before we move."

"I'd like to."

We talked for a little while more about Momma's health, about how his wife was doing, and about how Robert's partner had agreed to coach our recreation league team.

"Daddy told me houses are going up for sale everywhere," he said. "How are they doing with thinking about moving?"

"He probably told you they're looking at some property in Denham Springs."

"Yeah."

"He tell you he wants to move the house out there 'cause he's worried he can't build another one for what he'll get with this one?"

"He didn't mention that."

"He's bitching about it all the time."

"I'll have to talk to him about it. Anyway, he doesn't need you worrying him more, and you don't need to screw up that scholarship." I inhaled and kept quiet. "I think you're more cut out to be a lover than a fighter anyway." He laughed hard. I wanted to say it was better to fight than to run, but I knew he'd lecture me on how ridiculous that was. I knew I'd agree with him at least in how futile fighting seemed.

After we hung up, I headed toward the garage to finish the story for the third time. My parents' laughter, good belly laughs, came from the living room as I passed. I paused in the kitchen and listened. I couldn't remember them laughing like that in a long time, although maybe I just hadn't paid attention.

I hunched over my bedroom desk, drafting my indignant paper on the pitfalls of following tradition, a paper inspired by "The Lottery." I had been so agitated by the story that I hadn't actually formed ideas until in class Mike and Jan Small zeroed in on the theme of how blindly following superstition and tradition is destructive and unreasonable. I nearly ignited when they said it, but not yet out of self-awareness. As Shirley led the class deeper into the discussion, I tuned out and fixated on the wrongs done to *me* in the name of tradition, the guilt heaped on *me* for thoughts I couldn't help thinking, the pressures put on *me* to act a certain way. I hadn't yet admitted that my own hand had held a stone.

The physical world around me disappeared as I scrawled away, until a soft knock interrupted me. Daddy poked his head in. "We fixing to eat some ice cream," he said. I wanted to shove the paper at him, tell him how at fault he and the church were, tell him to leave me alone with an idea that wasn't claustrophobic. Instead, I looked up and tapped my pen.

"I'm busy," I said.

He opened the door completely. "You doing school work?"

"Working on a paper." I knew if I told him it was a paper for English and not math or chemistry homework, he would give me the look that said how impractical and useless it was. He nodded and didn't leave.

"You making out all right?"

"Fine."

"School's going all right?"

I breathed in and set the pen down. "Yes, sir." He took a step into the room.

"How's Gary's coaching?"

"Good. Our first game is in a coupla weeks."

"His daddy coached college, didn't he?"

"Yes, sir. He scouted for the Washington Bullets, too."

He put his hands in his pockets. "I think that'll be better than all them coaches at school. I hated to see you torn up about that."

I had the urge to yell why couldn't he see the real things I'd been torn up about, ask him why he could never let me know what he wanted from me, but I could see that he was trying hard, and for a moment I let go. "You gotta work tonight?" I asked.

"Old dog shift. Gunn and them coonasses said they gone cook a rabbit stew, so they'll probably be out back shooting the rabbits. I just hope they shoot away from the unit." He smiled.

"Make sure you don't hop around." He laughed.

"Well, I'll let you get back to it." He started to turn, then looked in again. "Oh, they's a good ball game coming on this weekend if you want to watch it. Ole Miss might win one. I'll check when it is." He paused. I could see that he was thinking about patting me or maybe even kissing me on the forehead like he used to, but neither of us moved. He closed the door behind him, and I listened to his footsteps move down the hall. "He's in there writing on something," I heard him say to Momma. "He might eat some ice cream after while." I wondered how this good man who loved so much could hold such pessimism and intolerance. I didn't take time to ask the question of myself. Then I picked up the pen and wrote again without a thought of the tradition that had just been in my room.

I peered through Mr. Shirley's classroom door window from the long, empty hall. He leaned forward over a paper, holding it in one hand, his red pen in the other, while he glared, as if the paper were the portrait of pure stupidity. I smiled, knocked, and poked my head in. "Am I bothering you?"

"Yes, and thank you. Come on in." He motioned to the chair next to his desk and laid down the pen. "You're here late."

"Had a meeting with Ms. Arnault and Mrs. Purdy about club stuff."

"I heard that our esteemed principal couldn't impeach you."

"Don't know about couldn't, but he didn't."

"That's very good." He ran a thumb beneath his tie and sat back. "How's your paper coming?"

"I think I've got a solid draft. It could still be bad though. Who knows?"

"I'm eager to read it."

"I hope it doesn't get the look you just gave that one," I said.

He slapped the edge of the essay with his pen. "Introductory Expository Writing, or Ignorant Scribbling for Non-Thinkers."

"That was me last year."

"Nowhere close. Your first one was a B-minus, wasn't it?"

"I'm glad you remember that."

"Let's just say I remember it as contrast to what came later." He tossed his pen onto the desk. "So, how are things?"

"All right. I know I don't need to, but I just dropped by to say thank you for not telling me how stupid I was when I got suspended."

"I didn't think it was necessary. I thought you'd discover it yourself when it was time."

"So you did think it was stupid?"

"The better question, I think, is why do you think you needed to fight?"

My face warmed. I shrugged. "I thought I needed to do something after they shot at Riche and messed with his grandmaw."

"Why?"

"To keep things from getting out of hand, I guess. To try and protect this place. The school. The neighborhood."

"Protect them from what?"

"From what's happening. What's changing so much that nobody will recognize it and take pride in it."

"And so it's up to you to stay here and make sure nothing changes?" He raised his eyebrows. Irritation swept over me. I glanced over the neat piles of papers and stacks of books on his desk, an orderliness I could only dream about having. I let the irritation go.

"I'd sit in the back," I said.

He linked his hands, let them rest on his belly, and swiveled his chair to see out the window to the small courtyard between buildings. "I'm going to miss you and your group. I suspect there may be one or two more classes as driven and dedicated to school as y'all are, but I doubt many after that."

I almost asked if he thought it was because the school was becoming mostly black, but I didn't like saying it—and I didn't want him to hear me say it. "Why do you think that is?"

He swiveled back towards me. "The condensed, global answer? Hundreds of years of disenfranchisement in terms of both race and class. A legacy of not having access to education and so not valuing education at home. For just the blacks, a history of not seeing any way out of poverty as the whites take off and the money goes."

"Jesus." I'd heard Ms. Arnault give versions of what he'd said, but more through implication in historical lessons rather than so compressed and direct. I couldn't really take it all in. A part of me still reacted with defensiveness that we whites were being blamed. Mr. Shirley slightly rocked his chair.

"Again, I'm not saying it's all racial. It's happening already, the pride in ignorance and devaluation of education, and I guess it's always happened because of people distrusting education and a perception of it as part of an elite system to belittle them. A lot of it is racial, though. I mean, I'm not letting anybody off the hook for their personal behavior, but there are larger reasons."

For the first time, I saw sadness cross his face. I'd seen his vulnerability, but most often it spun off as a side product of frustration or resentment or disappointment. I saw right then that he was losing a place and people, too.

"Will you stay here?" I asked.

"Probably not. A new magnet school is opening, and I have enough seniority to apply there in a year or so. I'm not interested in teaching remedial writing and reading, and that's where this place is already headed. Maybe I could help a few people if I stayed, but I want to teach people who are going to college, and I see fewer and fewer of those." He breathed slowly out and leaned forward, elbows on his desk. "I've thought a good bit about what I'm about to say. I believe that sometimes when one feels like he's running away, he's actually running toward something. At least I like to tell myself that."

I loved Mr. Shirley's love of words, even loved his sometimes stilted speech, because they showed his pride at being intelligent and articulate, things that were tricky for me to even intimate without being razzed. I nodded. Nonetheless, I resisted his words about running. They felt planned, and I wondered whether that made them less authentic. I wasn't ready to let go of all my defenses.

"We oughta play ball some time," I said. He sat back.

"I'd like that. Seeing me will make you appreciate your youth."

Spring 1976: Flight

Momma, Daddy and I rolled down Florida Boulevard through Denham Springs' main drag of tire stores and grocery markets. I hadn't been down this road in a year, not since Dyer had rocketed us in front of a train and pulled his .44. This time, I sat in the backseat, while most of the tension sat in the front.

Daddy turned off into residential neighborhoods of old ranch houses with sagging roofs and traveled on through even more worn-down houses until we entered the development where they'd been thinking of buying a lot. Scrub trees and thick vines snarled the land, most of which wasn't yet developed. It looked to me like barely reclaimed swamp. Deep in the subdivision, Daddy pulled to the side of the narrow road and shut off the engine next to the corner I'd seen twice before. Nobody moved or spoke. A muddy ditch fell sharply away from the edge of the curbless, asphalt street. From the ditch rose small mud columns built by crawfish. Even I could see that the lot, patchy with grass and thick with small palmettos, was low. No lush carpet of St. Augustine grass; no beautiful pin and water oaks; no azalea bushes. It was depressing, a piece of land I figured Daddy would have scorned.

"Well, let's get out," he said.

We stepped from the car into the hot spring sun. Momma scanned the neighboring mobile homes, one with a lean-to shed built above it. "Not much to see," she said to me under her breath. She glanced at her white sneakers and made a face as we headed toward the dirt drive that crossed the ditch atop a metal culvert. The flat ground sank a little as we entered the property. I slapped at mosquitoes. The lot seemed smaller to me than the one we had, even though I thought it should look larger without a house. Tiny pink flags created a house-sized rectangle, but I didn't think much of it. My mind was preoccupied with the dismalness of the place and with the mechanics of how we might move our house here, something Daddy seemed set on doing wherever they bought. It was as if he'd read my mind.

"I reckon we'd have to bring it in on that side without the ditch. Don't know how we gone get it situated right." He pointed. "The truck would have to come in the way we did and it'd have to maneuver onto that side and then back it in. Power line would have to come down."

Momma and I stared at where he pointed and at the seeming impossibility of his plan. Even if the truck could navigate the skinny streets and the house could be brought onto the lot, I imagined it sinking. But worse than that was picturing it here in this impoverished location. A poor, provincial place. A town with David Duke and another man vying to control the Ku Klux Klan. Neighbors whom I imagined as lovers of guns more than people, resentful of us as if we were carpetbaggers or at least too smart and, amazingly, too citified. People terrified of someone taking something, anything, everything. People like us in many ways, except ready to burn crosses and actually torch a house, something that seemed nearly impossible for me to believe I'd considered only a year ago. I had no proof of these stereotypes. I was ashamed to think of these people as trash. And yet I did believe these people weren't like my parents and weren't as proud of their homes as my parents were. I believed without reason that these people somehow chose poverty and ignorance, and I knew that my parents wouldn't be happy here.

"I still think we oughta look around and think about building, Hollis," Momma said.

"I don't see how we can build. It's gone cost a whole lot more and the house on Wyandotte is in good shape."

Momma pointed. "Who put up these markers?"

Daddy faced us. "I did," he said softly. "That's the size of our house. I staked it yesterday."

"You staked it?" Momma asked.

"The owner let you stake it?" I asked.

Neither of my parents spoke. Momma stared at the flags while Daddy stared at her. "You didn't," she said.

"Yesterday. I put the deposit down." He tried to smile. Momma's cheeks pinkened.

"We hadn't decided that."

"Hon, the man said it was fixing to sell."

"That's what a salesman is supposed to say."

"We couldn't wait, Rachel. Our place is dropping every day."

"You don't even know we can move the house." She glared at him, then turned and went back to the car. He watched until she dropped into the backseat. He wrung his hands and swallowed, then looked at me, his eyes desperate in a way that made me want to wrap an arm around him. "She'll see it's all right," he said. I nodded. He surveyed the lot and the surroundings like I'd done before. I knew he was seeing the conditions I'd seen, knew that he was thinking how

Spring 1976: Flight

he'd always wanted better for Momma than they'd had, and how he'd failed her. I took a step closer to him. He kept looking off.

"I don't know how we can afford to build another house or buy one in a new subdivision," he said. "We'll have to get ours in here." He put his hands in his pockets and made a divot in the ground with his toe. Then he peered toward the car.

"I guess I oughta go talk to her," he said, but he didn't move.

"You're bogarting, dude," I said to Virgil, and took the joint out of his hand.

"That's good shit, man, I can't help it."

"You've said that every time we ever got stoned."

"It's true!" His voice strained with the held smoke. He leaned his head out the window and exhaled as we passed City Park Lake, streaks of light shimmering across the dark water. "I'm feeling hiiigh," he said.

"Then stop smoking that shit and getting stink all over me," Mike said from the backseat. "I don't want to go to jail with you fools."

"I'm sure your old man would love bailing you out," I said.

"Shit, I'd rather stay in jail."

I took the joint back from Virgil, rubbed the fire into the wind, and put the roach in my pocket. Mike's daddy was a big man prone to high emotion. He hated our long hair and our love for any rock 'n' roll made later than Jerry Lee, Elvis, and Chuck Berry. His head would have blown off if Mike had been caught anywhere around pot. I didn't want to consider what he'd do to our heads.

I usually didn't smoke with Mike in the car, but tonight was special because he, Virgil and I were all out together, a rarity, and I didn't know how many more times there would be before we graduated. We had just left a motel room, where there was a post-meeting after party of Scholars' Club officers from around the state. Everyone in the room had been white except Virgil, and everybody seemed to like him until he chatted a good while with a couple of girls, and several guys in the room appeared to be bowing up, intensifying my paranoia and ambivalence. Mike was flirting, too, as I sat back and watched. When he caught on to the tension, he and I exchanged glances, ready to jump in if somebody came at Virgil, an irony of which I was completely aware, especially because as Virgil kept on, oblivious and easygoing, my insides squirmed and wrestled with imagining his black lips touching a white girl's lips. At least it was a somewhat different struggle than before, not over whether I should hate or not, but between racist feelings that had been wired into me and the lesser racist I had begun to be.

As we cruised, we talked about football and the coaches Mike had come to despise for urging him to play with his elbow swollen to the size of a softball before chastising him when he couldn't play because his injury became so bad he literally couldn't bend his arm. I told Virgil about our rec-league team, and Virgil talked about how the latest school coach actually coached and didn't scream. "Wish y'all had come out," he said. "We need some white people when we go to schools like Tara and shit."

"Yeah," Mike said, "but they'd just throw more rocks at the bus at Capitol and McKinley."

"They couldn't throw no *more*," Virgil said.

I laughed, glad to simply be bullshitting again, no pistols beneath seats, no metal stars or chains at the ready. I glanced in the rearview mirror at Mike. He had never been conflicted about race the way I was, evidently never afraid the way I was, and I wished I'd had his good sense. In seventh grade, he'd said "nigger" around Jason Stanley, seen Jason's hurt face, apologized, and then altered the way he thought. He wasn't free of prejudice—none of us was—but he never had the urge to prove anything because of it. I glanced at Virgil. I wanted to confess to him the conflict I'd had at the motel, but I knew his reaction would be that it was all cool. Everything was so much cooler than with Dyer, than even the start of this school year, those days often seeming far gone.

"Hey," I said to Mike, "I ever tell you that Virgil stole my bike when I was a kid?"

"Say what?"

"Him and a bunch of brothers rode through my neighborhood and stole my bike. He remembers 'cause it was such a pretty bike."

"I lied, man," Virgil said. "Your bike was too crummy to steal."

A Kind of Closure

About a month later, I lay dozing on the couch. I went there when I couldn't go to sleep in my own bed, which was more and more often, what with graduation approaching, my anticipation over going to LSU, and the anxiety over our moving. My parents had sold the lot in Denham and bought a larger, much nicer lot in Walker, even farther from town. Too far from any hospital, I thought. They increasingly debated how they would pay to build a house, when they would put ours up for sale, and how much they would ask for it. They also agonized over whether they would be the first among our close neighbors to sell to blacks. Daddy fretted over the uncertainty, his irritability nearly constant and always counterproductive, while Momma tired of trying simultaneously to reassure him and to help make good decisions. I tried, at times, to mediate, but the stress grinded me, too.

When the key turned and the front door opened, I swung my legs off the couch. I knew it was Robert and wondered what was wrong. He eased in and began toward the hall, his badge glinting in the slight light through the picture window. "Hey," I said softly so as not to surprise him, but he flinched anyway.

"What you doing out here?" he asked.

"Couldn't sleep. What are you doing here?" He came across the living room and sat next to me, the odor of cigarettes pouring off him.

"Heard you got that scholarship to study like brother Bigshot."

"They might take it back when they see what I get in advanced math."

"Fucking math. I had this math teacher who used to go off talking about dropping bombs in World War II. He'd just blank out and look out the window saying, 'The bombs falling, the bombs, the bombs, the bombs.'"

"Sounds like a blast."

"Smart-ass." He rummaged in his shirt pocket, brought out a matchbox, and handed it to me. "Thought you might want this *tonight*." I stared at it.

"Thanks. I was wondering where I could get some matches."

"Open it, dickhead." I slid open the tiny drawer and the smell of weed came up like a genie. He nudged me. "Jarreau's," he said.

"Jarreau's?"

"Took it off the asshole. It's probably shitty weed."

I pinched up a bit and rolled it between my fingers, trying to sort through what was happening. "You're shittin' me."

He settled back into the couch. "Me and Gary were patrolling Howell Park and we saw somebody blow and go across the road. We went after him in the unit and hemmed him up against a fence in our headlights. It was Jarreau."

"No way."

"Oh, yeah. Best part is, the idiot throws down a lid like we wouldn't see it was his, and me and Gary just broke up. I got out just right behind the car door and said, '*Mis*-ter Jarreau,' all glad to see him. I don't think he could really see me yet 'cause of the headlights and he was wasted too, so he goes, 'I ain't done nothing.' I go, 'You mudhead, we saw you throw your dope down and jackrabbit.' He starts looking around where to book but the big baseball fence is all behind him and I step up a little beside the lights so he can get a look at me. I say, 'You're busted.' He does his hand like a visor over his eyes and squints and then his eyes go big. Stupid fucker pulls a blade."

"He did?"

"Fuckin' A. Dumb bastard. We pulled our guns and Gary goes, 'Clean shoot, Robert.' Jarreau's arm sogged out like a droopy noodle. I asked him if he remembered me putting my boot on his neck and he nodded and dropped the knife. 'It's still clean,' Gary said. I thought about it, but Jarreau went to begging and saying he didn't do nothing. I went over and smushed his nose into the fence and put the cuffs on him real tight. He starts whimpering when I was hustling him over to the unit." Robert brushed at his pants leg. "Goddamn if he ain't clumsy. Tripped and fell down on the ground face first a couple of times right in front of me. Bammed his head on the car *hard* getting in the backseat, too. *Real* clumsy motherfucker."

I pictured it all, almost wishing Robert had shot him, yet glad for his sake that he hadn't. I wondered if Jarreau would come after me to actually hurt me when he got out, but I wondered only for a moment. That fear didn't have me anymore. Robert laughed.

"We took a little time with him at the jail and then told them to give him extra special treatment. Deputies are probably taking care of him about every hour."

I sat back and laughed. Robert took a straight-bladed knife from his belt and handed it to me. "I'm keeping that, so don't get any ideas."

"He was carrying a straight-blade instead of a pocketknife? What is he, fucking Jim Bowie?"

"Fucking Jim Dumbshit. His dumbshitness never ends. He probably stole it." I handed it back. He pointed at the matchbox. "We kept most of the weed for evidence, but I plucked that. Maybe we oughta smoke it together."

"You haven't smoked since 'Nam."

"I'm getting sick of all the bullshit. Brass has been fucking with me about all kinds of shit. Fuck 'em if they don't want me to do my job."

"That sucks, man."

"Fuckin' politics. What you gonna do?" He stood. "How's Momma?"

"Daddy's driving her crazy. They're all worried about moving and shit. I think she wishes you'd come around more."

"I get by at least once a week."

"She wants you here every day."

"Just like the old man."

"He's wishing you'd move back in."

He shoved my head. "I'd probly get the top bunk this time." He adjusted his gun belt. "Okay, gotta get back. Gary's out in the car."

I followed him to the porch and waved at Gary. Robert's career with the police was in its death spiral. Not far down the road, he'd end up on the night beat in dead downtown as punishment. After that he'd quit and go to work in a chemical plant, then on to other jobs before ending up on PTSD disability. It would be a struggle at times for us to stay close.

I watched until their unit turned the corner, then I rotated the matchbox like a diamond, sniffed it and shook it. I replayed the scene Robert had told me about and reveled in my picture of Jarreau about to shit his pants, just like me all those times. The breeze rustled the leaves. I took a seat on the steps and watched the reddish clouds move across the black sky. It would be pretty to say I recollected the past and came to some moment of forgiveness and redemption, but I didn't. I hoped that as Jarreau watched Robert's gun hand, he felt the same fear I had, hoped his forehead had split wide when it banged against the car, hoped the deputies at lockup were kicking him in the guts over and over. For a few minutes, I held onto the angry satisfaction of that. Then I listened to the neighborhood, quiet and filled with sleeping lives, and hoped I'd be able to sleep.

Epilogue

June 2006: Reunion

"Yeah, I saw Dyer just last weekend," a former classmate said to a group a few feet behind me. "He was fishing with us at my camp. Eight in the morning, and he was drinking beer and getting stoned and giving us shit. He's just like he was in high school." They all laughed with what I took to be admiration.

Anxiety and doubt flooded me with the old fears of humiliation, perceived weakness, and failures in judgment. I imagined Dyer at my future reading of this book in Baton Rouge. He stood in back behind the chairs, hands in his pockets, posture relaxed, mouth fixed in an inscrutable smirk, his eyes amused, perhaps even kind and sentimental, his whole self more the mystery and big brother who connected with me than the racist who led me toward my worst self. Amazingly, I was afraid of how I'd be judged, even by myself, and not primarily about my racist acts. I worried that others would see me as delicate or too sensitive, unmanly, because I take seriously what happened so long ago. Worried that I would be a hypocrite if I stood face to face with Dyer and denied through a grin and understatement the severity of the past. Wondered why I still cared that he and my classmates might think I'm a too-brainy, whiny coward? Then doubts about my writing this book tumbled in. Would I be fair and accurate to Dyer and to the people and past I was portraying? Was I exploiting my family? Would I hurt Daddy? Would Alan chastise me, as he did with my first book? And was this book simply a narcissistic confession of my own racism, shameful weakness, and continuing zealotry, the latter now in the form of some self-perceived enlightenment? The questions rolled me like a wave, and they still sometimes roll me. But at least I have some means to understand the roots of my doubt in a destructive past, as well as the means to trust my own motives in trying to get at a truth. Maybe not fully understand the motives, but at least to continue to try and understand.

My Process, In Brief

I'm sure there's much to say in general about fear, but I'm not the one to say it. What I can say is obvious. That listening to well-founded fear can protect us, while listening to irrational or manufactured fear cannot. Unfounded fear is the great perverter and thief. I have seen what it does. It breeds ignorance and violence; erodes us; separates us from one another and ourselves; destroys reason; and creates scapegoats. In its extremes, fear subverts love and trust, generates bigotry, takes us to war, and even causes genocide. As object lesson, we now have a government with ever-increasing police power and an unending, Orwellian war against "terror." All of which is to say that the above is easy to know, but harder to remedy, harder because actual threat is often difficult to separate from unlikely threat. We can only try, I suppose, not to be ruled by fear, not to allow rationality to be corrupted by it, and not to lose ourselves in the unlikely nightmare possibilities and long odds of harm. Danger is real, but for most of us, danger is not a constant reality. But, then, all of this is easy to say in the abstract; the specific is much more complex.

When I started this book, the old fears curdled into anger and shame. I wanted to kill Jarreau, Lassiter, and even Chandler, sometimes wanted to kill myself because I'd let them humiliate me, and humiliation, volatility and rage lived in me still. I'd anticipated struggling against shame at having been a racist and at having wanted to be a "purer" racist, and yet the anticipation didn't stop me from battering myself. Why hadn't I had better judgment? When teens commit crimes today, they're tried as adults, so why shouldn't I hold myself accountable and unforgiveable as an adult for what I did from thirteen to seventeen? Worse, why did I still struggle with the old racist reflexes, like a user struggles not to use? But the most unexpected shame, and maybe the most perverse, was my ongoing belief that I'd been a coward. I obsessed over why I hadn't fought Lassiter every day until some resolution, why I hadn't swung at Chandler and at Jarreau, or even alongside Dyer, no matter how morally sickening doing that would have been to me. Intellectually, I knew that fighting would have been futile, destructive, and wrong-headed, but the shame was still poisonous. I raked myself over and over the old misguided standard of manliness and retribution that had nearly erased me as a teenager; that had led me into fights and violent confrontations even as an adult; that percolates animosity in me still, and has undermined relationships and people I love. Even when I was furious over the fact that the same macho standard that had controlled me was keeping our country at war and leeching our rights, I couldn't forgive myself for not having acted like what some call a man.

Surprisingly, with each draft I gained empathy for the boys who'd hurt me the most. I saw Lassiter as an abused, unloved kid. An ass-hole, yes, but a confused teenager who probably hadn't savored our fight any more than I had; otherwise, why hadn't he come after me again? I doubt much good happened to him. It took longer to see Jarreau as the pathetic sociopath he was. My most intense hatred was for him—the Jarreau of *then*, the Jarreau in my memory who could never be changed, no matter what he'd become or even if he was dead. I had the same generalized insights into him that I had about Lassiter, but my hatred hung on.

I started with much less anger for Dyer. He manipulated me into complicity in horrible acts, lied to me, bullied me, often made me feel weak, but he did love me in his way, tried to tutor me in the way he understood, and led me on fun times that I've mostly left out of this book. He let me be as close to him as he could allow, took me in and tried to make me tougher, and he did make me tougher by making me deal with him. I wasn't forced to follow him; I chose to follow him. I still despise his brutality, but I don't despise him. And yet I don't easily forgive myself for what I did with him.

So, yes, I talked in therapy about Dyer, Jarreau, and Lassiter. I wrestled with self-loathing, perceived weakness, and vulnerability, wrestled with mistrust and paranoia. I was aware that my younger feelings and reactions were similar to those of post-9/11 Americans who believed terrorists were lurking in every mall and that the only way to be safe was to attack, and my knowing filled me with self-disgust. I'd scorned Americans who got in line to attack Iraq, to condone torture, to give up liberty for the guise of protection, and yet there I was still operating from the same fears in microcosm, allowing the past to dominate me. Slowly and in strange steps, I partially let go. I accepted that I couldn't go back and fight, accepted that even if I could, fighting wouldn't have given me self-respect or made me feel safer, accepted that I couldn't fight the past to save myself now. I began the work to stay aware. I began to reckon with my adversarial stance toward anyone with the power or potential to reject, belittle, or undermine me. But for a while I still couldn't forgive myself at all.

Then, on a trip to Baton Rouge, Robert played my girlfriend and me a tape Momma had sent him in Vietnam. On it, I talk in my high-pitched, silly drawl about myself being "live and in color," about the doings of our guinea pig and dog, and other juvenile fascinations. I felt my girlfriend's eyes on me as the tape chattered on. Finally, I looked at her. She said, "You hear that? That was a year before you fought Lassiter. You were a little boy." I snorted, smirked and nodded. I thought self-accusingly, Yeah, a *whole* year before. I thought, And only a couple of years before I raised a chain to hit a defenseless boy, before I thought about burning down a house, before I got into a gang fight with the belief that I was defending honor. Then I thought, I should have been braver and smarter. I considered how the impulses to be that kind of "brave" and to actually be smarter could not coexist. She touched my arm. "A little boy, Tim."

The "N-word," Art, and Anger

Well before I finished this memoir, I gave a public reading of its beginning. Afterward, a Jamaican-American student of mine emailed me, angry and disappointed that I had used "the N-word." I was on sabbatical writing this book, and I didn't want to engage in drama at school. But I wrote back trying to explain that I had to use the word in order to convey the reality of what I had lived through and to show my early immersion in a racist world. He answered that I should write about the "cured" me, as if racism had a vaccine, as if the fearful programming could simply be replaced with new software. I understood that he was hurt and struggling both with his own pain over racism and with how my reading had changed his image of me. Nonetheless, I wanted to lash out. Didn't he know how I agonized over how I'd acted; agonized over using that language again and again; agonized over the way I'd be seen? Couldn't he see that I had to write the repulsive language in order to dramatize the actual? I resisted responding angrily, turned the anger on myself for a brief while, and finally turned it away. I realized I had again become immersed in my fear of being belittled—a self-serving fear. I wrote that I'd heard him, respected his hurt and what he said, and would consider what he suggested in revising the book. But I'm still not completely sure how much of my anger at him had to do with the racism wired so deeply in me.

And now as I finish this, we have something I couldn't imagine when I began: an African-American president. Even as I worked hard to get him elected, I scoffed at the idea that he could. On election night, I hooted from the porch with my girlfriend and her daughter. Later I cried for the promise of an evolving America. Then I laughed when I heard the term "post-racial." Post-racial. Not now, not during my generation. Not in the South, not in the North, East, or West. The re-emergence of right-wing extremists—whether they're called birthers, militias, Tea Partiers, or Republican fringe— is only a half-step from what I still hear people say when I go home. Sometimes not even a half. I also hear it in Connecticut, even in the unaware language of white liberals and from my own mouth.

When Clinton was president, I thought that our country had crossed some boundary toward a less frightened America. Here was a governor from the south who didn't use as much veiled language about race as his predecessors, who seemed mostly to speak in a respectful, global, more egalitarian way. Not completely by any means, but more than the two previous administrations. Then Bush, Cheney, Rumsfeld, and their gang killed that belief, and even now the cultivation of fear and its destructiveness continues. Obama expands the drone wars, erodes judicial process in matters of "suspected terrorism," and expands his executive powers. Twelve years after 9/11, our nation is still in an official "state of emergency." Without perspective and reason, we'll always be attacking the other and ourselves. That's one of my fears.

My Parents

The year I started college, Daddy built a house thirty miles outside of Baton Rouge. I helped as much as I was capable and willing, but the process tested all of us. Bizarrely, Daddy formed up the house with wood from the reconstruction of his chemical plant unit, which exploded one night thirty minutes after he left, while I was on my senior trip. Once the house was finished, I moved there with my parents for a year, commuting to LSU, and then moved into town again. I dropped out of petroleum engineering and began work on a degree in secondary education. Some nights I got the call, rushed out to get Momma, and sped her back to Baton Rouge General or Our Lady of the Lake, trips that were most harrowing when I was on the way to pick her up and didn't know if she would still be alive when I arrived. Robert did the same.

In the early eighties, while I was teaching high school, I had a great bit of serendipity. A friend tipped me about a cheap apartment across the street from one of the hospitals. Momma was spending a lot of time there by then, and many nights I sat with her, tending to her when she was trying to shake fever and severe pain, bringing food when she was better. When she wasn't too sick, we ate, laughed, joked, and shared stories and gossip. She encouraged my being a writer and never worried that it wouldn't help me fix a lawnmower or drill an oil well. She gave me oblique advice about my constantly floundering relationships, and fretted over my edgy rock 'n' roll life and manic behavior, even though I tried to hide what I could. Her health worsened throughout the eighties, the cortisone swelling her, the lupus attacking her joints and organs.

Daddy did his best to take care of her, just as she'd always done her best to take care of him. When he turned sixty-two, BASF management locked out his union. After thirty-four years at the plant, he was forced to take early retirement at a much reduced pension in order to keep good medical benefits for him and Momma. At around the same time, he contracted prostate cancer and underwent massive radiation treatments. Some days he was so stubborn and determined that he would come home from the treatments and work in the hot yard until near collapse or until Momma made him come in.

Through my mid-twenties, he and I had rough times over my chaotic post-divorce life, my choice to switch majors from petroleum engineering to English education, my rejection of religion, my disdain for Reagan, my singing in punk and post-punk bands, and my going away to get a Master of Fine Arts in Creative Writing. I knew he was worried about me, but often it came off as rough criticism, and being a hothead, I didn't do well in smoothing things over.

Then one night in 1989, in a bar after a fiction workshop in Tuscaloosa, Alabama, I received a call from my sister-in-law telling me Momma had fallen into a coma due to a drug reaction. I rushed the six hours home. Two weeks later, I was in the room with her and Robert when she died. She was sixty-two.

During her last years, she became an accomplished painter of still lifes. Her most compelling work was primitive landscapes that sparked with bold strokes and bright, unexpected yellows, blues, and purples. She painted pictures of farmhouses based on the ones from her childhood and pictures of swamps lit by mysterious luminary sources. The swamp scenes hold eerie images, cypress stumps that look like robed children and nuns, and half-sunken boats that resemble floating coffins. They're visionary works, as if she were seeing her own mortality and a world beyond.

I've come to understand how hard it was for her, living in a world of volatile men, trapped by illness and the pressure to take care of all of us, repressed by a lack of any creative outlet, and powerless to protect me, or any of us. She was a more complicated person than I think I am capable of understanding because my interaction with her was clouded by her illness and my alienation. But I do understand that she had a powerful soul and spirit. Her encouragement to be creative bolstered me and let me know that there was a world of imagination and love. She shaped me as much as anyone. Still, I wonder what she would say about this book, whether she would say I shouldn't have written it because of what it reveals about us, especially Daddy, and how it doesn't protect him with silence. Then I think that, even if she believed that, she would most likely respect me because I've tried to be honest, to show both our flaws and our triumphs over our worst impulses, show how we loved each other through complication after complication and survived as a family. Also tried to understand the despicable things I thought and did.

2006: After the Reunion

"I wish they'd at least had good beer," I said to Robert as we stood in the super-heated garage of the small Baton Rouge house where Daddy and his wife lived. In 2002, Daddy had moved from Walker back to the opposite side of town from where we'd grown up, relieving Robert, Alan, and me of the worry over his driving on Highway 447 with its barreling gravel trucks and blind curves. "It was good seeing Mike and a bunch of them," I said, "but it felt cliquier than the twentieth."

Robert blew smoke and wiped sweat from his forehead. "It *was* a lot smaller this year, that's for sure. You hear Grayson yelling at me about have I been beating up any fucking queers and how 'bout them queers?"

"What was that about?"

"He's an idiot's what it's about. Maybe he thinks that's what I did when I was a cop and that's what he wants me to still do. He looks crazy as shit, like all his joints got popped out and they put slinkies in there, and his hair looks like Larry Stooge."

"Enough pot and your hair falls out, I guess. I tell you I got the speech about Katrina being God's punishment on New Orleans?" I asked.

"You lucky bastard."

"Yeah, this woman who was always drugged out of her mind in high school started going on about how they deserved it because they were a sinful city. So, of course, I tell her it's a pretty indiscriminate god if he wipes out families and people of every socioeconomic class and all walks of life and then includes all of the Mississippi coast, blah, blah, blah. She gave me that I-know-you're-an-atheist-liberal look and walked away."

"You should just wear one of those sandwich signs and have it say 'Commie Trash.'"

"Why don't I ever learn? Every time I come down here I spout all this lefty stuff and try to argue logically, and every time I go home feeling like a fool. I'm like one of those reformed alcoholics who turn loudmouthed Christian, except I'm the reformed Christian turned loudmouthed lefty."

"You hate Jesus." He took another long drag and smiled. "How you liking the Eagles' Jesi room this time?" Above the bed in Daddy's guest bedroom hung prints of three white, blue-eyed Jesuses with long, silky brown hair straight out of the seventies. I'd given them their country-rock, plural designation.

"Taking it easy, man." I gave him a peace sign.

"They oughta put up a picture of a Chevy van with galaxies painted on it and those Jesuses could all be riding in there smoking forgiveness dope." He laughed.

Robert took the last drag of his cigarette and pinched at the end to put it out. We'd had a good night at Daddy's. Our stepmother had fed us a great meal of meatloaf, mashed potatoes, field peas, and cornbread, and we were taking a break before dessert and coffee and some college baseball on TV. Daddy had been having stomach problems and he was pale and even thinner than usual, but my being home had him spinning old stories on request and laughing his big laugh. Plus, he and his wife had cut back on the blaring Rush Limbaugh on the radio and the grating Fox News on TV, and I had backed off on expressing my outrage over Bush.

"Hey, look," Robert said, "there's your book." He pointed at a stack of books up against the garage wall. I knew a bunch of books had been moved out to make room for a new piece of furniture, but I hadn't looked closely before. And there it was, one of two copies of my short story collection that I had given Daddy.

"At least it's on top of Bill O'Reilly and Ann Coulter," I said.

The next day, Robert, Daddy, and I headed back into town on Highland Road. We winded past houses built on the sloping trough that was once the Mississippi's bed, past mansions with their sprawling lawns festooned with azaleas and magnolias. Among the older houses, new homes of rich, post-Katrina expatriates from New Orleans had sprung up. The road took us through LSU's campus, the viney tails of Spanish moss again on the trees after years when the moss had nearly disappeared. Near Robert's house, we hit I-10 and traveled north. Ahead of us the smokestacks of Exxon and Dupont trailed streamers of white smoke. Eventually, we veered off the Chippewa exit toward Plank Road.

Daddy sat in the backseat, smaller and grayer and much less hard than he'd been in those days of turmoil. "They closed this part of the interstate down for that movie," he said.

"The *Dukes of Hazzard*?" I said. "They closed I-10 for *The Dukes of Hazzard*."

"Hey," Robert said, "they had to do a car jump. They can't just do a car jump anywhere."

We turned onto Plank, the stores that thrived when I was a kid now closed, run-down, or changed into heavily barred, check-cashing places, or convenience stores. Daddy and Robert reminisced about changes as we drove down Winbourne Avenue, past Istrouma High, but their nostalgia was edged with disgust and fresh loss more than I felt, this place still part of the town they lived in. When we were closer to our street, Daddy pointed out houses and named the people who had lived there, all of the houses shaggier than they were then, smaller with each visit than I remember them from growing up, the energy and money needed to keep them from sagging in the tropical stew gone. I know that it had been gone for some people there even when I was a kid, but in those days I saw mostly our house and our yard—the well-kept paint, the gleaming white ironwork, the carefully edged lawn.

"Do you know what happened to Jarreau?" I asked Robert, even though I'd asked him this before.

"Last thing I heard was when I was a cop. He was hiding behind a couch with a .22 rifle when some officers showed up on a disturbing the peace call and they hauled him in. Then he tried to rob a store across the river and the owner booked and Jarreau couldn't get the register open, one of them big heavy old-timey registers, so he picked it up and ran outside. Dumbass's car wouldn't start, so he took off out in the swamp still lugging the register. Sheriffs found him out in a bog hanging on to it."

"You think that's true?" I said.

"Oh, yeah. Remember when me and Gary busted him and his girlfriend when you were in college? They were trying to steal a car by pushing it."

"Genius."

"Big brain. He kept getting out of jail for a while. I figure he's dead or in Angola now."

We turned onto our short street. The houses looked even more derelict in the blasting sun than they had during my last trip only a year before. Dyer's house, like several others, was boarded up and going to mildew. The houses of other friends looked barely inhabitable, yet people were obviously living there. We crawled along, swapping information about people we knew who had died or moved, and then Daddy said, "The Haines still live there. He been barely able to get around for a long time." I was shocked. I used to visit their place, flirting and fooling around with their daughter. Their house had been cluttered and unkempt yet scattered with books—it had hummed with strange literate intelligence from Mr. and Mrs. Haines, both teachers. That they still lived there struck me as tragic, their inability to leave with the rest of us whites, their being left amidst this new poverty and crime and black people, nearly a curse. The irony of my feelings quickly followed. Me, lefty and semi-enlightened, starting a book to investigate fear's creation of racism in my life, now thinking how bad it was for whites to be left behind. But I couldn't help think it. Life is harder there, and the Haines are weighted in every way possible, all of their old neighbors gone, the neighborhood nearly unrecognizable. But I knew, too, that everyone there is weighted.

Four houses down, we slowed to a stop. Our cheerful light green paint had been replaced by chocolate brown, the ironwork lining the sidewalk removed, the ironwood tree near the house cut down, Momma's monkey-grass-bordered garden let go to weeds, my basketball pole rusted and without a backboard. It made me both proud to recall how lovely my parents had made this place and sad to see it like this.

"Two murders in there," Daddy said, something else we all knew but often ritually repeated. "Fourteen-year-old killed his stepfather in one, I think. Another woman shook her baby to death. They all messed up with that dope."

"I think one of 'em happened in the hall," Robert said. "I used to get a spooky feeling in that hall, like I knew something bad was gonna happen."

"That was just you knowing you wasn't 'sposed to be turning that attic fan on and off to pull y'all's hair up," Daddy said.

Across the street, in the yard where I'd run to escape Chandler, three older people drank beer at a card table in the shade of a pecan tree. We waved as we sped up and passed them. They lifted their chins to us, I suppose wondering who the hell we were. At the end of the street, a house lay caved and burnt. "I don't guess anybody'll ever tear that down," I said.

"I don't reckon," Daddy said.

We turned at the intersection where Jarreau had stood as Chandler came down. The reek of poverty hit me even more, money and any outside hope seeming abandoned. I knew this wasn't fully true, but I suspect that many of these parents don't believe, as mine did, that their kids will go to college and move on, suspect that their world is even smaller and more enclosed than mine was. Many of these children grow up without even the benefit of immigrant parents from farms, bayous, and small towns who came to Baton Rouge to find something better, who expected their kids to do better than they had done. These parents, I imagine, are trapped in the ever-deepening destitution on the north side of town. And even though I know I'm projecting, I believe I'm right; I believe that the impoverishment here is not simple proof that the dire expectations that made us flee were well-founded, but rather that the impoverishment is the offspring of the larger forces of class that kept my parents struggling and fearful of blacks in similar circumstances. It's also the offspring, in part, of our own moral poverty, ignorance, and racism.

We drove on. Up ahead a young woman in a prim white shirt and red skirt walked through the 94-degree heat and humidity as slowly as if moving across the floor of the Mississippi. She didn't even glance as we passed her and turned onto Eaton. The route that took so long those months I dreaded Jarreau is so short in actual distance that it did not take me back to those days. Instead, I tried to imagine how it would be to walk here now. At worst, the dangerous route Robert described; at best, awkward and rife with paranoia. We went past the old cut-through to the convenience store where Lassiter and the others had hung out, the path overgrown with vines and brush and still blocked by a metal rail greened with mildew. At the next corner sat a house with no screens in its open windows, its door swung wide, a box fan chugging against the heat. A young man with braids rising like knotty snakes strode out of the house and glared as he strutted in front of our car, making us nearly stop. Then we turned again and quickly again, and ahead stretched the road where I fought Lassiter.

A car or two passed in the opposite direction. The air held a deadness as we eased closer to the parking lot where Lassiter pulled the knife I never even saw. "Daddy," I said, "you remember in eighth grade when I got in the fight with that kid? We fought out into the street and stopped traffic. We got so exhausted we fell down on the cement right over there. The kid tried to pull a knife and this other guy pulled him away."

"I don't remember that," he said.

The convenience store and bar were deserted, but two young men stood in the sun next to the store, attentive to us. "Want some crack?" Robert asked.

"I'll pass," I said. "Daddy?"

He evidently didn't hear. We drove past my old junior high. Daddy said they were closing it, then talked about how his present wife's family grew up across the street and owned a lot of the land when there were almost no houses.

"Is it really that bad around here?" I asked, already thinking there was something racist in what I'd said about the crack a minute before. Too much thinking, Dyer would say.

"Why don't you get out and we'll pick you up back at the house," Robert said.

We cruised back toward our street, passed down the street behind our old house, one we'd always thought of as lower class. Robert pointed out two more murder houses, one in which five people had been killed in a drug dispute. Then we were back on Wyandotte. We pulled up next to the people still drinking beer and stopped.

"Y'all got some for us?" Robert asked through the open window. They laughed.

"Y'all got the right idea," Daddy said and they nodded, looking at us as if we'd dropped from the sky.

"We grew up in that house," I said.

"Uh-huh," the woman said. On their card table sat a twelve-pack and a number of empties. The three of them looked buzzed by beer and heat, and I wished I could sit with them and swap stories of then and now. But after a little more chat we all said goodbye, and went on our way to the other side of town.

I wondered if Alan were there whether he would want to take this drive with us. He seems to have shaken it all off, escaped the nostalgia and puzzling over the past that Robert and I do. He thrives. He worked for oil companies, became an executive, bought and sold his own company, and now operates in the world of big-money deals. He cruises the world on a sailboat he designed and stays in close touch with Daddy, helping out with funds, an attentive son. He stays in touch with me, too, despite my self-righteousness and disapproval of his politics. He probably won't approve of this book either, but that's his right and his way of protecting Daddy.

I glanced back at Daddy again, almost incomprehensibly frail. He hadn't expressed much vulnerability in his life, almost none at all until the night Momma died. That night, after they had taken her from her room, he and I sat on the bed in another empty room. He looked both weighted by the years of caring for Momma and somehow relieved that she'd been released from so much pain. He stared at the floor and began describing the horrible night two weeks earlier when Momma had reacted to the drugs. He described how helpless and frantic he'd been. "It was terrible, Tim," he said and cried. I'd only seen him cry once before, when he and I had argued while building the house in Walker. We'd said terrible things to each other and I told him he could build the house on his own and headed for my car. He'd followed me, yelling, and when I turned he fell to his knees and wept. "Everbody hates me. You and your momma. I'm afraid she's gone leave me and I'm doing the best I can." I hadn't been able to move.

In the hospital, I put my arm around his shoulders. He looked at me. "I'm glad you're okay, son. There was nights back when you were struggling after your divorce and all agitated and down . . . You'd leave the house and I worried I wasn't gone see you again. I wanted to stop you from going, but your momma told me I had to let you do what you was gone do. I was too hard on you."

Near LSU, we went to a buffet for lunch, bowls of chicken-sausage gumbo and salads. I don't know why, but I recalled an old story. "Hey, Daddy, you remember that mynah bird Grandaddy Upton had?"

"Sure do. That bird was special. He was a mimic, could mimic anything. I'd come in and say one word and he'd drop his voice way down," Daddy lowered his voice even more, "*and talk like this.*"

"Didn't that bird rat out that crazy wife of Grandaddy's?" Robert said. "Hadn't she been going around all day saying, 'I'm gonna poison that son of a bitch, I'm gonna poison that son of a bitch,' and the bird said it to Grandaddy in her voice and he kicked her out."

"I don't know about that, but I wouldn't doubt it," Daddy said. "That bird'd hear a lawnmower or a mockingbird or a cat and he'd go to it. He like to drove Tim crazy. Tim thought it was a human. I 'member you standing there and it asking you, 'Where'd you get the purdy bird?, Where'd you get the purdy bird?' and you saying, 'We got it to the store,' for about a half-hour, until you finally said, 'I'm gone tell you one more time, we got him to the store, and I'm throwing you out in the yard.'"

We laughed, ate and talked for a little while more, then I told Daddy about some of the things I've told in this book. How I fell in with Dyer; how dangerous he was; how he wanted me to help burn somebody's house. I told him I felt lucky not to be dead or in jail. Daddy had never heard these stories. He shook his head, chewing.

"And y'all get on me for saying things," he said. "I never did anything like that, and I'm from Mississippi."

Robert and I looked at each other and smiled. I patted Daddy on the back.

Acknowledgments

This is not a book I wanted to write. One of my mentors, Ted Solotaroff, told me "to write toward the pain," and I did for seven years. I stayed after it when I wanted to abandon this memoir and write other things, and I did so because more people than I can name (and here I obviously name many), or who do not wish to be named, encouraged me, advised me and loved me when I was least able to accept their support. I hope this book lives up, at least in part, to their high expectations.

Thanks especially to Brock Clarke, Steve Almond, Elise Blackwell, and Paul Solotaroff, who helped me with the earliest versions of the book and then some. Thanks always to Bill Black, Sarah Gardner Borden, Dan Hall, Michael Griffith, Steve Larocco, Erin McGraw, Jeff Mock, Bob Pellegrino, Jim Rhodes, Tony Rosso, Geoff Schmidt, Margot Schilpp, Mike Shea, Boykin Short, Robin Troy, Colleen Tully, and Valerine Vogrin for their support, friendship, and wisdom in life and in art. Thanks also to Brad Watson, Audrey Petty, Josh Russell, Kim Trevathan, Inman Majors, Nanci Kincaid, Ilene Crawford, Cindy Stretch, Robert McGuire, Thuan Vu, Xhenet Aliu, Jeff Voccola, Jessica Forcier, Penelope Pelizzon, Steve Davenport, Kathy Pories, Tim Huggins, Vivian Shipley, Nicola Mason, Alli Payne, Melissa Easton, and Ray Murray, who all gave suggestions, bucked me up and/or promoted me when writing and publishing this book felt like a Sisyphean endeavor. My appreciation as well to my constant advocate, Dean DonnaJean Fredeen, and to Marianne Kennedy, the SCSU Arts and Sciences Research Reassigned Time Committee, the English Department Reassigned Time Committee, the Connecticut State University Research Grant Committee, and the Southern Connecticut State Sabbatical Leave Committee. For their inspiration, thank you to numerous colleagues and friends not mentioned above, to many current and former students, to Mary

Nicholas, David Tate, Jane Shepard, Lydia Dixon, Laki Vazakas, Bill Haydon, Judy Kahn, Nolde Alexius, and The Group. Great appreciation to Craig Gill, Steve Yates and all the wonderful folks at the University Press of Mississippi, who saw something worthwhile in this book and were willing to take a chance. And finally to Peter Tonguette for his excellent copyediting.

Excerpts of this book have appeared in slightly different form in *Cincinnati Review* and *Ninth Letter*. Beth Ann Fennelly's poem, "Elegy for the Footie Pajamas," from the book *Unmentionables* (Norton, 2008), is used with permission of the author.